Please renew/return this item by the last date shown.

So that your telephone call is charged at local rate, please call the numbers as set out below:

	From Area codes 01923 or 0208:	From the rest of Herts:
Renewals:	01923 471373	01438 737373
Enquiries:	01923 471333	01438 737333
Minicom:	01923 471599	01438 737599

L32b

Yorkshire Through
Place Names

Yorkshire Through Place Names

R. W. MORRIS

David & Charles
Newton Abbot   London   North Pomfret (Vt)

To the memory of my parents

British Library Cataloguing in Publication Data
Morris, R. W.
    Yorkshire through place names.
    1. Names. Geographical—England—Yorkshire
    I. Title
    914.28'1'0014   DA670.Y6

    ISBN 0-7153-8230-6

Typeset by ABM Typographics Limited, Hull
and printed in Great Britain
by Redwood Burn Ltd., Trowbridge, Wilts.
for David & Charles (Publishers) Limited
Brunel House   Newton Abbot   Devon

Published in the United States of America
by David & Charles Inc
North Pomfret   Vermont 05053   USA

Contents

Preface

This book began as an inquiry into the origins of the place-names of the new Cleveland County, on behalf of a local conservationist group; it was to be a small contribution to the group's laudable effort to increase interest in the environment among the people of the district. Though the study has grown in scope and widened its area, that original purpose remains. It is intended for all who have a deep and abiding concern for the landscapes of their neighbourhood, whether that finds expression in rambling, cycling or motoring through the local countryside, in its protection and preservation, or in an interest in its history. The book is designed to acquaint them with the progress made in the study of English place-names during the present century, and also to suggest some of the many aspects of local development – historical, geographical, scenic, economic and social – on which such studies have thrown fresh light.

Yorkshire is an appropriate area for such a review, a compromise between a local neighbourhood which would have induced too parochial a treatment, and the whole of England which would have provided too large a canvas to show realistic detail. For centuries Yorkshire has been the largest of English counties; and, though its local administration has been rearranged since 1974, it preserves a strong sense of regional patriotism, of which the county cricket club is by no means the only manifestation. Geographically it contains a wide variety of environments in which our ancestors made and named their settlements – limestone and sandstone moors, chalk wolds, lowland plains. Most of its area is naturally drained by an extensive river system that flows into the Humber. It contains three industrial regions and two National Parks. It

7

offers visible remains of most periods of English history – pre-historic stone circles and earthworks, Roman villas and roads, medieval castles and abbeys, Jacobean and Georgian mansions, mines and railways of the Victorian Age – periods which have left indelible marks upon the place-names of Yorkshire.

The Local Government Act of 1974 has imposed upon me one major decision: whether to base this book upon the former Ridings or upon the subsequent administrative divisions. The overriding factor that led to my decision in favour of the former was that the bulk of the information is grouped according to the three Ridings, and only in that arrangement is it available to anyone wishing to consult the authorities.

I
Introducing Place Names
—and Yorkshire

Place names rank high among the many things we tend to take for granted, such as clean water from the kitchen tap and light at the touch of a switch. Some odd ones may attract our attention – like Ugglebarnby, the name of a hamlet near Whitby, and Crigglestone, south of Wakefield. The stone cross that marks the site of the Battle of Towton, fought in the Wars of the Roses near Tadcaster, stands in a parish named Saxton-cum-Scarthingwell. The name Hanging Grimston has sinister overtones that contrast with the pleasant downland of the Yorkshire Wolds. On the North York Moors above Guisborough is a remote farm bearing the name Tidkinhowe and a more accessible one called Kateridden.

Place-names often provide material for jokes. Others puzzle us. Blubberhouses has an odd ring for the name of a Pennine hamlet and of a moorland pass near Ripon, so far from a whaling port. People from southern England are likely to wonder why the ancient burial mounds which they have been calling 'barrows' on Salisbury Plain bear the name 'howes' on the North York Moors. Crackpot and Booze, the names of hamlets in Swaledale and the tributary valley Arkengarthdale, arouse our curiosity. We wonder what Penhill, a name borne by summits both in the Pennines and the North York Moors, has to do with writing. Probably, we rightly suspect, as little as laughter has to do with the coining of the name Giggleswick in Wharfedale or secret conclaves with the formation of Whisperdales in the North York Moors.

The modern form of a place-name is more likely to mislead than guide us to the original meaning. No sound of 'battles far ago'

9

ever disturbed the quiet of the peaceful villages of Upper and Lower Slaughter in the Cotswolds. Leake Hall and Church on the A19 some five miles north of Thirsk do not owe the name to bad plumbing. The name Haltemprice in the East Riding has nothing to do with the control of Tudor inflation. The Danes Dyke at Flamborough Head was not dug by the Danes – even in their day the dyke belonged to a long distant past and probably puzzled them as much as it does us. The name Menthorpe, a hamlet on the River Derwent east of Selby, is still more deceptive. Far from referring to a male community, it commemorates the name of a Scandinavian woman, *Menja*.

Thus to guess a place-name's meaning from its present-day form is to invite disaster, though we may be tempted occasionally into a lucky speculation. Oxford seems so obviously 'the ford of the oxen' that one might assume that Cambridge originated from 'bridge over the Cam'. But this could not have been so, for when the settlement was founded and first named, the river there was called not the Cam but the Granta – a name still preserved in the title of Rupert Brooke's poem 'The Old Vicarage, Granchester'. In the eighth century, Bede, writing in his monastery at Jarrow, recorded the name as *Grantacaestir;* in the ninth century, the *Anglo-Saxon Chronicle* called it *Grantebrycg*. The change in the river name from Granta to Cam did not begin until after the Norman Conquest and was not completed till the sixteenth century.

Yorkshire sets similar traps. Northallerton has a suburb called Romanby. But the name has no link with the Romans, whose relics are confined to the opposite end of the town; it preserves the name of a viking settler, *Hromund*. On the North Yorkshire coast, Sandsend obviously got its name from its position where the fine two-mile stretch of sand northwards from Whitby ends abruptly against the high sandstone cliffs near Lythe Bank. But to make a similar facile assumption concerning Robin Hood's Bay to the south of Whitby will only lead us into error. The association is completely fictitious. There is no evidence that the outlaw ever visited the spot, and the name does not appear until three centuries

10

after his death; his visit to the bay occurred only in popular ballads of the Tudor period.

It might be thought reasonable to assume that Wooldale in the old West Riding derived its name from some activity connected with the woollen industry or referred to sheep rearing on the neighbouring Pennine moors. But for our ancestors who first named the valley the meaning was more sinister – to them it was 'the wolves' dale'. In the Vale of Pickering, midway between Malton and Helmsley, lies the village of Salton. Important though the trade in salt was in early times, it in no way contributed to the naming of the settlement. The feature that most impressed the first settlers in this neighbourhood, apparently, was the prevalence of willow-trees that flourished on the flat, marshy terrain, for they named the settlement from their word for willows – *sealh*. As 'the farmstead among the willow-trees' the name was intelligible. The land has since been drained and the willows have disappeared, but the place-name still preserves their memory and gives a passing glimpse into the landscape of those bygone days.

Too many factors have changed since those far-off times when so many of our place-names were first coined for any reliance to be put upon the present-day form of any name. Even the landscape has altered. The major topographical features – the hills, plains and rivers – of course remain, but 2,000 or more years of increasingly intensive farming have clothed the physical landscape in a different garment of vegetation. Of the great Forest of Galtres that once covered so much of the countryside north of York, only small, scattered fragments – and the name – remain. In the Vale of Pickering the marshes have been drained and replaced by arable and pastoral farmlands. In all parts of Yorkshire four or more centuries of enclosures have covered most of the once open countryside with a patchwork pattern of fields, bounded in the uplands by stone walls and in the lowlands by hedges – 'little lines of sportive wood run wild', as Wordsworth saw them.

Urban change has been even greater. The built-up area of York today is at least a dozen times larger than that of the medieval city whose boundaries are still traced by the ancient walls. Hull has developed from a medieval port based on the Baltic trade into one of international status. In the valleys of the old West Riding steam power founded on local coal has transformed the early rural woollen industry into an urban factory system based on busy industrial towns; these have engulfed most of the villages upon which the earlier industry was centred. The great conurbations of our own age along the Tees and Humber and in South Yorkshire have, in their unremitting expansion, absorbed many of the villages of the neighbourhood and obliterated local features formerly distinctive enough to become elements in place-names.

In addition to these environmental changes, the very place-names themselves have undergone alteration which has been none the less striking because the process has often been imperceptible. For instance, the Anglo-Saxon word *stan* meaning stone, has retained the early pronunciation in Stainmore, 'the stony moor', crossed today by the A66 between Bowes and Brough; and in Stainburn, 'the stony stream', the name of a village between Huddersfield and Otley. But the vowel has been shortened in Stanley, north of Wakefield – the stony clearing. Stonegrave, the name of a village at the western end of the Vale of Pickering to the north of Hovingham, embodies a change in pronunciation to the modern form. Changed spellings have naturally followed in the wake of changed pronunciations, and as the forms slowly altered the original meanings have been lost.

This process helps us to interpret many of the strange place-names quoted in the opening paragraphs of this chapter. The settlement in the Cotswolds that later developed into the Upper and Lower Slaughter of our day derived the name from *Slohtre*, an Anglo-Saxon word indicating a muddy place. We still retain the meaning, though not the pronunciation, in our word 'slough', as in Bunyan's Slough of Despond. The further change of the pronunciation to Slaughter not only altered the spelling but also suggested a wholly misleading meaning. Similarly, the name Crigglestone is no longer puzzling when we realise that the original village overlooked the Calder valley as the *tun* (settlement) on a ridge our Anglian ancestors called *Cryc-hyll*. Booze began quite simply from *Bowehous* – the house by the bow or curve. The hamlet can still be seen in Arkengarthdale where the northern side-slope curves round to form the steep edge of the tributary valley of the Slei Gill. The farm-name Tidkinhowe preserves the pet-form of an Anglian farmer's name *Tydi*. Blubberhouses derives its name not from whaling but from a medieval word *blubber* which was used to express the foaming or bubbling of the sea, and probably referred to the turbulent flow of the River Washburn. The hamlet of Leake preserves in its modern form the ancient *loekr*, a brook. Whisperdales originated as 'the White Spot Valley'. When the Danes established their Kingdom of York in the ninth century, the personal name *Guthrum* was very popular among them. And as *gata* was their word for a road, *Guthrumgate* made sense as *'Guthrum's street'*. Since those days the name has imperceptibly changed its form until we know it today as Goodramgate, with a meaning more distorted than the timbers of the old houses along its frontage.

It follows that the etymology – the history of these changes in pronunciation and spelling – of a place-name is essential to the unravelling of its meaning. That the name Oxford originated as 'the ford of the oxen' is vouched for, in part at least, by Chaucer's fourteenth-century reference in *The Canterbury Tales* to the 'Clerke of Oxenforde.' The argument is strengthened by the recording of *Oxeneford* in Domesday Book at the end of the eleventh century, and confirmed by a reference to *Oxnaford* in the *Anglo-Saxon Chronicle* in the early tenth century. Similarly, the name Haltemprice, of a village near Kingston-upon-Hull, makes little sense until it has been traced back to a taxation record of 1340, in which it was entered as *Hautempris*. This gives the clue; it represents the Norman-French *Haute Emprise*, High Enterprise, and refers to the foundation of a monastery there in 1322. In like manner, the name Giggleswick becomes intelligible from its entry in Domesday Book as *Ghigeleswic* – the *wic* or farm of a man called *Gikel*. In short, all is guesswork unless the interpretation is based on the detailed etymology and the earliest ascertainable spelling. As Professor K. Cameron has said: 'The study of place-names is

13

based on an analysis of the early spellings of names in the light of the historical development of English sounds.'

Etymologies are printed at the end of chapters 1–8 in order to illustrate both the modifications that can occur to place-names in the course of time and the process of removing the accretions of the years to restore the original version. Of those at the end of this chapter, this is most easily done in the case of Huddersfield, for apart from the addition of an initial aspirate, the form of the name has changed little since it was first recorded – in Domesday Book in 1086 – as *Oderesfelt*, 'Huder's feld'. The only source of difficulty arises from the meaning of the final element *felt* or *feld*. This term in those early days did not carry its modern meaning of a field enclosed by hedges or stone walls: it then denoted an open space of uncultivated country, where presumably Huder had settled. The name is also interesting as an illustration of the evolution of our apostrophe 's'. Following the practice of the Anglo-Saxons, the Domesday clerks recorded the possessive case by adding the final syllable 'es', and wrote *Oderesfelt* – the *feld* of *Huder*. In the course of time the 'e' in the 'es' has become discarded, though we still acknowledge its omission by inserting the apostrophe, as in '*Huder's feld*'.

Little difficulty is posed by the etymology of Rievaulx once it is realised that the abbey there was founded by French monks. They took the name from the valley of the river in which they built it – the Rye valley, which they translated literally into their mother tongue as *Rievalle*.

The etymology of Kingston-upon-Hull is somewhat more devious. When the later forms are stripped away we are left with the twelfth-century recording of the Old English *Wyk*, a word that carried a variety of meanings. In Anglo-Saxon times it meant a village or, more likely, a dairy-farm. Later the Danes used a similar term to indicate a creek. The settlement must have prospered, for in the thirteenth century it became known as *Burgus super Humbre* – the borough upon the Humber. This latter name Humber was even older, for Bede mentioned it about AD 730. In 1292 the prospering town was taken into the hands of

Edward I, and from the thirteenth century onwards it became known as 'the king's town', with all the associated privileges. The Hull mentioned in the later forms of the etymology referred to the stream of that name that still flows into the Humber from the north. It may well have been the creek implied in the earliest form *Wyk*.

The etymology of York is more complicated and illustrates the modifications in a place-name that could be brought about by racial changes. A glance at the etymology will show that the name York did not come into general use until the Middle Ages, over twelve centuries after the Romans had constructed an important legionary fortress there as early as AD 71. For the first four centuries of its history it was known as *Eboracum*, and this was the name that appeared on the public inscriptions of the time and in the works of the contemporary Roman and Greek historians and geographers. When Roman rule in Britain ceased in the fifth and sixth centuries, *Eboracum* was taken over by the Angles, who changed the name to *Eoforwic*. There is no logical reason for the change, but it is thought that the old name, though incomprehensible to them, reminded them in some obscure way of their own word *eofor*, a wild boar. This explanation is not unreasonable – centuries later the same mocking instinct led Londoners to convert the Norman-French word *Bocage*, applied to the shady, wooded walk from Whitehall past St James's Park, into the derisive *Birdcage Walk*, a name it retains to this day. Bede, working in the ecclesiastical tradition of the Roman Church, continued to use the old Latin name *Eboracum* in the eighth century; and even in the ninth the memory of the Roman past was acknowledged by the addition of *ceaster*, an Anglo-Saxon term derived from the Latin *castra*, fortress, to their *Eoforwic*. The Scandinavian invasions of the ninth and tenth centuries brought further changes. In their turn, the Danes and Norwegians adapted the Anglian name to a form more familiar to their ears. The etymology shows that at this period the form *Euruic* came into use, while the contemporary sagas record the name *Jorvik* and *Jork*. The French influence that followed the Norman Conquest favoured the change

15

from '*j*' to '*y*', and the modern form York began to establish itself. But the etymology shows that the old Anglian form still persisted. The use of the Latin term *Eboracum* also continued, aided by the conservative habit of the minster in keeping its records in Latin. To this day the Archbishop of York signs himself *Ebor*.

From this examination of the etymology, it appears that when all the later accretions are stripped away, we are left with the early name *Eboracum* from which to gauge the original meaning. At this point the study moves from the historians to the linguists, who alone can provide an answer to the question – from what source was the Latin *Eboracum* derived? Expert students of sound changes in language are generally agreed that the Romans took their Latin word from a Celtic personal name *Eburos*, which in turn can be traced by experts in the Celtic tongues to an old Celtic word meaning yew-tree.

The etymology of York illustrates some of the changes in place-names brought about by the several waves of immigrant peoples who have crossed from the continent to settle in Britain. Place-name formation did not end with the Middle Ages: it continued into modern times. The eighteenth century contributed Ironbridge in Shropshire, where the first iron girder bridge ever constructed in this country was laid across the River Severn near Bridgnorth. In the late nineteenth century came such names as Port Sunlight on the Mersey and Bournville in the Midlands near Birmingham, given to the new towns erected by William Lever and George Cadbury to house their workers under improved conditions. Yorkshire followed with Dormanstown, built by the firm Dorman Long for their steel-workers at a suburb of the seaside resort of Redcar. Another influence was that of Ebenezer Howard, under which garden cities were laid out at Letchworth in 1903 and at Welwyn in 1920. These were the forerunners of the 'new towns' of today, of which no less than twenty-three have been planned in England alone since the passing of the New Towns Act in 1946.

But the spontaneity that characterised the coining of the place-names of the earliest periods has disappeared. The names of today's new towns are almost invariably given after much deliberate thought by the owner or the administrative body responsible for them. They are either taken directly from villages to be obliterated by the new developments, as at Milton Keynes, or are such unfortunate artificial creations as Teesville, a recent suburb of Middlesborough. When, a score of years ago, the two East London boroughs of East and West Ham were amalgamated into one single authority, the two councils concerned deliberated for nearly a year upon the name for the combined town, finally deciding upon nothing more original than Newham.

Only a minority of the older place-names in England were deliberately coined by their owners or inhabitants. It is unlikely that *Huder's feld*, which opens the etymology of Huddersfield, was so called by its owner *Huder*. That designation more probably sprang from his neighbours, wanting to distinguish that site from others. When the Danes settled at a village in the Esk valley, they could not themselves have named it Danby; the name only becomes intelligible when we realise that it was coined by the English inhabitants of the valley to mark a new and alien intrusion. The frequent use of nicknames in the formation of place-names further suggests that such names were given by the owner's neighbours rather than the owner himself.

Since Latin was the first language in use in Britain to produce written records, the earliest place-names available for modern study are those of the Roman period. Celtic names have come down to us only through Latin transcriptions. But the builders of Stonehenge and Arbor Low in the Bronze Age and Neolithic period must have had a language even though they left no inscriptions. It is interesting to speculate whether any of their ancient place-names have not been wholly lost, but instead have descended to us in distorted versions passed down the ages in oral tradition, unexplained elements in today's place-names.

Pioneers in Place-Name Study

Detailed study of the place-names of England on scientific lines, applying the known laws of sound changes to the development and interpretation of those names, has been essentially a work of the twentieth century. After pioneer work by such grammarians as Wyld and Skeat, the English Place-Name Society was formed in 1923 to further this research. The work was organised on a county basis, a linguistic expert being appointed to carry out the research and to edit the findings for each county. The task was formidable: the county records had to be searched for the early forms of place-names, and these forms had to be arranged chronologically for each name, traced back to their origins and interpreted. The research called for familiarity with the medieval Latin, the Anglo-Saxon and Scandinavian languages involved, combined with a background of extensive historical knowledge. Under the inspired and scholarly leadership of the late Sir Frank Stenton of Reading University and Sir Allen Mawer of Liverpool University – who themselves were responsible for several of the earlier volumes and guided the subsequent ones – expert and authoritative surveys of the place-names of most of the counties of England are now available to the public. In addition, Eilert Ekwall of London University employed his expert knowledge of the old Germanic tongues to publish *The Concise Oxford Dictionary of English Place-Names* in 1936 – a monumental work that treats most of the towns and villages of England, and one that has deservedly gone into four editions. It is difficult to express an adequate appreciation of the vast quantity of detailed work and of the erudition and thought that have gone into these studies.

The volumes especially concerned with the place-names of Yorkshire are those issued by the English Place-Name Society and edited by the late Professor A. H. Smith of University College, London. The first volume, *The Place-Names of the North Riding of Yorkshire*, was originally issued in 1926 and was revised and reissued in 1969. The second, *The Place-Names of the East Riding of Yorkshire and York*, followed in 1937. Since then, the eight volumes of *The Place-Names of the West Riding of Yorkshire* have appeared. As all these books are available to anyone within reach of a good reference library, it is no longer necessary to be a linguistic expert or even a humble student of languages for a study of place-names to be rewarding. All who are interested in the history, geography or social life of past ages will find much that is illuminating in the development of local place-names. No one suggests that place-names can replace written records as a source of historical material, but place-name study can supplement, support or challenge accepted views.

Subsequent chapters in this book, for instance, will discuss the evidence provided by place-names in relation to such historical problems as the fate of the Britons under the impact of the Anglo-Saxon invasion, and the influence of Scandinavian settlement in Yorkshire and northern England. As Dr Gillian F. Jensen, an expert in place-name studies currently working in Denmark, observes: 'To the historian, toponymy, like archaeology, is the handmaid to be employed whenever more conventional sources of information are absent or inadequate.'

But one need not be a professional historian to consult the volumes of Ekwall and the English Place-Name Society with interest and profit. Anyone interested in local history, however vaguely, will find in these volumes many a fascinating illustration of bygone life in his or her neighbourhood. The amateur archaeologist as much as the professional may find that local place-names indicate sites where a dig might prove rewarding. The general reader will find that place-names, properly interpreted, throw a light on the social and economic life of former days. If his interests lean towards geographical and landscape features, he will find that place-names not only illuminate the old farming practices, but also help him recreate the scenery of earlier days, which in many parts of Yorkshire was by no means the same as it is today. Many a country stroll has been enriched by an imaginative restoration of the former landscape as suggested by the original meanings of local place-names. The new interest that a study of place-names can bring to the exploration of one's home ground and the new perspectives that emerge from familiarity with the original meanings of those names are well worth acquiring.

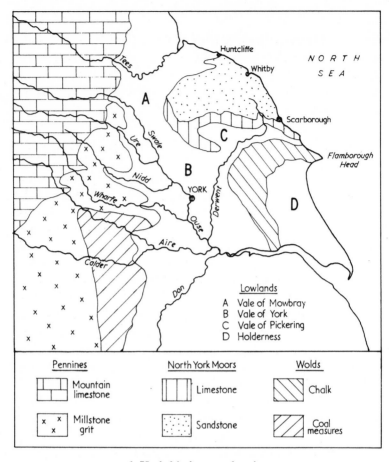

1 Yorkshire's natural regions

The Basic Scenery of Yorkshire

Yorkshire is a large county, and few can be expected to be familiar with all its 5,000 square miles. As place-names reflect settlement patterns and as settlement is greatly influenced by the natural environment, some idea of the basic features of the structure and scenery of the county is a helpful, even necessary, preliminary to an understanding of its place-names.

The main geographical regions that have broadly influenced settlement – and hence the distribution of place-names – within the county are set out in map 1. The threefold regional division is apparent to any traveller entering Yorkshire from the north by either the A1(M) or inter-city train. As soon as the River Tees has been crossed shortly after leaving Darlington, the basic three regions lie open to view. Ahead are the gently undulating lowlands of the Vale of Mowbray. Away to the west, the foothills of the Pennines can be seen rising against the skyline. Eastwards, the steep escarpment of the North York Moors abuts sharply against the edge of the plain, near enough for the white horse cut in the limestone edge above Kilburn to be plainly visible. This general pattern of broad lowland sandwiched between lateral uplands continues southwards throughout the county as the Vale of Mowbray merges imperceptibly with the Vale of York. To the west the Pennines continue to border the central lowland, extending as far south as Derbyshire. Only on the east is the bordering upland interrupted, the low flat Vale of Pickering separating the North York Moors from the Yorkshire Wolds.

The lowland of the vales of Mowbray and York has long provided a major north-to-south line of communication. The Romans followed it with their main road to Hadrian's Wall, taking advantage for much of the way of the drier route offered by the outcrop of magnesium limestone on the west. The Great North Road of coaching days and the modern A1 (M) have closely followed the same route. This lowland has a gently undulating surface that rarely rises above 200ft and is formed by an uneven spread of clays, gravels and sands left by the ice-sheet as it retreated at the end of the last ice age some 20,000 years ago. The underlying sandstones and marls are deeply buried beneath this glacial drift and can only occasionally be seen at the surface. A notable exposure of the basal red sandstone can be seen by railway travellers in the cutting at Doncaster railway station. Today mixed arable and cattle farming flourishes, barley and sugar-beet being important crops. But in former times, before the farmland was drained and the prevailing forests cleared, the patches of glacial gravel and sand played an important part in attracting settlement, as shown in the subsequent chapters dealing with the

21

distribution of the Anglian and Danish place-names.

The Pennines provide three distinct types of terrain. South and east of an imaginary line drawn from Richmond in the north to Skipton further south, the Pennine moors are formed of a sandstone known as millstone-grit. This rock gives rise to high, treeless moors where the thin, acidic soil supports only coarse grass, bracken and heather. Since millstone-grit is impermeable, extensive peat bogs are found on the plateau tops. The local term is 'moss', which preserves the Old English term *mos*, meaning bog or swamp. Down the precipitous edges of the gritstone outcrops amber-coloured streams descend in rocky ravines known locally as 'cloughs', again preserving an Old English term, *cloh*.

North and south of the gritstone moors the Pennine limestone replaces their sombre tones by the rich green of the short, springy turf, and the dark-brown gritstone walls around the fields give place to the more cheerful white and grey limestone ones. Surface water is almost completely absent, for the streams plunge down potholes to pursue their courses underground. This term also comes unchanged from the medieval word *pot*. At the foot of Ingleborough and in the neighbourhood of Malham extensive limestone pavements form a striking feature, in which the rain, rendered acidic by carbon dioxide from the air, has dissolved 'pipes' several yards deep, leaving a surface etched into 'clints', a term drawn from the Old Scandinavian word *klint*.

The third type of Pennine landscape is found in the Dales National Park, where the rivers Ure, Swale, Nidd and Wharfe descend the eastern flank of the moors in broad pastoral valleys – or dales as our Anglo-Saxons ancestors called them. Rich pastures encourage cattle-rearing, dairying and cheese-making on the broad valley floors. On both sides of each dale the stone walls of the eighteenth-century enclosures climb up the slopes to the plateau top, where the sheep graze.

The North York Moors are mainly of sandstone – a softer and less coarse stone than the gritstone of the Pennines, but one which also weathers into a thin, infertile, sandy soil. The area has been designated a national park in an endeavour to preserve one of the few large natural moorlands left in England today from the dual threat of industrial development and afforestation. These moors rise steeply from the Vale of Mowbray in a western escarpment nearly 1,000ft high, to a summit plateau largely covered with bracken, heather and coarse grass. Arable farming and cattle-rearing are confined to the valleys. In the east the moors meet the sea in an imposing line of sandstone cliffs that provided few landing beaches for earlier settlers.

To the south, however, the moorland landscape changes: limestone beds rise, overlying the sandstone, in an imposing escarpment. The fertile, tawny-coloured soil formed by the weathering of this limestone carries rich crops of barley, wheat and roots. The broad valleys of the sandstone moors give place to the narrow gorges cut by the streams as they flow across the limestone outcrop to the lowlands of the Vale of Pickering. Once the bed of a post-glacial lake, this vale rarely rises much above 100ft. In former days its marshy surface gave little encouragement to settlers, but today its silts and clays have been drained to give good farmland, with the result that, viewed from its bordering heights, the vale presents an intricate pattern of fields and hedges.

The Vale of Pickering is bounded on the south by the north-facing escarpment of the Yorkshire Wolds. These form the most northerly extension of the belt of chalk-land that extends from Salisbury Plain and the Chiltern Hills into the East Riding of Yorkshire via the Lincolnshire Wolds. They display many of the features characteristic of the chalk downs of the south. The gently rounded, rolling hills offered little physical barrier to movement; the permeable nature of the chalk provided naturally drained sites for settlement. The short turf still forms rich grazing for sheep, while grain and root crops are grown in the valleys.

The Wolds make only one contact with the sea, to form the chalk cliffs of Bempton and Flamborough Head. Inland they curve southwards to enclose the low-lying flats of Holderness, where the chalk is deeply overlain with glacial drift. Here the land rarely rises above 75ft, and the soils are damp and marshy. But in the low-lying shore that extends from Spurn Head to Flamborough Head the immigrants of earlier times had no difficulty in pulling their ships up on to the land, while patches of glacial sand in the interior gave relatively dry sites for settlement.

Abbreviated Etymologies

Huddersfield (WR, now West Yorks)
DB 1086 Oderesfelt
1121 Hudresfeld
1297 Huderesfeld
OE personal name *Huder*
OE *feld*: open land
'*Huder's feld*'

Kingston-upon-Hull (ER, now Humberside)
Bede 730 Humbrae Fluminis
1160 Wyk
1239 Burgus super Humbre
1306 Kengeston-on-Hulle
1407 Villa Regia super Hull
1493 Kengstown super Hull

York
71–410 Eboracum, Eburacum
Bede 730 Eboracum
895 Eoferwicceastre
1053 Eoforwic
1070 Everwic
DB 1086 Euruic
1100 Eoforwic
1150 Eoferwic stole★
1176 Ewerwic
1251 Eboracum
1330 Jorc
1344 Yorke
1393 Yhorke
★*stole*: stool, archbishop's see

Rievaulx (NR, now North Yorks.)
1157 Rievalle
1226 Ryvalle, Rivalle
1252 Ryevallis
1301 Ryvaus
1390 Ryvaux
N-Fr: 'valley of River Rye'

DB: Domesday Book   OE: Old English, Anglo-Saxon
N-Fr: Norman-French

2
The British (Celtic) and Roman Place Names

The Celtic language had been spoken in what is now Yorkshire for several centuries before the rulers of the ever-expanding Roman Empire began to cast acquisitive glances upon distant Britain. As early as 500 BC Celtic-speaking groups from the continent had begun to land on the southern and eastern coasts of England and to spread inland. The Brigantes settled in Yorkshire and soon established a loose confederation of tribal groups, superimposing their Iron-Age culture upon the Bronze-Age culture of the native peasantry.

Archaeological research has shown that in general the Brigantes lived in small, circular, thatched huts, built on a framework of timber pillars around a central hearth. Such huts were often grouped to form a small village, protected by a surrounding palisade and outer ditch against predatory animals and humans. They settled down as farmers, growing corn on the more southerly lowlands, but rearing cattle, sheep and horses on the extensive uplands of the north. The pattern of their small, rectangular fields – still known as Celtic fields – can be traced to this day on the Pennine moors above Grassington and in the neighbourhood of Malham.

These Celts brought to Britain two interests that changed history – a skill in working in iron and an obsession with war. The former accounts for the variety of their household and workshop tools for carpentry, farming and general purposes, fashioned in iron and not dissimilar in shape to many in use today. The latter produced the numerous Brigantine hill-forts, the ramparts and ditches of which can still be seen on the summit of Ingleborough and many another Yorkshire hill.

In about the year 300 BC, more than two centuries before the coming of Julius Caesar, a second immigration of Celtic peoples took place, this time from north-east France. The Parisii settled in the East Riding, bearing a tribal name that is still preserved in that of Paris. With them they brought a still more advanced Iron-Age culture. Their skill in decorative art in general and iron work in particular was remarkable, and was applied to all kinds of objects – shields, swords, pottery, even to the backs of mirrors. The characteristic design – the returning spiral line and the lively portrayal of moving animals – is recognisable on many an exhibit of their work displayed in local museums. They were no less skilful in the arts of war. Julius Caesar himself praised the Celts for this, admiring the mobility of their horse-drawn chariots and the dexterity with which the charioteers handled their vehicles on the battlefield. On the death of a chieftain it was the practice of the Parisii to bury the body with the chariot and war trappings under a circular tumulus. No less than nine such chariot burials have been unearthed in the Yorkshire Wolds.

The Celtic language was destined later to separate out into various forms – Welsh, Breton, Gaelic and Cornish. But at the time of the Roman invasion the Old Celtic language was in general use in Britain, with the sole exception of the extreme north, where the Picts continued to speak their own even more ancient tongue. Of the many place-names that must have been used by the farming and warrior communities of Yorkshire in Celtic times, those that have survived in one form or another into our own day are marked in map 2. At first sight the scatter may not appear impressive. But no less than 1,500 years have elapsed since Celtic place-names were in daily use. Further, since the language then had no alphabet, no Celtic place-name could expect to survive unless it aroused the interest of the Romans sufficiently for it to be preserved in a Latin form. It then had to survive no less than three mass-migrations – of the Anglo-Saxons in the sixth century AD, the Danes in the ninth and the Norwegians in the tenth.

26

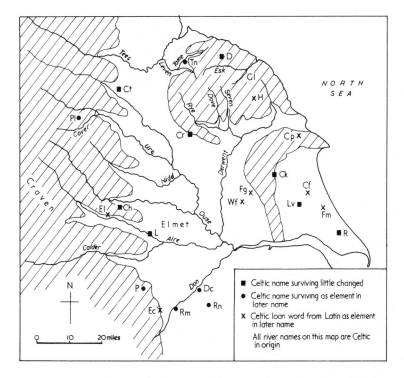

2 Place-names of Celtic origin. Key: Cf Catfoss; Ch The Chevin; Ck Craike Hill; Cp The Camp; Cr Crayke; Ct Catterick; D Dinnand; Dc Doncaster; Ec Ecclesfield; El Eccleshill; Fg Fangfoss; Fm Fosham; Gl Glaisdale; H Hole of Horcum; L Loidis, Leeds; Lv Leven village; P Penistone; Pl Penhill; R Roos; Rm Rotherham; Rn Rossington; Tn Tanton; Wf Wilberfoss

Despite this, the names of at least two districts of modern Yorkshire – Elmet and Craven – have been traced back to Celtic sources. Motorists travelling between Tadcaster and Pontefract today pass through Sherburn in Elmet. This name preserves that of the Celtic kingdom of Elmet, which resisted the subsequent invasion of the Angles for over a century. We still refer to the region of the upper Aire as the Craven district, a name that has probably descended to us from the Old Celtic word for garlic, *craf*. In the previous chapter the origin of the name York has been traced through the many changes of a complicated etymology back to the Old Celtic personal name *Eburos*.

The number of river-names in Yorkshire that we owe to the Celts is remarkable. Of the several words in the Old Celtic language that carried a general meaning of water, *isca*, *dana* and *usso* in particular have entered into the formation of Yorkshire river-names. *Isca* has given us the modern river-name Esk for the stream that flows eastwards through the North York Moors to enter the sea at Whitby. The Exe in Devonshire and the Axe in Somerset draw their names from the same source. The River Don, on which Doncaster now stands, shares with the mighty Danube an origin from *dana*. The Yorkshire Ouse has its origin in *usso*, in company with other rivers of that name in Sussex and Cambridgeshire. Ekwall gives this as an example of those words of a prehistoric tongue that have filtered through via Celtic from a still more ancient Sanskrit root-word for water, *udan*. There is in Yorkshire no river bearing the name Avon, but readers acquainted with Wales will recognise its association with the Modern Welsh word for river, *afon*, from the Old British *abona*. The name of the river by which Rievaulx Abbey was later to be built, the Rye, has not wholly lost its identity with the Welsh *Rhiw*.

Other Yorkshire river-names stem from the names of Celtic nymphs and goddesses, then commonly associated with watercourses. The River Leven, from the Celtic *Leuan*, the name of a Celtic water-nymph, is an example. But the majority of the Celtic river-names preserved in modern Yorkshire are purely descriptive, as summarised in the table on page 27. The River Ure, for instance, takes its name from the Old Celtic *isura*, swift-flowing, a derivation shared by the River Isar, a tributary of the Danube. The poet Campbell must have been impressed by this characteristic when he wrote of 'the flow of Isar, rolling rapidly'. The Calder bears an Old British name, originally formed from a compound of the Old Welsh *caled*, hard, violent, with the Old Celtic word for stream, *dwfr*. The River Dove, the small stream that flows among the daffodils which attract visitors to Farndale every spring from far and wide, has emerged from the Old Celtic word *dubo*, black or dark – the *ddu* of Modern Welsh. The Tame, a tributary of the Leven, shares with the River Thames an origin which Ekwall traces back through the Celtic *tam* to the Sanskrit *tamas* – darkness. The Brigantes knew the Aire as *Isara*, 'the strong, powerful river'. In all, of the forty-four Yorkshire river-names examined, no less than twenty-four have been found to stem from Celtic origins. As Yorkshire was subsequently invaded first by the Angles and then by the Danes, both of whom utilised the rivers for penetrating into the interior, this rate of survival is remarkable.

Several Yorkshire hill-names contain elements of Celtic origin. A popular excursion in Otley, the metropolis of Wharfedale, is the walk from the railway station to the top of the Chevin, the steep ridge that overlooks the town, to enjoy the extensive view from its summit. The earliest recorded version of this name is to be found in a tenth-century document as *Scefine*. *Cefine* is associated with the Welsh word *cefn*, a ridge. Ekwall sees in the initial 's' a relic of an original Welsh preposition *is*, below. *Scefine* would accordingly have referred to 'the place at the foot of the ridge', an exact description of the site.

YORKSHIRE RIVER-NAMES OF CELTIC ORIGIN

River	Celtic Origin	Meaning	Other Examples
Esk	Isca		Exe (Devon)
		General meaning	Axe (Somerset)
Ouse	Usso	of 'water', stream	Ouse (Sussex, Midland)
Don	Dana		Danube
Leven	Leuan	Celtic water-nymph	
Calder	Caled	hard, swift	
Derwent	Derua	oak tree	
Dove	dubo	black, dark	Dovedale (Derbyshire)
Aire	Isara	strong	
Nidd	Nouijos	new, fresh, bright	R Neath (South Wales) (Welsh Newydd)
Tame	tam	dark	Thames, Tame (Oxon)
Ure	Isura	swift	Isar (tributary of Danube)

29

Pen is another Old Celtic word that has survived in the modern place-names of both England and Wales. It marks a summit or high point, often well worth a visit for the panoramic view therefrom. The name is today found as an element in Penyghent and Pendle Hill, both famous Pennine summits. In the case of Pendle Hill, the later addition by the Angles of their word *hyll* to the earlier Celtic *pen* illustrates a form of tautology that is not uncommon among place-names. It suggests that though the Angles accepted the term *pen* from the native Celts, it held no meaning for them. To make it intelligible they added their own word. There is another Penhill between Aysgarth and Middleham in Wensleydale.

There are many *pen* names on the North York Moors – Pen Hill, near Sutton Bank; a Penny Hill, east of Stokesley; Pen Howe, a tumulus just off the road between the top of Sleights Hill and Goathland. In the 1930s the archaeologist Elgee printed a comprehensive list of these *pen* summit names found on the North York Moors in his authoritative work *Early Man in North-East Yorkshire*. A. H. Smith, however, excludes most of them from his equally authoritative work *The Place-Names of the North Riding of Yorkshire*, presumably since they do not appear in any historical record and consequently cannot be vouched for with certainty. For this reason they are omitted from map 2. But all the summits that Elgee quoted have the characteristic attributes of a *pen*, each rising to a distinct summit height above the moorland plateau, and there is therefore considerable topographical support for a claim to authenticity.

Modern Welsh distinguishes between *pen*, indicative of a distinct summit point, and *bryn*, applied to gently rounded, dome-shaped hills. Elgee applied the same distinction to the North York Moors and suggested that the many Brown Hills found thereon derived their names from this Celtic *bryn*. Certainly none of the Brown Hills of the Moors is named after its colour – predominantly black and gold in winter from the dead heather and bracken, bright green in spring and summer from the fresh bracken, and purple in autumn from the flowering heather. Topographically, all fit so comfortably into the meaning of the Welsh term *bryn* that Elgee's surmise may well have been correct.

Place-names are often classified into two groups: habitative names, which refer to the type of settlement concerned, and topographic names, descriptive of landscape features such as rivers, rocks, marshes and hills. Few of the Celtic place-names that have come down to us are habitative in type; almost all are topographic. In addition to those quoted is Roos, the name of a hamlet in Holderness between Hull and Withernsea. This name is identical with the Welsh *rhos* – moor or heath – and throws light on the natural vegetation of this part of Yorkshire in Celtic times. The same stem forms the first element in Rossington, the modern coal-mining village south-east of Doncaster, and bears the same interpretation.

There are in Yorkshire two place-names Crayke and Craike. Both are derived from the Old Welsh *creic* (Modern Welsh *craig*), rock. The first is of a castle perched upon a steep cliff in the Howardian Hills near Easingwold. The other is the name of a hill in the Wolds near Driffield which later became the regular meeting place for the Anglo-Saxon folk-moot and in medieval times of the Shire or Riding Court. Across the Wolds, on the northern face above Folkton, two ancient earthworks are today known as 'The Camp'. The topography would, as A. H. Smith observed, fit an origin of the name from the Celtic *camb*, a hill-crest or ridge.

There was a similar Old Celtic word *cumb*, applied to a deep valley, which provides the final element in the name Hole of Horcum, the deep depression that often puzzles motorists on the moorland road between Pickering and Whitby. Those who pull up their cars on the grass verge to look down into the deep hollow will at once realise how appropriate the term was. The inclusion of the word Hole in the modern place-name is another example of place-name tautology. The first syllable Hor is a relic from an Anglo-Saxon word *horh*, muddy, a description rendered out-of-date by modern field drainage. Off another moorland road, the A171 between Whitby and Guisborough, not far from the Scaling reservoir and yachting marina, two ancient boundary stones still stand among the heather and bracken of Danby Moor. They are known as the Great and Little Dinnand, from the Old Celtic word *din*, hill.

Usually, however, Celtic names survive only when compounded with an element of a later period. The name Tanton, of a small hamlet on the River Tame near Stokesley, combines the Celtic name of the river with the later Anglo-Saxon *tun*, farmstead. Doncaster similarly combines the Celtic river-name *Dana* with the Anglo-Saxon term *ceaster*, frequently applied to remains of Roman fortifications.

There are in the East Riding a number of place-names in which the term foss appears as an element. Catfoss, Fangfoss, Wilberfoss and Fosham are marked on map 2. The term was derived from the Latin *fossa* and originally meant a ditch. This Roman word was borrowed by the Britons and subsequently absorbed by the Angles. It is significant that all four examples quoted belong to hamlets situated in damp, low-lying lands where field drainage is a necessity.

In all, few will disagree with the conclusion of A. H. Smith when he wrote: 'The river-names of England are an enduring memorial to the Celtic tribes so little known to us, who are none the less our ancestors as well as the Angles, Saxons, Danes and Normans' – except possibly to add 'hill-names' to complete the tribute.

Place-Names of Roman Yorkshire

The Roman conquest of AD 43 brought Britain into the age of recorded history for the first time. From the subsequent four centuries of Roman rule a variety of written sources are still available to us for the study of the place-names of Roman Britain. For the first two centuries of the period we have the historical works of Tacitus, Dio Cassius and Suetonius, the secretary of the Emperor Hadrian. For the last two centuries there are the writings of Ammianus Marcellus and Zosimus. Two official documents, the *Antonine Itinerary* and the *Notitia Dignitatum*, add greatly to the list of known places. The *Itinerary* was a kind of Roman AA book, compiled in the third century to list the main routes used by the imperial postal and administrative services throughout the Roman Empire, and recording the towns and posting stations along them where horses could be changed and accommodation found for the night. The British section included sixteen routes, of which three passed through the area of modern Yorkshire. The *Notitia Dignitatum* was compiled in the late fourth and early fifth centuries, and listed the officials and military officers with their respective units and stations. These sources are supplemented by official engravings on the ruins of public buildings, private dedications on tombstones, military plaques, commercial stamps on metal ingots and graffiti.

Map 3 plots the main Romano-British sites known today within the traditional area of Yorkshire. The main supply road to Hadrian's Wall entered the region from the south, where the fort at *Danum*, now Doncaster, guarded the crossing of the River Don. *Lagentium*, now Castleford, and *Calcaria*, now Tadcaster, protected the crossings of the Aire and Wharfe respectively. *Calcaria* drew its name from the magnesian limestone quarries in the vicinity which produced the stone used in the fortifications of *Eboracum*. Further north, *Isurium Brigantum*, now Aldborough, grew up at the crossing of the River Ure. This was an important civilian settlement, which became the cantonal capital of the territories of the Brigantes. Still further north, at the crossing of the River Swale, was *Cataractonium*, now Catterick. Beside the military fort that defended the crossing, a thriving civilian settlement was located – where the road over the Pennines by Stainmore to Carlisle branched off from the main artery northwards to the eastern end of the frontier wall.

Further east, the road from *Lindum* (Lincoln) led northwards to the important ferry-crossing of the Humber. There, on the northern bank, flourished the small town of *Petuaria*. The military road ran on northwards to *Deventio*, where, on a site now occupied by Malton, an important military station and a civilian settlement developed at the crossing point over the River Derwent. Shortly after leaving *Petuaria*, another road branched off to *Eboracum*, now York. At this strategic point, where several cross-country (*opposite*) 3 The Roman period

Initial Letter on Map	Present-day Name	Name in Roman Times	Type of Settlement
A	Aldborough	ISURIUM BRIGANTUM	Walled town, Cantonal capital
B	Brough-in-Stainmore	VETERAE	Fort
Ba	Bainbridge	VIROSIDUM	Fort
Br	Brough-on-Humber	PETUARIA	Town
Bs	Bowes	LAVATRAE	Fort
C	Catterick	CATARACTONIUM	Fort and civilian town
Cd	Castleford	LAGENTIUM	Fort
Cl	Cleckeaton	CAMBODUNUM	Fort
Cs	Castleshaw	——	Fort
Cw	Cawthorne	——	Practice camps
D	Doncaster	DANUM	Fort
E	Elslack	——	Fort
F	Filey	——	Signal station
G	Goldsbrough	——	Signal station
GB	Greta Bridge	MAGLONA	Fort
H	Huntcliff	——	Signal station
HB	Healam Bridge	——	Mansio (posting station)
I	Ilkley	OLICANA(?)	Fort
M	Malton	DERVENTIO	Fort and town
Mi	Millington	DELGOVICIA	Mansio
R	Ravenscar	——	Signal station
S	Slack	CAMULODUNUM	Fort
Sc	Scarborough	——	Signal station
T	Tadcaster	CALCARIA	Fort
Th	Thornton-le-Street	——	Mansio
Y	York	EBORACUM	Colonia and legionary fort

roads took advantage of the dry approach provided by glacial gravels to converge on the crossing of the River Ouse, *Eboracum* developed as the legionary fortress and headquarters of the Roman army in the north.

Not only were these centres situated at strategic river crossings, but several actually took their names from the Celtic appellations

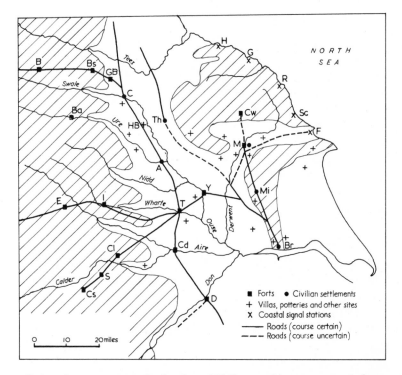

of the river concerned. *Isurium* (Aldborough) was named from
Isuro, the Brigantian name for the River Ure. The name *Danum*
(Doncaster) was taken from the Celtic *Dana*, the name by which
the Brigantes knew our River Don. Our River Derwent clearly
preserves its Celtic name *Derventio*, and gave its name to the
Roman station on its banks. The fact that *Eboracum* did not follow
this practice and was not named after the Celtic *Usso* (our River
Ouse) has been quoted to support the suggestion that some form
of Celtic settlement preceded the Roman one there. *Cataractonium*
probably derived its name from the Latin word *cataracta*, waterfall, a reference to the swirling rapids of the neighbouring River
Swale.

Still more striking is the extremely small number of Roman
names that have survived, even in part, to be used today in Yorkshire. Map 3 is accompanied by a scheme that gives, in alphabetical

35

order, the present-day names side by side with their Roman ones. If these are compared, only two out of the twenty-six listed will be found to have preserved even the slightest vestige of their Roman names. *Cataractonium* survives recognisably as Catterick. *Danum* is preserved in the first element of our name Doncaster. All trace of the Latin names of the other twenty-four settlements has vanished; their present names belong to another language. *Isurium Brigantum* has become Aldborough. *Petuaria* and *Veterae* have both changed to Brough, the one on the Humber, the other at the western end of the A66 over Stainmore. The forts of *Lagentium* and *Lavatrae* have become Castleford and Bowes respectively. Since even the name of the capital of northern Britain in Roman times, *Eboracum*, has vanished from the map, it is not surprising to find that none of the Roman names of the signal stations erected along the Yorkshire coast has been preserved. Of the sixty-nine occupied sites listed for Yorkshire in the Topographical Index of the OS Map of Roman Britain, the names of only two – Catterick and Doncaster – have survived in recognisable form.

Several reasons can be offered for this sweeping replacement of Romano-British place-names by others of Germanic origin, not only in Yorkshire but over much of Roman Britain. The very fact itself furnishes a powerful argument for concluding that the subsequent Anglo-Saxon invasion was so overwhelming as to wipe the slate clean – a question which is examined in the following chapter. This chapter is confined to those factors which lay within the nature of the Roman rule itself in Britain, for the Roman conquest differed from the folk migrations that preceded and followed it. It was essentially a military operation, inspired by imperial ambition, undertaken for political purposes and achieved by a trained army. No land-hunger drove hordes of Roman citizens to seek farmlands across the Channel; there was little in the bleak climate of Britain to attract many settlers from the warm Mediterranean lands. The number of Romans from the seven hills of Rome or from the plains of Latium was never large. Even the army was recruited from the barbarian tribes of the continent. Latin-speaking immigrants were largely confined to army officers, the higher ranks in the civil administration and a few merchants and financiers. Throughout the four centuries of Roman rule the overwhelming mass of the population remained Celtic. The survival of Latin place-names, indeed their very acceptance in the first place, therefore depended on the extent to which this native Celtic population could be persuaded to adopt a Roman way of life and speak the Latin tongue.

The Roman authorities were very conscious of their civilising mission, which they interpreted as extending beyond the 'To reduce the proud and to spare the defeated' of Virgil's lines. The Celtic tribes, both within and outside the imperial frontiers, were their 'third world'. Once the army had brought them within the orbit of the *Pax Romana*, the civil authorities sought to introduce them to the polish of civilisation. To the Romans this meant a cultured life in a *civitas* – a city or town – as distinct from the bucolic and boorish life of the rural peasant. To this end they encouraged the building of towns laid out in the characteristic Roman chessboard pattern of streets around a central market place (*forum*) and townhall (*basilica*). In such towns as *Isurium* the more wealthy tribesmen were urged to take a town house equipped in Roman fashion with mosaic pavements patterned with scenes from classical mythology and warmed by underfloor heating from hypocausts. Archaeological evidence suggests that in general the upper classes of Celtic society responded. Several tribal chiefs became quisling kings, and many a Celtic aristocrat moved into a town house and served on the *ordo* or town council, administering justice as a magistrate in the basilica.

Excavations show that Latin was everywhere the language of officialdom. Inscriptions on the gates of Eboracum and in other towns proclaimed the titles and status of the reigning emperor in Latin in that style of lettering still called 'Roman'. Temple dedications, memorial valedictions on tombstones, legionary records carved in the stones of Hadrian's Wall were all inscribed in Latin. Within the influence of Roman officialdom and upper-class Celtic society, Roman place-names were readily accepted.

The business men seem to have followed suit, as Latin became the language of commerce. Wooden writing tablets, once lined with a thin layer of wax, have been found in several Romano-British towns, especially in London which was even then the chief trading centre of the province. Messages were scratched in the wax by a pointed stylus, and whenever the stylus was too heavily impressed it scratched into the wooden base, thus unwittingly preserving the writing. Most of the impressions of business letters that have been found were written in a cursive Latin.

How far the bilingualism of the merchants and of the upper classes of Celtic society extended to the working classes of the towns may be gauged from the evidence of graffiti – a couple of examples are quoted in illustration. From the excavations at Silchester came a broken tile with the Latin word for girl – *puella* – scratched upon it, presumably by some lovelorn swain. In London, a tile was unearthed on which a workman had scratched a note about a companion: *Austalis dibus XIII vagatur sibi cotidim* – 'Augustalis has been going off on his own every day for a fortnight' – thus providing what is probably the earliest record in this country of industrial absenteeism. The fact that such trivial scribblings were made by workmen of none too high a grade in their idle moments, on broken or discarded tiles, suggests that, in the town at least, quite ordinary Celtic people used Latin with some familiarity.

But most of the native Celts lived in the countryside. A few of the leading tribal families and progressive native farmers might have been beguiled by the persuasions of the fashionable builders of the day to convert their rough wattle and daub huts into stone-built Roman-style villas. But there is no evidence to suggest that the mass of the peasantry was so influenced. They continued to live in their squalid huts, tending their flocks and herds on the hillsides and tilling their small rectangular fields, largely unresponsive to Romanisation. Their main contact with Roman influences was probably restricted to their annual visit to the nearest military establishment to pay the 'Annona' – the grain levy imposed upon the tribesmen for the upkeep of the garrisons. Over extensive areas of rural Britain the language and the place-names in current use by the local inhabitants remained Celtic.

This did not, however, prevent a number of common Latin words being absorbed into Celtic speech, from which they later passed on into Anglo-Saxon place-names. An example is the Latin word *castra*, used of a legionary camp or fortification, which subsequently entered into Anglo-Saxon place-names in the form of *ceaster*. Map 3 shows *Danum* emerging as Doncaster, and *Calcaria* as Tadcaster. Visitors to North Wales will recall how frequently the word *eglwys* appears in the names of the chapels; this is derived from the Latin *ecclesia*, church, which passed into Old Welsh. Yorkshire provides Ecclesfield, on the northern fringe of Sheffield, and Eccleshill north-east of Bradford. The Anglo-Saxon origin of these names is revealed by the other elements, hill and field; and as the Angles did not embrace Christianity for two centuries after Roman rule ended in Britain, it is highly likely that they acquired the word from the native Celts among whom Christianity was well established.

Among these Celtic loan-words from the Latin, the word *strata*, street, has entered into many place-names in Yorkshire. On the northern edge of the Howardian Hills west of Malton there are the neighbouring villages of Barton-le-Street and Appleton-le-Street. On the high Wolds between Driffield and Malton lies Wharram-le-Street and three miles north-east of Tadcaster is the hamlet of Streethouses. So many of these *street* names are located on the course of a Roman road that the connection cannot be doubted. Recently, Dr Margaret Gelling has argued cogently that the first element in such names as Wykeham, a village a few miles inland from Scarborough, is derived from the Latin word *vicus* – a term applied to those settlements of wives of legionaries, tradesmen and other camp-followers that commonly sprang up on the fringe of a military station. As the Roman legions had left Britain long before the Angles settled in Yorkshire, it is reasonable to assume that the term reached them via the native Celts who had absorbed it into their vocabulary.

The circumstances of the closing period of Roman rule in Britain favoured the Celtic language as an intermediary in the transfer of Latin terms into Anglo-Saxon. Though beset by increasing raids by Picts from the north, Scots from Ireland in the west and Angles and Saxons from the east, the Wall and the interior forts were repeatedly denuded of trained legionaries who were transferred to the continent either to further the imperial ambitions of their generals or to defend the empire nearer Rome. The Roman authorities in Britain consequently relied more and more upon a local militia, termed 'foederati' (allies) and composed of local inhabitants. This arrangement provided ample opportunity for the Celtic foederati to become familiar with such Latin terms as *castra*, *strata* and *vicus*.

The situation was realistically acknowledged by Emperor Honorius in his letter of 410 AD, in which he officially invited the Britons to see to their own defence. Out of the obscurity of the Dark Ages we get occasional and vague glimpses of an Artorius who led a successful campaign at the head of a mobile field army in the tradition of the late-Roman times, and of a number of Celtic tribal chieftains reverting to the style of inter-tribal warfare of their ancestors, the story of Vortigern introducing the Jutes of Hengist and Horsa into Kent as foederati being the best known.

This was the confused Britain upon whose shores the Angles and Saxons landed over half a century later. By then the villas had long been abandoned, the forts were in ruins and the towns silent, uninhabited and desolate save for an occasional band of robbers. It is not surprising that few place-names of Roman Britain survived, or that such Latin words as did were largely the loanwords from the Latin that had passed into Celtic speech.

Abbreviated Etymologies

River Tees
1026 Tesa
1050 Tese
1090 Teisa

River Ure
1142 Jor(e)
1175 Yor
1202 Yhor
1295 Your(e)
1530 Yeure

River Ouse
1066 Use
1286 Huse
1314 Ouse, Ouze

River Esk
1109 Esch
1129 Esc
1204 Esk(e)

Catterick (NR, now North Yorks)
Ptolemy *c* 150 Katouraktonion
4th century Cataractone
Bede 730 Cataractam uicum
DB 1086 Catrice
1198 Cateriz
1231 Kateric
1238 Catrich
1308 Katrici
1362 Catrik
1396 Catteryke
1536 Catheryk
Latin *cataracta:* waterfall

The Chevin (Otley, WR, now West Yorks)
972 Scefinc
1030 Scefinge
Welsh *cefn*: ridge

DB: Domesday Book   OE: Old English, Anglo-Saxon

3
The Anglo-Saxon Place Names

'Hengist and Horsa fought King Wyrtgeorn in the place called Agaeles threp and Horsa his brother was killed. After that Hengist took the kingdom, and Aesc his son.' In these words, under the year AD 455, the *Anglo-Saxon Chronicle* recorded the conquest of eastern Kent by the Jutes. This marked a significant change of barbarian policy from raiding for loot to conquest for settlement. After the middle of the fifth century AD boat-loads of Jutes, Angles, and Saxons began to arrive in family or tribal groups. If necessary they would fight for territory, but the main purpose of the majority was to seek the best farmland they could find, settle on it and cultivate the soil.

Under the year AD 477 the *Chronicle* records the arrival of the Saxons: 'Aelle came to Britain and his three sons, Cymen, Wlencing and Cissa with three ships at the place called Cymenes ora and there they slew many Welsh.' The coming of the people later known as the West Saxons is recorded under the year AD 495, when 'The chieftains came to Britain, Cerdic and Cynric his son . . . and fought the Welsh'. A whole generation was to pass before northern England appeared in this catalogue of landings. Then the record for AD 547 reads: 'In this year, Ida, from whom the royal family of the Northumbrians took its rise, succeeded to the kingdom. And he reigned twelve years and he built Bamburgh which was first enclosed with a hedge and afterwards with a wall.' This was over a hundred years after the departure of the legions and the end of Roman rule – ample time for a Celtic resurgence.

The *Anglo-Saxon Chronicle* was not compiled until the ninth century; but it was written in Anglo-Saxon and its writers, in the Wessex of King Alfred, drew upon oral traditions that had been

42

cherished by generation after generation of their race, preserved by bards and minstrels, and listened to with critical attention by the descendants of those same pioneers. Doubtless the records are as biassed as they are tantalisingly short, but they give a vivid picture of a migration commencing with the arrival of small groups of warriors, a few shiploads at a time, under leaders of established reputation whom they had chosen voluntarily to follow. The significance of this in the formation of the place-names of the pioneer age is discussed later.

The settlement was a long one, continuing through several centuries, the pioneer phase being followed by phases of colonisation and consolidation. By the eighth century AD the scattered settlements of the pioneer stage had merged to form the seven kingdoms of the Anglo-Saxon Heptarchy. In the north the Anglian kingdoms of Deira and Bernicia had amalgamated into the realm of Northumbria, then extending from the Humber as far north as the Forth. Other bands of Angles had worked their way up the Humber and Trent, eventually forming the midland kingdom of Mercia. This name came from the Old English word *mearc*, a boundary, for Mercia was the frontier state, confining the Celtic lands to the west. To the east the kingdom of East Anglia had been formed by a merger of the North Folk and the South Folk – the Norfolk and Suffolk of today. The Saxon kingdoms lay to the south: Essex, Sussex and Wessex, the lands of the East, South and West Saxons respectively.

In all these kingdoms a common Anglo-Saxon – Old English – tongue was spoken, wholly superseding the Celtic speech of Roman Britain. Britain, the land of the Britons, became England, the land of the Angles. The weekdays acquired new names based on the Germanic pantheon – Wednesday from Woden, the chief of the gods; Thursday from Thor, the god of thunder and war; Friday from the goddess Friga. In all parts of England small villages arose in which the wooden dwellings were grouped around a village green or, later, around the church. New social ranks appeared, distinguished by graded 'wergilds' – compensatory payments due to a family for the murder of a kinsman. By the eighth century the paganism of the earlier phase had been replaced by Christianity and the Old English word *cirice*, church, was becoming an element in place-name formation.

Some Common Anglian Place-Names

To stress the density of Anglo-Saxon settlement in southern England, the late Sir Mortimer Wheeler once remarked that the destination-board of every London bus was covered with Anglo-Saxon place-names. A similar claim might be made for those of the Yorkshire buses but for the many Scandinavian place-names introduced subsequently by Danish and Norwegian immigrants. Nevertheless, the number of Anglian names still surviving in Yorkshire is considerable. Three-fifths of the place-names recorded in the Domesday Book folios for the county stem from Anglian origins.

Once an Anglian family had taken over its share of land the prime need was to get a roof over its head, the characteristic type of house having a timber frame with walls of packed clay and a roof of rush-thatch or turf. There was a variety of terms for such dwellings – *tun, ham, worth, burh, cot*. These were then not mere synonyms, though today we are not familiar with the differences implied. All have entered widely into place-name formation, and as these terms refer to habitations of one sort or another, the place-names of which they form an element are classified as habitative, as distinct from names descriptive of local geographical features.

The element most widely found in the place-names of today is *tun*, A. H. Smith listing no less than 180 in the area of the West Riding alone. The term originally denoted an enclosure, a homestead, or farmstead, though its meaning soon broadened to include a village or even a town. Thus Sutton Bank, that steep hill between Thirsk and Helmsley so well known to motorists, derives its name from the *Sudtune* of Anglo-Saxon days – the south homestead. It shares this derivation with many other Suttons: Sutton-on-Derwent, some six miles south-east of York; Sutton-on-the-Forest, a similar distance north of York; a Sutton north of Doncaster;

and many others. Almost as frequent is Norton – the north homestead.

Hutton is another place-name in *-tun* that frequently occurs. There are no less than eighteen in the North Riding area. All were recorded in Domesday Book as *Hotun*, from the Old English (Anglo-Saxon) *hoh* and *tun*, high farmstead. Hutton-le-Hole, the pretty village near Lastingham which attracts so many summer visitors to the North York Moors, entered history as 'the farmstead on the hill'. The element appears in slightly modified form in Hooton Roberts, the name of a hamlet on the Rotherham–Doncaster road. The term was often treated as relative: the parish of Huttons Ambo, for instance, which straddles the A64 three miles south-west of Malton in the Vale of Pickering, contains within its boundary the village of High Hutton which is only 150ft higher than Low Hutton on the bank of the River Derwent.

Other names in *-tun* or *-ton* apply to lowland sites, as in Marton, a place-name which also occurs frequently. In many such cases the first element originated in the Old English word *mere*, which denoted 'a pool or lake', the full name referring to 'the homestead by the pool'. Long Marston, a village seven miles west of York, was recorded by the Domesday scribes as *Mersetone*, from the Old English (Anglo-Saxon) words *mersc* and *tun* – the *tun* on the marsh. The term often enters into the names of settlements on streams. Compounded with *ea*, the Anglo-Saxon word for stream, it has given us Great Ayton on the River Leven south of Middles-brough, and West and East Ayton, twin villages on the Derwent west of Scarborough. Airton on the upper Aire similarly began as 'the farmstead on the Aire'. Bolton Abbey, whose ruins attract visitors to Wharfedale, appears in Domesday Book as *Bodeltune*, of which the first element came from the Old English word *botl* or bothl, 'a dwelling'. The addition of *tun* to this name is another instance of place-name tautology.

Place-names in *-ham* occur less frequently in Yorkshire than those in *-tun*, not because they denoted less important places, but because the term ceased to be used in place-name formation relatively early, falling out of use by the eighth century; *tun* continued to enter into place-names for another century or more. Like *tun*, *ham* first meant homestead but later widened its meaning to include village settlement. As this element is the subject of discussion in the following chapter, only a few illustrative examples are mentioned here. Middleham Castle, which commanded the entrance into Wensleydale, was built in the twelfth century. But a more peaceful settlement existed there long before that, for in 1086 Domesday Book records a *Medelei*, which had become *Middelham* by 1184 – the middle settlement. The Domesday version of Rotherham was *Rodreham*, which was known as 'the settlement on the Rother' from the start. Examples from East Yorkshire relate mostly to villages. A well-known one is Kirkham, between York and Malton, famous for the ruins of its old priory at the entrance to the picturesque gorge cut in the local limestone by the River Derwent. The first syllable originated from the Old English *cirice*, church – a village with a church. Harpham, between Bridlington and Driffield, became known as 'the harpist's homestead', from the Old English *hearpe*, harpist.

The element *worth* frequently appears in the place-names of the former West Riding, though rarely elsewhere in the county. This absence from the North and East Ridings is not necessarily proof that settlements so named were not made there in Anglo-Saxon times; it probably means that the names were modified later by the Scandinavian immigrants. The term *worth*, with the allied *worthig*, denoted an enclosure or dwelling. There is extant a law of Ine, a seventh-century king of Wessex, ordering the husbandman 'to keep his *worthig* fenced', to prevent damage caused by escaping animals. The term appears in Haworth, the name of the village where the Brontës lived. The first element is probably derived from the Old English word *haga*, a hedge, the full name thus indicating 'a hedged enclosure'. Ackworth, known for its Quaker school near Pontefract, is thought to have drawn the first element of its name from the Old English word for oak-tree, *ac*. Heworth, on the north-eastern fringe of the City of York, formed its name from a compound of *worth* with *heah*. The latter was an Old English word meaning high; but as there is little high ground around York, the term in this instance is best interpreted in the sense of 'the chief' – the main enclosure or dwelling.

In many place-names of the West Riding the element *worth* is compounded with Anglian personal names. Cudworth and Hemsworth, both north-east of Barnsley, and Wadworth, south of Doncaster, began as the enclosures of *Cutha*, *Hymel* and *Wadda* respectively. This frequent association with personal names calls for comment, for it implies that the enclosures so named were in individual possession at a time when it is generally assumed that village farming was a communal activity in the common fields of the village community.

The suffix *cot*, often used in the plural *cotes*, was an Anglo-Saxon term denoting the smallest, humblest and roughest of habitations. It is usually translated as cottage, though the word was normally applied to any rough wooden hut, or even to a shelter for sheep and other farm animals. A simple illustration is in the name Coatham, the western suburb of Redcar. Today the new steel complex of the twentieth century looks across the sand-dunes towards the spot known in the twelfth century as *Cotum* – at the cottages. The same element is hidden in the name Cargo Fleet, today an industrial suburb of Middlesbrough, a few miles away. The name was first recorded in the thirteenth century as *Kaldecotes*, from the Old English words *cald* and *cotes*, the cold huts. The 'Fleet' is the modern form of the Old English *fleot*, stream, a reference to the River Tees. The name thus denoted 'the cold huts by the river', in vivid contrast with the steel furnaces there today.

Another habitative element appearing in Anglo-Saxon place-names is *burh* or *burg*. It was commonly applied to any form of fortified site, whether of contemporary construction, the ruins of a Romano-British fort, or even the earthworks of prehistoric times. It enters into the place-names of today in several forms – borough, burgh, brough and, through the dative form *byric*, as bury. A number of these names are associated with the sites of Roman settlements. The Romano-British ferry-town on the Humber was known as *Petuaria* while it was thriving and full of activity; the

47

Angles found it a heap of ruins when they arrived and applied to it their term *burh*, which has now become Brough. There can be little doubt about the derivation of the name Aldborough, the township just off the Great North Road by Boroughbridge. It occupies the site of the Romano-British town *Isurium Brigantum*, already mentioned in the previous chapter as the cantonal capital of the Brigantes. By the time the Angles arrived on the scene it was already in ruins, and they called it the '*eald burh*' – 'the old fort'.

The Angles came upon another 'old fortification' in Holderness, to which they gave the same name, though we spell it today as Aldbrough. About 60 miles further north, on the moorland coast, at the south-eastern side of Runswick Bay, the basal mound of one of the Roman signal stations can still be discerned on the cliff-top near the disused railway station. As might be expected, the site commands extensive views in both directions along a magnificent coastline. The Roman name for the station is not known; its present one is Goldsbrough. It was noted in Domesday Book as *Golborg*, and in another, contemporary document as *Goldeburg*, from which the name has been traced back to an original Anglo-Saxon personal name *Golda*. The *burh* element suggests that in Golda's day the ruins were still recognisable as some form of military site. In general, however, the term was not restricted to Roman remains. The second element in the name of the Pennine peak Ingleborough refers to the Celtic ramparts still visible on the summit.

In the West Riding, a group of borough names appears west of Doncaster, comprising Conisbrough, Sprotbrough, Mexborough and others. The etymology of Mexborough printed at the end of this chapter shows that the name originally came from the Old English personal name *Meoc* and marked '*Meoc*'s fortified site'. Conisbrough was entered in Domesday Book in 1086 as *Cuninges-berg*, from the Old English *cyning*, king – the king's stronghold. Dewsbury preserves the dative form *byric*, though the derivation of the first element is less certain. Knaresborough on the River Nidd was known in Domesday times as *Chenaresburg* – the *burh* of a man known as *Cenheard*. Almonbury, now the southern suburb of Huddersfield, was entered in Domesday Book as *Almaneberie* – the *burh* of all the men. This looks like a reference to the site of one of those popular assemblies or folk-moots that were a feature of Anglo-Saxon life.

But more than normal caution is needed in attaching a date to the formation of place-names in -*burh*. They can, and often do, indicate a quite early formation, as illustrated by Aldborough, which merited such a name even when the Angles first came to the district. But *Meoc*'s *burh* at Mexborough and the *burh* at Dewsbury may well have denoted fortified manor houses built at a much later date by two prospering medieval farmers or merchants. A royal fortification, such as *Cuningesberg*, might have been constructed and named at any time. Hillsborough, now part of Sheffield, has little to do with any fortified site of any age. The name does not appear in the records until the sixteenth century, and then simply as *Hylls*, from the Old English word *hyll*, hill. The element 'borough' is a deliberate addition of modern times. Equally suspect is the name Templeborough in the area of the West Riding. Today the name certainly applies to the site of a Roman fort on the south bank of the River Don, and to that extent the derivation of the *burh* element may be justified. But as late as the eighteenth century, the name remained as simply Burgh Hill. The addition of 'Temple', suggested A. H. Smith, was an antiquarian invention of that century.

Another habitative word used by the Angles and Saxons that may cause confusion is *wic*. In most cases it is synonymous with homestead or farm, and often came to denote a certain degree of agricultural specialisation. The term survives in the final element of such names as Burstwick in Holderness and Earswick near York, but it is impossible to tell whether it was used in its special sense of 'a dairy farm' or in its more general sense of 'a dwelling'. The other elements incorporate the Anglian personal names *Brusti* and *Aethelric* respectively. Berwick, a small hamlet in the West Riding, shares an origin with Berwick-on-Tweed as a *bere-wic* – a corn or barley farm. But *wic* has recently been shown to have entered into the Anglo-Saxon vocabulary as a loan-word from the Britons who in their turn had borrowed it from the Latin *vicus* of Roman times. The significance of this aspect of the word will be treated more fully when the place-name Wykeham is examined in the following chapter. Further, any of these meanings of the Anglo-Saxon word *wic* can easily be confused with the Scandinavian word *vik* which was introduced several centuries later, and which denoted a bay or creek. Dairy-farm, however, is the normal translation, as in Butterwick, the name of a hamlet on the River Rye in the Vale of Pickering. The name comes from two Old English words, *butere* and *wic* – the dairy-farm with rich pastures.

Anglo-Saxon Topographic and Descriptive Place-Names in Yorkshire

As countrymen our Anglo-Saxon ancestors had keen eyes for landscape, and their place-names abound with allusions to scenic detail. The name of the new County of Cleveland preserves almost intact the Old English word *clif*, used of steep, rocky slopes and cliffs. Nothing could be more appropriate as a description of the North York Moors, in both their moorland and coastal aspects. More subtle was the observation of the ridge of volcanic rock that can still be traced crossing the North York Moors in a surprisingly straight line from west of Great Ayton near Middlesbrough to the coast by Robin Hood's Bay. The hard volcanic rock that welled up and solidified in this ancient fissure has been so vigorously quarried in recent years for road-metal that the ridge today has become a deep cleft throughout its length. This cleft is clearly visible above Great Ayton; beside the railway station at Castleton; and at Sil Howe, the tumulus beside the road to Goathland from Sleights Hill. The Angles appropriately called the ridge the *lang beorg* – the long hill – a name that has come down to us little changed as Langbaurgh, now revived in the title of an administrative district within the new county.

Anyone familiar with the upland areas of Yorkshire will not be surprised to find that the Old English word *hrycg*, ridge, appears as an element in many a place-name. Rigton derives its name from a simple combination of the two Old English words *hrycg* and *tun* – the farmstead on the ridge. It was an apt name for a settlement situated on the high ground between the depression that today carries the railway from Harrogate to Otley on one side and the valley of the Nar Beck on the other. A similar derivation accounts for the name of the coastal village of Reighton, between Filey and Flamborough Head, on the ridge that ends in Speeton Cliff. Askrigg in Wensleydale was entered as *Ascric* in Domesday Book – the ash ridge. The second element of Marrick, the name of a village in Swaledale, is probably the Anglian word *hrycg* in disguise, for Ekwall explains this name as a Scandinavian version of the Old English *(ge)maer-hrycg* – the boundary ridge.

Sites on the side-slopes of hills and ridges were often favoured for settlement. Liversedge, between Leeds and Huddersfield, was recorded in Domesday Book as *Livresec*, from a combination of the personal name *Leofhere* and the Old English word *ecg*, also meaning a ridge – *Leofhere*'s ridge. On the eastern fringes of Halifax the twin villages of Southowram and Northowram occupy sites opposite each other high up on the flanks of the deep valley of the Red Beck. In Domesday times there was only one village, recorded simply as *Oure* or *Overe* from an old word *owram*, which in turn had been developed from the earlier Old English form *aet uferum* – on the slope.

Often a ridge slope descends by one or more steps, the more resistant strata standing out in a series of natural benches. These more or less level terraces provided sites for many an Anglian settlement. The Old English term for such natural terraces was *scylf*, and frequently settlements upon them were recorded in Domesday Book as *Schelton* – the *tun* on the shelf or terrace. The later hardening of the soft 'sch' sound under Scandinavian influence has produced the modern form of Skelton. Places of that name are found in all parts of Yorkshire today: on the north bank of the lower Ouse near Goole; north-west of York; between Boroughbridge and Ripon; and on the Pennine moors between Richmond and Reeth. The original Anglian term *scylf* is preserved almost intact in the place-name Shelf, borne by a village situated at a height of 850ft between Halifax and Bradford. It can be traced in Shelley, the name of a village some five miles south-east of Huddersfield. Entered in Domesday Book as *Sciuelei*, the name had become *Scheflay* by the thirteenth century. The original name was compounded of *scylf* with *leah*, an Anglian word for a clearing, to give the full meaning as 'the clearing on the terrace'. The curious name of Crigglestone, given to a village on the high ground above Wakefield, is explained by its upland situation. Entered in Domesday Book as *Crigestone*, it embodied the Old English words *cryc*, *hyll* and *tun*. Each of the first two elements meant a hill, *cryc* being a loan-word from the Celtic *cruc*, hill. The whole name meant 'the farmstead on the hill'.

Valleys had a special interest for Anglian settlers, since they provided relatively easy routes among the uplands while offering well-watered, flat land for cultivation and cattle-raising. Consequently their word *dael* occurs frequently in the place-names of today as the modern ending dale. It is especially common in the area of the West Riding, where streams descending the eastern flanks of the Pennines have eroded many a valley. Unfortunately, it is rarely possible to distinguish between names derived from the Old English form *dael* and those from the Scandinavian form *dalr*, introduced some centuries later. Airedale is likely to have been an Anglian formation, and we have the authority of A. H. Smith in tracing back the name North Dalton, between Driffield and Market Weighton, to the Old English *dael* – the *tun* in the dale. There is another example in Farndale in the North York Moors, where people from all parts of Yorkshire gather each springtime to admire the impressive show of wild daffodils. What impressed our ancestors, however, were the wild ferns, for their name combined the Old English elements *fearn* and *dael* – the valley of the ferns.

But the alternative Old English word for a valley – *denu* – is free from such ambiguity, and many a place-name ending today in *-den* can be traced back to this term. Hebden Bridge in the upper Calder valley developed its name from a combination of the Old English *heope* and *denu*. We still retain the former in our word for the fruit of the wild rose – hip. To our ancestors it was a 'valley of wild roses'. Still further upstream is Todmorden, a small town of character close to the Lancashire border. Its name originated from a combination of three Anglian words – *Totta*, a personal name; (*ge*)*maer*, a boundary; and *denu* – *Totta*'s boundary valley. Marsden, a village between Huddersfield and Bradford, similarly began as another 'boundary dale'.

Rivers were equally important to Anglian settlers. They were sources of water-supply, without which no settlement could survive; their water-meadows gave lush pastures and hay for those animals that could be kept through the winter; and their valleys provided flat land for tillage. Negatively, they were obstacles that had to be crossed by fords or bridges. It is not surprising, therefore, that place-names contain many references to streams and waterways. Linton, near Skipton in upper Wharfedale, where the infant stream flows swiftly, was originally 'the *tun* on the *hlynn*', an Old English word for torrent. Reeth, in upper Swaledale, has a name which has descended virtually unaltered in pronunciation if not in spelling, from the Old English *rith*, a small stream. The reference was probably to the Arkle Beck on the banks of which Reeth stands, a little above its confluence with the Swale. The Prissick Farm Estate, where until recently Middlesbrough held its international eisteddfod each year, incorporates another Old English word for stream, *sic*, combined with *preost* – the priest's stream. Three villages in the area of the former West Riding share the name Sykehouse, 'the house on the stream'. Elland, on the River Calder south of Halifax, seems to have developed from an early site on an island in the river, for the name *Elant*, as it is recorded in Domesday Book, is derived from the Old English word *ealand*, an island. Riverside pastures were especially important, and in northern England the Old English word *halh* or *healh*, which carried a variety of meanings, developed a special one, being applied to a piece of alluvial land beside a river. We still use the word 'haughs' for these water-meadows. The term forms the final element in the names of Killinghall, between Harrogate and Ripley, and Burnsall, in upper Wharfedale. A. H. Smith lists

53

over fifty place-names from the former West Riding area alone that incorporate this element.

Even small riverine features were used to coin distinctive local names. The North York Moorland stream, the Esk, provides several examples. It has no single source, but is formed by the convergence of several small headwaters at the upper end of Westerdale. Visitors to the ancient monument called Ralph's Cross or the neighbouring memorial stone erected recently to the local archaeologist Elgee on Castleton Rigg can look down into the combe where these streams merge. The present name is Eskletts, the final element of which is drawn from the Old English (ge)laete, a term applied to just such a junction of headwater streams. A little further downstream is Dibble Bridge, a mile west of Castleton. This name has been formed from three Old English words: bryc, bridge; deop, deep; and hylr, pool. The 'bridge by the deep pool' is to this day a perfect description of this delectable spot. Still further downstream, as the Esk approaches the leafy village of Lealholm, its course is deflected from the relatively broad and flat vale through which it has been flowing, into a narrow ravine with steep, wooded side-slopes, known today as Crunkley Gill. Our ancestors may not have known that this diversion had been caused 20,000 years ago by a thick deposit of boulder-clay blocking the normal channel at the end of the last ice age, but they noticed it as an unusual feature. They called it Crubeclif – the ravine of the crooked cliff.

Before the development of agricultural drainage much of the low-lying land was damp and marshy, a feature reflected in many an Anglian place-name. Marske today is a popular dormitory town attractively placed by the sea amid the farmlands of the coastal flats between Redcar and Saltburn. Its site was less alluring in the days of its first Anglian settlers, who referred to the area quite bluntly as Mersc – the marsh. The neighbouring farmlands are still criss-crossed by drainage ditches dug in the eighteenth and nineteenth centuries to bring the marsh under cultivation. The hardening of the soft Anglo-Saxon 'sc' sound in the original name, as indicated in the accompanying etymology, is the subject of discussion in a later chapter. The Old English pronunciation still persists in The Marishes, the name of a parish in the low-lying alluvial flats at the confluence of the rivers Rye and Derwent in the Vale of Pickering, once covered with extensive marshes.

Marston Moor, the site of the Roundhead victory near York in 1644, derived its name from a combination of *mersc* and *tun* – the homestead in the marsh. Sledmere House is popular today as part of a visit to the High Wolds. The name comes from the Old English words *slaed* and *mere*. *Slaed* was another of the Anglian synonyms for valley, while *mere* has retained both spelling and meaning, to justify a rendering of Sledmere as 'the lake in the valley'. Seamer, a short distance inland from Scarborough, has not greatly changed its name since the end of the eleventh century, when it was entered in Domesday Book as *Semaer*, from the Old English *sae*, lake, and *mere*, pool. The second element was added presumably as the first passed out of common use. The same source *mere* has given us Semer Water, the name of the largest natural lake in Yorkshire, in the heart of the Pennine moors south of Bainbridge in Wensleydale. In this name we have an instance of triple tautology, all three elements *sae*, *mere* and *water* having the same meaning.

The Personal Element in Anglo-Saxon Place-Names

As might be expected, personal names enter frequently into the formation of Anglo-Saxon place-names, and several examples of both habitative and topographical names have already been quoted in illustration. East of Barnsley, for instance, lies the mining village of Silkstone which has given its name to a famous seam of coal. The settlement here began as *Sigelac's Tun*. Royston, north of Barnsley, appears in the Domesday record as *Rorestun(e)*, from an Old English nickname *Hror*, meaning strong, vigorous, and *tun*. Sheltering at the foot of the north-facing escarpment of the Wolds lies the village of Ganton. It was recorded in Domesday Book as *Galmeton* – the *tun* of *Galma*, an Anglian settler. Those who have travelled on the picturesque railway line on the North York Moors between Pickering and Grosmont will recall two stations named Lockton and Levisham. The villages served by those halts began as 'the *tun* of *Loca*' and 'the *ham* of *Leofgeat*' respectively.

The personal name is not always compounded with *tun* or *ham*. Pudsey, to the west of Leeds, was registered in Domesday Book as *Podechesaie*. The first element was a personal name, *Pudoc;* the second comes from the Old English *eg*, island. The neighbouring Ossett was recorded by the Domesday clerks as *Osleset*. Here Ekwall suggests that the personal name *Osla* is compounded with the Old English word (*ge*)*set*, denoting a fold or enclosure for keeping sheep in. Similarly, the name Wakefield is thought originally to refer to the *feld* of an individual called *Waca*.

Personal names are also found attached to the Old English word *leah*, applied to clearings and glades in woodland, as in Ilkley and Helmsley. Ilkley derives its name from *Illica's leah* – *Illic's* clearing. Otley began as '*Otta's* clearing'. In the Aire valley, clearings by *Cyhha* and *Gislica* have given us the names Keighley and Guiseley. Similarly, Helmsley, the small but attractive market town picturesquely situated where the River Rye emerges from the North York Moors to enter the Vale of Pickering, derives its name from a clearing made by a man named *Helm*.

Several Yorkshire place-names are formed by the linking of a personal name to the Anglo-Saxon *halh*, which we have already seen was applied in northern England to haughs or water-meadows. Killinghall and Burnsall have already been quoted as examples. Bedale, a typical small Yorkshire market town at the eastern approaches to Wensleydale, has a name which has scarcely changed since the time of William the Conqueror, for it was recorded in Domesday Book by a spelling identical with that of today. Its name has been formed from a combination of the Old English personal name *Beda* with *halh* – *Beda's* water-meadow.

The late Sir Frank Stenton, an authority on both Anglo-Saxon history and English place-names, long ago expressed the conclusion that the large proportion of place-names in which personal names form an important element illustrates the strongly individual aspect of Anglo-Saxon rural society. They present, however, a more difficult problem when we come to consider the status of the individual in the settlement to which he gave his name. If the settlement was that of a simple farmstead, it is likely, but by no means certain, that the personal name belonged to the individual who first possessed or developed the site. It is reasonable, for instance, to suppose that when Illic and Helm cut down the trees and cleared the undergrowth and brushwood from their chosen *leahs*, their neighbours called the newly-made clearings after them. It is equally tempting to see the family name of the hero who led a pioneer band – such as those quoted in the extracts from the *Anglo-Saxon Chronicle* with which this chapter opened – in the personal element in some of the earlier Anglo-Saxon place-names. It is likely that the warrior who had successfully seized some territory would continue to lead his followers in establishing their settlement, as *Hasta* seems to have done at Hastings and *Wurth* at Worthing. But even with early place-names there is little certainty; and still less in the case of the many settlements formed in the later phases of the migration.

Reference to the etymology shows that the first element in Northallerton, the name of the county town formerly of the North Riding and now of North Yorkshire, was added in the fourteenth century. In Domesday Book it was entered as plain *Aluretun*, a name which had developed from the personal name *Alfhere* and *tun* – *Alfhere*'s settlement. It is interesting to speculate upon the part that Alfhere played in the life of the early village: there are several possibilities. It is likely that in some manner or other he was a conspicuous figure in the village that bore his name. He may have been the leader of a band who seized the land and settled thereon. He may have been an ordinary Anglian peasant who was the first to set up a farmstead there – a farmstead that flourished enough to attract so many neighbours that a village grew on the site. He may in some other manner have impressed his neighbours to such an extent that they began to refer to the settlement as '*Alfhere*'s *tun*'. Another possibility is that he was a later arrival, one who subsequently acquired legal and economic power over the settlement and its inhabitants as lord of the manor.

The speculation is not an idle one. Historians have long debated whether the social life of Anglo-Saxon England began in servitude to powerful leaders and slowly grew in course of time towards individual freedom, or whether an original freedom that may have characterised the pioneer stage was gradually eroded away, lost to manorial overlords whose power increased during late Anglo-Saxon times until it was finally established by the Norman barons. Place-names sometimes throw light on this problem. H. P. R. Finburg has called attention to the large grants of land made by the Anglo-Saxon kings from the royal domain – to establish their sons in life, and to the gesiths of the royal bodyguard and the Church. From one cause or another, the royal domain thus became increasingly alienated. But as Finburg points out, though this process may have impoverished the Crown it greatly enriched local nomenclature, as the personal names of the new owners so often became attached to the existing names of the villages. Margaret Gelling quotes an example for which there exists confirmatory evidence from written records. It is known that Edward the Confessor granted the manor of East Garston in Berkshire to his 'staller', an officer in charge of the royal stables, Esgar by name. This personal name became thus attached to that of the *tun*, to give the first element in the name we know today. The connection is clearly recognisable in the Domesday record, *Esgareston* – *Esgar*'s *tun*. But this is only one of many ways in which a man could achieve a personal eminence which would lead to the linking of his name to that of a village. The conclusion reached years ago by the late Sir Frank Stenton still holds good: 'The essential fact is that in regard to numberless English villages we have to reckon with a lord of some kind as an integral and original force in the development of the agrarian community.'

Sources for Anglo-Saxon Place-Names

For the earliest, pagan phase of the Anglo-Saxon migration the written materials that have survived are so few and obscure that we speak of the fifth and sixth centuries AD as belonging to the Dark Ages. This is especially unfortunate for place-name study, since it denies knowledge of the earliest forms of the names of places involved in these critical years when the invaders were landing and establishing their first settlements. For such early forms we have to rely upon chance references in the works of later writers. For the later phases of the settlement the flow of contemporary material increased, reflecting the growth of learning in the monasteries established after the age of conversion, and the increasing use of written records by the secular authorities.

For the earlier phases we have the place-names that are mentioned in the biographies of such Anglo-Saxon ecclesiastics as Cedd of Lastingham, Wilfred of Ripon and Hild, Abbess of Whitby. Of the monastic writers of this period, the most famous was Bede, who achieved a European reputation as a historian. Though he spent all his life in the monastery of Jarrow on the Tyne, he not only had access to a variety of ancient writings in the monastery library, by Celtic as well as Anglo-Saxon authors, but he also gathered information from the various monasteries with which he corresponded. His *History of the English Church and People* was completed in AD 731, shortly before his death. Though written in Latin it gives the names of the Anglo-Saxon settlements in the forms used in the eighth century. But on occasion Bede refers to a locality in a still more archaic form. When he wrote of a monastery as situated *Inhrypum*, he was using a form embodying the ancient tribal name of *Hrype*, thus carrying our knowledge of the origins of the name Ripon back to the very earliest phase of the migration, when tribal bands were settling themselves in this country. Similarly his reference to *Ingetlingum* used a form of the place-name known to us as Gilling that was already ancient in his day, taking us back to the early days of the settlement by the Anglian band who called themselves the *Getlingas*. His writing the name *Lastingas* assures us that such a form of the present-day name Lastingham was in general use within a century of the foundation of the monastery there by St Cedd. Bede's term for the place we know as Catterick was *Cataractam uicum*, confirming that the name if not the occupation of the Romano-British town continued into the Anglo-Saxon era.

After the eighth century the monastic material was augmented from several sources. The *Anglo-Saxon Chronicle*, begun towards the end of the ninth century under the inspiration of Alfred of Wessex, not only recorded the West Saxon traditions, but continued the annals throughout the rest of the period into Norman times. At about the same time, the Anglo-Saxon 'charter' came into general use – a royal document issued to authenticate a grant of land by the king. Applied at first mainly to ecclesiastic bodies, such charters were soon extended to lay recipients. As many of these documents, especially those of later years, included detailed descriptions of the boundaries of the estates concerned, they provide a valuable source of place-names from all parts of the country.

By far the most useful source of information on the place-names of Anglo-Saxon history, however, was compiled at the end of the reign of the Norman king, William I. The *Chronicle* tells us that while spending the Christmas of 1085 at Gloucester, 'William held important deliberations and exhaustive discussion with his council about this land.' As a result, commissioners were despatched to every part of his newly-acquired realm to collect information, village by village, as to its value. The investigation was so detailed that in many areas the route taken by the investigating clerks can still be traced from the information recorded. Though Domesday Book was essentially a record of the taxable wealth of England at the end of the eleventh century and in no way a gazetteer, it is still a rich source of place-names. It has been estimated that more than two-thirds of the names of places still inhabited today are recorded in it, all in their eleventh-century forms.

But the use of Anglo-Saxon language did not come to an end with the Norman Conquest. Many a village was given a name in the early Middle Ages by communities familiar with the Anglo-Saxon tongue. It follows that the records from the Middle Ages are not to be despised as sources of information on place-names, even for those dating back to Saxon times. For a medieval source may mention a name that has never before been recorded. Moreover, while it is obviously safer to infer the original form of a place-name from a form recorded in the Anglo-Saxon period before the eleventh century, trained philologists are able to trace the sound changes back from a later record when no other is available.

A brief mention of the main post-Domesday records may help one to understand how the dates have been assigned to the forms quoted in the etymologies printed in the standard reference books which may be consulted on the subject. The early Middle Ages saw the Chancery and Exchequer courts slowly emerging from the amorphous writing departments of the earlier Saxon kings. Each began to keep its own records. Those of the Exchequer became known as the Pipe Rolls, from their appearance after they had been rolled up for storage at Westminster. They recorded revenue payments made to the king through the sheriff of each county, and so include references to place-names from all parts of the realm. Other details of royal business were similarly recorded in the Close Rolls and the Patent Rolls. As the judicial system of the realm was developed, the records of the Curia Regis and of the Judges in Circuit provide place-names in contemporary form. The Inquisitions Post Mortem and the Coroner's Rolls are important sources of minor names, and, sadly, of river-names. As commerce developed and towns grew in wealth and importance, urban archives provide a valuable additional source, to which can be added the increasing number of manorial court rolls and surveys of private estates, both ecclesiastical and lay.

Finally, parish surveys and accounts of the perambulations of parish boundaries, so necessary in days before maps were common, add to our list of place-names in their medieval forms.

Abbreviated Etymologies

Cleveland
1104 Clyveland(a)
1304 Clieveland
Klifland in a
  Scandinavian saga
OE *clif*: land
district of steep slopes
**Great Ayton (NR, now North
Yorks)**
DB   1086 Atun(a)
     1129 Aton(a)
     1160 Etonam
     1202 Haiton
     1226 Atton
OE *ea*: river
OE *tun*: farmstead,
       settlement
**Masham (NR, now North
Yorks)**
DB   1086 Massan
     1153 Masham
     1233 Mesham
     1251 Masseham
     1286 Massam
OE personal name *Maessa*
OE *ham*: homestead
**Ackworth (WR, now West
Yorks)**
DB   1086 Aceuurde
     1201 Akeworth
OE personal name *Acca*
OE *worth*: homestead
**Dewsbury (WR, now West
Yorks)**
DB   1086 Deusberia
     1202 Deubir
     1226 Dewesbiri
     1267 Deaubir
Old Welsh personal name *Dewi*
OE *burh*: fortified place

**Langaurgh (NR, now
Cleveland)**
DB   1086 Langeberg(e)
     1166 Lankeberga
     1226 Langebrigg
     1231 Langebergh(e)
     1273 Langeberewe
     1599 Langbarffe
     1612 Langbarghe
OE *lang*: long
OE *beorg*: hill

**Marske (NR, now North
Yorks)**
     1043 Merscum
DB   1086 Mersc
     1180 Merske
     1218 Mers
     1285 Marske
OE *mersc*: marsh

**Bridlington (ER, now
Humberside)**
DB   1086 Bretlinton
     1119 Bridelinton
     1203 Breddelington
     1235 Briddelington
OE personal name *Beorhtel*
OE *tun*: farmstead

**Mexbrough (WR, now
South Yorks)**
DB   1086 Mechesburg
     1119 Mekesburc(h)
     1196 Mekeburc
     1263 Mikesburg
     1362 Mexseburgh
Scandinavian personal name *Meoc*
OE *burh*: fortified place

DB: Domesday Book   OE: Old English, Anglo-Saxon

4

The Anglian Settlement

At the beginning of this century it was generally thought that the Britons, having mounted a feeble resistance to the invaders, escaped death at the hands of the Angles and Saxons only by abandoning their farms and fleeing to the west where the Celtic kingdoms in Wales and Cumbria continued to offer a measure of protection. The historian Freeman had written: 'There is every reason to believe that the Celtic inhabitants of those parts of Britain which had become English at the end of the sixth century had been as nearly exterminated as a nation can be.' But the publication in 1928 of Ekwall's impressive study *English River Names* rendered that view untenable. In this work he convincingly demonstrated that in many parts of England, especially in the North, Midlands and Wessex, the Celtic names of innumerable rivers and streams had survived the Anglo-Saxon invasion and had passed into the Old English speech. He concluded that 'the old theory of a wholesale extermination or displacement of the British population is no doubt erroneous or exaggerated'. He wrote as a philologist, and since then a growing body of evidence has been gathered by archaeologists and historians, as well as by place-name scholars, which suggests that a considerable number of Britons survived the invasion and even entered into the social and economic life of the Angles and Saxons, not always in a servile or semi-servile position.

To the evidence for the survival of Celtic place-names given in Chapter 2 and map 2 can be added that of English place-names which specifically refer to Britons or Welshmen. The Germanic peoples had encountered Celtic tribes on the continent and had already coined a word for them – *wealh*, plural *wealas, walas* –

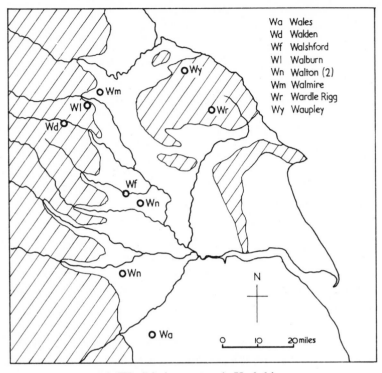

Wa	Wales
Wd	Walden
Wf	Walshford
Wl	Walburn
Wn	Walton (2)
Wm	Walmire
Wr	Wardle Rigg
Wy	Waupley

4 'Wealh' place-names in Yorkshire

foreigners. On their arrival in Britain, the Angles and Saxons applied this word to the Britons, and it is found in various forms in many place-names of today. It survives in its plural form *walas* in the name of the country Wales. It is to be found as the first element in such place-names as Walton and Walden. There are no less than nine examples in Yorkshire, the locations of which are plotted on map 4. The name Wales is actually borne by a village west of Worksop, just off the M18 between roundabouts 30 and 31. Two miles further west there is a neighbouring Waleswood. There are two places named Walton – one to the east of Wetherby, the other to the south-east of Wakefield. The Domesday Book entry gives the former as *Walitone* and the latter as *Waleton* – names which indicate an origin from 'the *tun* of the *Walas*', the settlement of the Welshmen or Britons. At a crossing over the lower Nidd is the village of Walshford, which is still recognisable in the present form of the name as 'the ford of the Welshmen', an interpretation confirmed by its earliest recording in the thirteenth century as *Walesford*.

In the neighbourhood of Catterick, itself bearing a Celtic name, are Walburn and Walmire. The former marked 'the brook of the Welsh', the latter 'the moor of the *Wealas*'. A mile or so below Aysgarth Falls in Wensleydale the River Ure is joined by a Walden Beck, which rises in Walden Moor and descends by the hamlet of Walden Head. The name is derived from *weala* and the Old English *denu*, a valley – the Welshman's or Welshmen's vale.

In the examples provided by the North York Moors the element is somewhat distorted. In the north it survives as Wapley or Wauple near Loftus. This name was first recorded in the early thirteenth century as *Walepol*, from which it has been traced back to a combination of *wealh* and *pol*, the Old English for pool – the pool of the Welshman or Welshmen. The other survival is in Wardle Rigg, on the southern moors. Its first recorded form, in the thirteenth century, was *Waldalerigg*, which is thought to stem from a combination of the Old English words *weala*, *dael* and *hrycg*, to denote, in reverse order, 'the ridge above the dale of the Welshmen'.

The argument is strengthened by linguistic evidence. As Stenton reminded the Royal Historical Society in 1938: 'the mere reproduction of isolated sounds conveyed in an unintelligible language would be very unlikely to preserve the original plural form of the British stream-name which has given rise to the place-name Wendover'. Such respect for grammatical niceties, which is to be found in examples from Yorkshire as well as from the Chilterns, suggests that, during the early period of the Anglian immigration, at least the bare elements of the Celtic tongue spoken by the native Britons were understood by many of the English newcomers. It supports the view that far from expropriation and extermination being the fate of the Britons, there must have been a good deal of economic and social intercourse.

In addition, there is historical and archaeological evidence to disprove the extermination theory, especially in northern England, where Celtic resistance was tenacious. No excavation of Romano-British villas so far undertaken in Yorkshire has shown that any of them came to a violent end; all seem to have become derelict from internal economic forces a generation or more before the Angles arrived from overseas. For a century after Ida had established himself and his followers in his stronghold at Bamburgh (AD 547), the Angles of Bernicia were confined to the coastal belt by the strong Celtic kingdom of Strathclyde, whose territories then extended from its capital at Dunbarton on the Firth of Clyde, across Cumbria and the Pennines to include northern Yorkshire. In South Yorkshire the Celtic kingdom of Elmet, centred on the magnesian limestone outcrop around Leeds and the lower Aire, retained its independence till well into the seventh century. There were, in effect, more than a hundred years during which contacts of a military, diplomatic, economic, commercial and even social nature could have been established, if only on a local and temporary basis, between the two races.

The historical evidence further suggests that the relationship was not necessarily hostile. In the south at least, the Britons enjoyed a special niche in the legal systems set up by the Germanic kingdoms. The early law codes of the Jutish Kingdom of Kent made provision for a special class of *laets* – British peasants descended from the native Romano-British population of the time of Hengist and Horsa. In Wessex, the laws of Ine show that in the seventh century there existed a class of free Celtic peasants who possessed the hide of land which was the normal holding of a Saxon freeman. In both realms the Britons, though regarded as of inferior status, were free men in no servile position. Like their Saxon and Jutish neighbours they were entitled to a wergild, and though this payment was fixed at a lower amount in their case, they had a legal right to the protection it was designed to give.

The genealogy of the West Saxon royal house, moreover, contained names that betray more than a slight element of Celtic influence; for example, *Cerdic* and *Cadwalla*, the latter an English version of the Celtic personal name *Cadwallon*. In Yorkshire, Caedmon, the humble cowherd of Whitby Abbey who was inspired to sing of the Creation in Old English verse to the astounded monks and nuns, bore a Celtic name. The historical record, no less than the place-name evidence, points to a lengthy period of linguistic contact between Britons and Anglo-Saxons – a period during which a not inconsiderable number of British families survived to be absorbed eventually into Anglo-Saxon society.

The Early Place-Names and Chronology of the Anglo-Saxon Immigration

The problem of tracing the course of the Anglo-Saxon invasion and of distinguishing areas settled by the pioneers from regions of later settlement has long exercised the minds of historians. Since the texts for the period significantly known as the Dark Ages are so few in number and obscure in matter, the hope has long been cherished that the developing study of place-names might shed some fresh light from a novel angle upon the chronology of the Anglo-Saxon migration. For instance, the practice of incorporating the term *ham* in place-names seems to have died out fairly early, in general by the end of the seventh century, while the element *tun* continued in use thereafter for several centuries. It follows that, as a very rough-and-ready guide, an area in which names in *-ham* are frequent is more likely to have been settled earlier than a region in which *tun* names predominate.

Some very early forms of place-names have been preserved in documents of a later period. Bede, for instance, writing about AD 730, referred to a gift by Oswy, King of Northumbria, to St Wilfred in AD 664 of a monastery with 40 hides of land. Bede gave *Inhrypum* as the location of this act. Bede's eighth-century use of a place-name in the form used a century earlier has preserved the ancient tribal name *Hrype*. Elsewhere Bede states that his own monastery of Jarrow was situated *juxta amnem tinam in loca quie uocatur in Gyrrum* (near the River Tyne where are the Gyrwe), thereby similarly preserving another ancient tribal name *Gyrwe*.

Such prefixes as *in* and *aet* are characteristic of archaic Anglo-

Saxon place-names and take us back to the earliest years of the migration. They often extend over a wide area and refer to the territories settled by a tribal group bearing that name. The present-day name Ripon thus indicates the area of settlement of an Old English folk-group known in their day as the *Hrype*. This is the only example of an Anglo-Saxon tribal name that has survived in Yorkshire. Hitchin in Hertfordshire and Wychwood in Oxford-shire preserve the names of two other early folk-groups – the *Hicce* and the *Hwicce* respectively.

Much more common than these relics of ancient tribal names are place-names ending in *-ing* and *inga,* or incorporating the dative form *ingum* or the plural *ingas*. Such Anglo-Saxon terms also indicate a folk-group, but one much smaller in size and associated by family as much as tribal ties. These elements are frequently found in combination with a personal name, in which case the place-name probably dates from an early phase in the migration. Pickering, the market town of the vale that bears its name, is entered in Domesday Book as *Piceringa* – a name that reverts to the *Piceringas*, 'the followers of *Picer*', so named in much the same manner as the Harrovians, Etonians or Mancunians of today. Gilling, today the village that gives its name to the gap between the North York Moors and the Howardian Hills, similarly derives its name from the *Getlingas* – the band of *Getla*. We have already seen that this name goes back to the early pioneer days as confirmed by its occurrence in Bede as *Ingetlingum*. Fylingdales, now known for its nuclear early-warning station on the moors between Whitby and Scarborough, was originally 'the settlement of the *Fygelingas*, the followers of *Fygela* or *Fygla*'.

The East Riding provides examples in Gembling and Fitling, both hamlets in Holderness. Gembling appears in Domesday Book as *Ghemelinge*, a reference to the *Gemelingas* – *Gemela* and his band. The name Fitling similarly takes us back to the *Fitlingas* – *Fitela*'s folk. In the West Riding, Headingley, now the home of Yorkshire cricket, was recorded in Domesday Book as *Hedingeleia*, originating from 'the *leah* or clearing of the *Hedingas*, the followers of *Hedde*'. Some four miles east of Barnsley the name of the village of Billingley is similarly interpreted as formerly 'the *leah* or clearing of the *Billingas*, the people of *Billa*'. Knottingley, on the Aire near Pontefract, originated as 'the *leah* of *Cnotta*'s people'. The unusual name Killinghall, of a village two miles north of Harrogate, can be interpreted as 'the *halh* (water-meadow) of the followers of *Cylla*'.

Not infrequently the element *inga* is found combined with the Old English *ham*, as in Lastingham, the name of the attractive village in the North York Moors where Cedd founded the monastery to which he retired to die in AD 664. We have seen that this name belonged to an early phase in the migration, borne out by its earliest surviving form found in Bede's *History* from where it appears as *Laestinga* – the *ham* of the *Laestingas*, 'the settlement of the leader *Last* and his dependants'. In the East Riding, Brantingham, a village to the north of Brough-on-Humber, similarly preserves the name of another Old English folk-group, the *Brantingas*, as 'the settlement of the followers of *Brant*'. Cottingham, the name of the northern suburb of Hull, was probably derived from 'the *ham* of *Cotta* and his followers'. The history of the name Goodmanham suggests that there were formerly many more such place-names than now survive. Today this name is borne by a small village on the edge of the southern Wolds near Market Weighton. In the seventh century it was important enough to have been the site of the royal residence of the kings of Deira. It is only by a single and chance reference to the place as *Godmundingaham* by Bede, writing in the eighth century, that the name is revealed to us as originally one of the *ingaham* type, denoting 'the settlement of the *Godmundingas*' – of *Godmund* and his followers.

From the place-name studies of the earlier decades of the present century a chronological pattern emerged, by which it seemed that the first settlements were marked by place-names ending in *-ing*, those of a later phase by names ending in *-ingaham*, while names in *-ham* and *-ton* were taken to indicate the foundation of still later settlements. The County of Sussex – the ancient kingdom of the South Saxons – was often quoted in illustration of this hypothesis. A line of *ing* names along the coast seemed to mark the sites of the first landings – of *Haesta* and his *Haestingas* at a spot we still call Hastings; of *Wurth* and his *Worthingas* at Worthing; of *Wlencing* at a spot that still preserves his name in Lancing. Names ending in *-ham* and *-ton* (*-tun*), such as Horsham and Clapham, were held to reflect the later settlement of the interior. Names in *-ington*, such as Storrington, Ashington and Chiltington, were regarded as intermediate in chronology as well as in situation.

The theory was not without support from recorded history. Haesta and Wlencing, and the latter's father Aella, were all mentioned by name in the accounts of the first landings given in the *Anglo-Saxon Chronicle*, which embodied the earliest traditions of the invaders. But after nearly fifty years of general acceptance, this hypothesis has come under heavy criticism from place-name scholars. One line of criticism has shown that the element *ham* in a place-name does not invariably indicate a settlement; it may have come from the equally common Anglo-Saxon word *hamm*, which was a descriptive term referring to a variety of natural features, such as the land enclosed in a river meander or a water-meadow. So far, Yorkshire has been found exempt from such confusion, except possibly with regard to some of the place-names in *-ham* in Holderness.

Yorkshire, however, is closely involved in the criticism of the hitherto accepted interpretation of the *ing* names as indicating a war-band of the heroic age. Research by Dr Margaret Gelling into the early place-names of Berkshire and Essex has shown that the term often carried a purely topographical or vegetational meaning. Clavering village in south-east Essex, for example, derived its name not from a band of early settlers but from the Old English word for clover, *claefre*. Other names in *-ing* in the neighbourhood referred to the creeks that abound in the marshes of the Thames estuary. She has shown conclusively that at least in some localities the *ing* element is descriptive of local landscape rather than indicative of a folk-group.

This has brought under review certain Yorkshire place-names

in -*ing*. One of the wapentakes – ancient administrative divisions of the East Riding – bears the name of Dickering. This was formerly thought to have indicated a folk-group known as the *Dikeringas* – followers of the leader *Diker*. It is now considered much more likely to be a descriptive name, compounded of the Old English words *dic*, dyke or ditch, and *hring*, ring, the whole name denoting 'a circular earthwork'. The many ancient ditches and ramparts in the vicinity, some circular and others straight, favour this new interpretation. Similarly, the -*ing* ending of Cleaving Grange, near Market Weighton, is now thought to be derived not from an Anglian folk-group but from the Old English topographical word *cliofung*, a cleft or fissure, a reference to the steep-sided ravine that is still visible in the Wolds at this spot. In the West Riding the name Cowling is no longer thought to represent an early settlement by a folk-group, especially as it lies so far inland. It probably took its name from the hill which rises behind it to a height of over 1,000ft, for Domesday Book records the name as *Collinghe*, from the Old English hill-name *Coll*, or possibly from the later Scandinavian version *Kollr*. In some instances the critical review has gone further, seeing in the *ing* element nothing more than a connecting particle between other elements in the name. Though the interpretation of the names Knottingley and Headingley as originating from references to the followers of *Cnotta* and *Hedde* carries the authority of Ekwall, it has recently been argued that the *ing* element in both these names has no greater significance than that of a connecting syllable. Under this new interpretation, *Cnotta* and *Hedde*, far from being warrior leaders of the heroic age, may have been only ambitious peasants who did not shrink from the labour of cutting down trees to enlarge their farmland.

A second line of criticism has directly challenged the previously accepted chronology of the Anglo-Saxon immigration. The earlier bands who invaded Britain in the fifth and sixth centuries were pagan, burying their dead according to heathen rites. Christianity was not introduced into Anglo-Saxon England until AD 597, when Augustine's missionary band landed in Kent. Pagan burial sites, therefore, may be taken as an additional indication of areas of early, pioneer Anglo-Saxon settlement. Maps of their distribution should tally with those of the place-names in *-ing*, *-inga* or *-ingas*.

Far from this being so, the researches first of J. N. L. Myres and later of John M. Dodgson over a wide area of south-eastern England have revealed instead a widespread disparity between the two distributions. Barrie Cox, who in 1972 published the results of an exhaustive investigation into the place-names of the Midlands and East Anglia, reported a similar discrepancy there, where the *ing* names were found mainly in areas apart from the pagan burial sites. As Dr M. Gelling somewhat tartly remarked: 'The maps which have been compiled of both types of evidence suggest that, if we must regard them as contemporary, there was a law in operation from AD 400 to AD 600 which said that people of English descent might either have a pagan burial or live in a place with an *ingas* name, but were to be strongly discouraged from doing both.'

Barrie Cox took the discussion a step further by observing that the distribution maps showed that the pagan burial sites were often located near Romano-British settlements and on or near Roman roads, suggesting an association, tenuous but not unlikely, between the pioneer arrivals and the sub-Roman culture of those centuries. By contrast, the *ing* names were in general found at some distance from these relics of Romanisation. The maps showed that the late Romano-British sites correlated rather with those of the names in *-ham* than with those in *-ing*. He concluded that such patterns could not be fortuitous, and suggested a new interpretation of the chronology of the Anglo-Saxon settlement. He argued that the first settlements, those of the early pioneer invaders, near Roman roads that offered convenient lines of advance into strange and hostile territory, were marked not by place-names in *-ing*, but by those in *-ham*. He observed, too, that settlements bearing *ham* names were often located on better soils and upon naturally drained farmlands – sites that would attract the attention of the firstcomers.

The names in *-ing*, *-inga* and *-ingas* he regarded as marking a much later stage, when settlers were moving away from Romano-British sites and Roman roads to open up the virgin lands of the interior. He observed that settlements bearing such names were often located peripherally to the more desirable soils, often being found on damp, low-lying ground, as in the Fen District south of the Wash – inferior farmlands that would have been bypassed by earlier immigrants.

The -*ingaham* names he regarded as marking an intermediary phase of settlement in which the settlements partook the characteristics of both earlier and later phases. As an approximate chronological guide he suggested the fifth century for the pioneer *ham* names; the sixth century for the beginning of the intermediary *ingaham* period; and the seventh and later centuries for the colonisation period marked by the *ing*, *inga*, and *ingas* names.

More research is needed on the *ham*, *ingaham* and *ingas* place-names of Yorkshire to determine which of the two suggested chronologies applies in the county. A tentative observation, however, may be made concerning the Vale of Pickering. This region contains one name in -*ing*, two in -*ingaham* and one in -*ham*. The *ham* name is that of Wykeham, a village on the Scarborough–Pickering road. The site satisfies the criteria thought by Barrie Cox to indicate an early Anglian settlement. Dr Margaret Faull has called attention to several considerations which suggest there was a Romano-British settlement there in late Roman times. She observes that it lay on the Roman road that connected the signal station at Scarborough with the legionary fort at Malton. She quotes the first element *wyke* in the place-name as stemming via a Celtic loan-word from the Latin *vicus*. This term originally applied to the native and civilian settlements that often grew on the outskirts of a legionary fortress, but was later applied to any unwalled township. Domestic pottery has been unearthed on the site dating to the late fifth century. She also observes that the round shape and method of construction of the Anglian dwellings whose remains have been examined do not conform to the normal Anglo-Saxon type of house. If this evidence is too weak to sustain an argument for continuity of occupation from later Romano-

British to early Anglian times, it at least suggests some Romano-British influence upon the minds of the invading Angles. Agriculturally the site is well endowed, for it lies at the junction where the limestone strata of the southern part of the North York Moors dip beneath the clays of the Vale of Pickering. Here a powerful dip-slope spring provided an ample and perennial water-supply. The site gave ready access both to the fertile limestone soils to the north for arable farming and to the natural grassland of the low-lying claylands to the south for cattle-rearing. The evidence is therefore strong that this *ham* place-name marks an extremely early Anglian occupation during the first phase of the invasion.

The *ingaham* names are represented by Hovingham in the Howardian Hills and Yedingham in the heart of the Vale. Hovingham lay on the Roman road from Malton and Roman remains have been excavated there, so the name is typical of those *ingaham* names that Barrie Cox found shared the advantages of the earlier *ham* sites. The site of Yedingham, far out in what were then the marshes of the Vale of Pickering, represents the movement outwards from the earliest sites to less favourable and less accessible sites characteristic of later Anglian settlement.

It is, however, difficult to relegate the *ing* name of the district, Pickering, to a late stage in the Anglian settlement. We have seen that its name, drawn from the *Pikeringas*, takes us back to a folk-group characteristic of the pioneer phase; while the site, only ten miles from Wykeham, lay on the same Roman road and enjoyed the same agricultural advantages.

The evidence over the whole county is equally inconclusive. Map 5 is based upon one in which Dr Gillian F. Jensen has plotted the locations of the place-names in -*ham*, -*inga*, -*ingas* and -*ingaham* against the pagan burial sites and the Roman roads. It is difficult to detect from it any of the correlations that elsewhere have impressed place-name scholars. Only in very localised areas – for example at York, or near Castleford, or at the mouth of the Esk – are *ham* names found near pagan burial sites, and then only in a few instances. For eighty miles the main Roman road supplying the Wall ran from south to north through the area covered by the

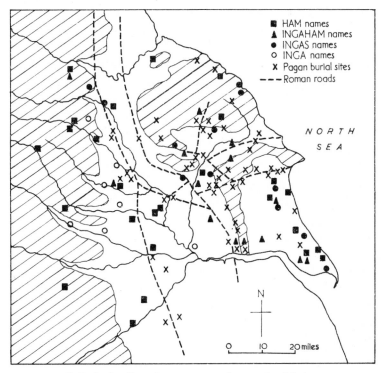

5 Early Anglian place-names and pagan burial sites

map, yet less than half-a-dozen *ham* names appear close to it. An equally meagre correlation is offered by the Roman road westwards from York. This general lack of correlation also extends to the *ingaham* names: only north of Brough-on-Humber can these be associated with pagan burial sites. This widespread disparity may be due to inadequate archaeological investigation in the county, but it can give little support to the view that *ham* and *ingaham* names mark areas of early Anglian settlement in Yorkshire.

The claims of the older hypothesis, however, that the early settlements are marked by names in *-inga* and *-ingas*, gains even less support from map 5. Only rarely are *ing* names found near Roman roads or in association with pagan burial sites. Instead of cor-

75

relations the map shows a tendency for all types of suspected early place-names to cluster together, though often in the neighbourhood of pagan burial sites and Roman roads. Such clusters can be seen around the present site of Driffield, northwards along the Roman road from Brough-on-Humber and eastwards on the Roman roads between Malton and the sites of the coastal signal stations. So far as Yorkshire is concerned the chronology of the early Anglian settlements is still an open question and its resolution awaits further research and discussion.

Some conclusions may be drawn from the map, however, concerning the routes by which the immigrants penetrated the interior. Entry seems to have been by the Humber, and thence up the Ouse and its tributaries. The River Derwent led them to the Vale of Pickering, where they could have encountered other immigrants coming inland from the beaches between Flamborough Head and Filey Brigg. The Ouse gave easy access to the vales of York and Mowbray. The scatter of early place-names in the valleys of the Swale, Ure, Nidd, Wharfe, Aire and Calder suggests that all these valleys were used. The correlations previously referred to between early place-names and the Roman roads are a reminder that those roads were still in a condition good enough to offer overland routes.

Place-Names and the Former Landscape of Yorkshire

It has long been assumed that the main features of the present landscape of Yorkshire, briefly outlined in the first chapter, have existed largely unchanged throughout historic and for much of prehistoric time. But recent research by archaeologists and still more by botanists has thrown doubt upon this surmise. To this debate, place-names can make an illuminating contribution.

When in 1936 Elgee wrote his well-known book on the archaeology of the North York Moors, a subject on which he was an acknowledged authority, few questioned his view that the Moors had been for thousands of years a wild upland, largely treeless, a tract of heather and bracken, as today. This, it was generally thought, was the 'natural landscape' of that region. It was assumed that over Yorkshire as a whole the landscape which the Angles and Saxons, and later the Danes and Norwegians, found on their arrival did not greatly differ from that seen by the holidaymaker of today. Of course, the main relief features – the uplands and low-lands, the major rivers and their valleys – have existed since they emerged from the last ice age some 20,000 years ago. But questions are now being raised about the vegetational cover. Have the rolling chalk downs of the Wolds and the high plateau of the limestone Pennines always been covered with miles of springy turf that makes them today the sheep-walk of England? Have the vales of York and Mowbray always been predominantly pastoral? The botanists are painting a different picture and the archaeologists are accepting its validity.

The botanical technique behind the change of view is that of pollen analysis. Pollen grains are virtually indestructible, and as each species of plant produces grains of unique shape, easily recognisable under the microscope, they can be used by botanists as a distinguishing token, as finger-prints are used by the police. So far this technique has been mainly applied to pollen preserved in ancient fens or beneath Bronze Age tumuli on the Moors. Surprisingly, the pollen found in such moorland soils is not that of heather, bracken and grass, but of trees – birch and pine in the most ancient soils, changing slowly to oak, ash, elm, willow and alder in the later ones. These investigations have demonstrated that throughout prehistoric times upland and lowland areas alike, not only of the Moors but also of most of Yorkshire, presented a landscape of extensive woodland. In these forests the Neolithic farmers who arrived in about 3000 BC began to make clearings by burning the trees and felling them with their stone axes. The process was continued even more effectively with the metal implements of their successors in the Bronze and Iron Ages. Only as the cleared areas increased did the pollen count begin to show signs of the emergence of the typical natural vegetation of the heather moorland landscape of today.

But since no botanical study of this nature has yet been made of the soils of the Dark Ages, we do not know how far such clearances had proceeded by the time of the Anglo-Saxon immigration. It is instructive, therefore, to investigate what Anglo-Saxon place-names can reveal about the sort of landscape the *Laestingas*, the *Piceringas* and the *Getlingas* encountered after they had beached their ships, and what proportion of trees they subsequently cleared for their farming.

Our word moor makes a convenient starting point. It has descended to us little changed from the Anglo-Saxon word *mor*. Even today it has no single meaning. To a Yorkshireman 'moor' calls up a picture of a typical high, heather moor where grouse shooting takes the place of cultivation. A native of Somerset, however, thinks in terms of the marshes of Sedgemoor, now drained, in which Monmouth's rebellion was literally bogged down. Our ancestors were equally ambiguous in the use of their word *mor*. But though, like us, they applied it to both types of landscape, its use usually involved a treeless, uncultivated expanse, as distinct from wooded tracts.

Several place-names can be quoted in support of the opinion that the North York Moors presented to our Anglian ancestors an appearance not unlike that of today. The term *mor* forms an element in three moorland place-names: Gillamoor and Fadmoor in the south, Moorsholm in the north. Gillamoor appears in Domesday Book as *Gedlingesmore* – the *mor* of the *Getlingas*. The meaning of the first element in Fadmoor is uncertain, but the suffix originated clearly enough from the Anglian *mor*. Moorsholm was recorded in Domesday Book as *Morehusum* – the houses on the moor. In no way can the *mor* element in these names be interpreted as denoting a fen. Fadmoor stands about 500ft up on the limestone slope above Kirby Moorside. Gillamoor is situated a mile or so away at a still greater altitude on the upper rim of the limestone escarpment, from which a spectacular view can be enjoyed into Farndale 300ft below. Moorsholm stands 600ft above sea-level, on the coastal moorland inland from Boulby Cliff. The only interpretation that can reasonably be put upon the element *mor* in each of these three place-names is that of the modern, north-country meaning of an uncultivated heather upland. To this evidence can be added the old term '*blackamoor*', a traditional name for the sandstone moors that died out during the eighteenth century. It first appeared in the records in the twelfth century as *Mora de Blachou*. If the Old English element *blaec* referred to the dark and even forbidding appearance of a heather moor in winter, this name supports the view that by the early Middle Ages parts, if not all, of the North York Moors presented the appearance of a typical modern heather moor.

On the other hand, many place-names, drawn from various parts of the area of the North Riding, point to the opposite conclusion. North of York such names as Sutton-on-the-Forest and Marton-le-Forest recall the extensive Forest of Galtres of medieval times. Bede tells us that when (in the seventh century) Cedd, Bishop of the East Saxons, decided to build a monastery at Lastingham in the North York Moors for his retirement, 'he chose a site . . . among some high and remote hills, which seemed more suitable for dens of robbers and haunts of wild beasts than for human habitation'. The statement gives no direct information about vegetation, but a dense forest is more likely to have provided shelter for thieves and wild beasts than an open moor.

The Anglo-Saxons had several synonyms for woodland – *wudu*, *hyrst*, *sceaga*, *weald* – and these have entered so frequently into place-name formation that they provide impressive evidence for a widespread woodland cover throughout the county. *Wudu* has given us the modern suffix wood, as in Harwood Dale, inland from Scarborough. Though there is uncertainty about the meaning of the first element – it may come from *hara*, hare, or *har*, rock – there is no doubt about the origin of the final element. We meet the same element *wudu* in the name of Lockwood Reservoir, still ringed with trees beside the A171 a few miles out from Guisborough. The name was formed by a combination of the Old English words *loc*, enclosure, and *wudu* – the enclosure in the woodland. The site is within a mile or so of Moorsholm, and the name implies a narrow limit to the open country or *mor* suggested by that place-name.

Other evidence of the ancient woodland cover comes from the western side of the county. At the entrance to Wensleydale stand the villages of East and West Witton. A twelfth-century spelling *Widtona* suggests a derivation from *widu* or *wudu* – the *tun* in the wood. Further up Wensleydale, across the valley from Aysgarth Falls, is Woodhall Farm, formerly an old hall, the name of which was formed from a combination of the Anglian terms *wudu* and *heall* – the hall or residence in the forest. Ekwall offers 'building where the forest courts were held' as a possible meaning.

Another Anglo-Saxon word for woodland was *weald* or *wald*, a term generally applied to high forestland. It has survived in the terms Yorkshire Wolds and the Cotswolds of Gloucestershire, suggesting that in Anglo-Saxon times both these uplands were forested. The word appears in the North York Moors in the name Coxwold, a pleasant stone-built village on the south-western flank of the Moors, much visited by sightseers because of its interesting church and Shandy Hall where Laurence Sterne, the writer of *Tristram Shandy*, lived. Domesday Book gives the name as *Cucualt*, but a still earlier charter of the mid-eighth century renders it more revealingly as *Cuha-walda* – *Cuha's* woodland.

By no means are all these forest names confined to the uplands. In the Vale of York is Easingwold, recorded in Domesday Book as *Eisincewald* – Esa's *wald* or *weald*. Inland from Scarborough, Sawdon Dale takes its name from *sealh* and *denu*, Anglian terms meaning 'the valley of the willows'. Salton, on the lowlands of the Rye in the Vale of Pickering, began similarly as *sealh* and *tun* – the *tun* or farm by the willows. Place-names in *-hyrst* add to the evidence. The area of the West Riding contains over a score of such names, including four names 'Hirst' or 'Hurst'.

The place-names of the East Riding provide a similar divergence of evidence. Several suggest that open countryside predominated in their neighbourhood. The Old English word *feld*, for instance, enters into at least two place-names – Driffield and Hatfield. This word originally denoted an expanse of open countryside, possibly covered in brushwood and scrub, but largely free of trees. It therefore carried a meaning almost the opposite of the 'field' of today, enclosed behind its walls or hedgerows. Hatfield was recorded as *Haifeld* in Domesday Book, from the Old English *haeth* and *feld*. The name Hedon, in Holderness, provides more convincing evidence: it derives its name from the Old English *haeth* and *dun*, the first syllable of which referred to uncultivated or heather-covered land – our word heath. Many names refer to scrubland; for example Thicket, the name of a hamlet in the lower Derwent lowlands, and Bracken between Great Driffield and Market Weighton. In the lowland flats of Holderness the two hamlets of Rise and Long Riston both have names that stem from the Old English *hris*, brushwood. The neighbouring Roos has already been quoted as coming from a loan-word from the Celtic, referring to moor or heath.

Equally numerous, however, are place-names indicative of true woodland in the East Riding, where the name Wolds preserves the Old English *wald*, used of high tracts of forested country. Bede, writing in the eighth century, located the monastery that was later to become famous as Beverley Minster as situated *in silva Derorum* – 'in the forest of Deira'. The Wolds were formerly part of this great Forest of Deira and still contain much residual woodland. Harwold Farm stands about 500ft high on the central Wolds near Huggate. Whether it derives its name as Ekwall suggested from the Old English *hoh* and *wald* – the high woodland – or, as A. H. Smith thought, from *haugr*, tumulus and *w(e)ald* – high forest land – the name is proof that in those days the Yorkshire Wolds were well wooded. Hessle, between Brough and Hull, was originally formed from the Old English *haesel*, the hazel-trees. Place-names Norwood and Westwood explain themselves, and contribute to the evidence for thinking that as Yorkshire emerged from the Dark Ages the East Riding was much more wooded than today.

The dichotomy in the evidence extends to the West Riding. Here several place-names include the suffix 'field', from the Old Anglian word *feld*, denoting open, treeless country. Sheffield derives its name from the Old English *sceath* and *feld* – the *feld* or open country along the River Sheaf. The northern suburb of Sheffield, Ecclesfield, was recorded in Domesday Book as *Eclesfeld*, which may fairly be rendered as 'open countryside where the church stands'. The name Mirfield – *Mirefelt* in Domesday times – referred to 'the pleasant countryside', from the Old English word *myrge*, merry. The clue to the meaning of Nesfield, the name of a hamlet in upper Wharfedale a mile upstream from Ilkley, is given not so much by the Domesday version *Nacefeld* as by a later recording as *Netfeld*, from the Old English *neates* and *feld* – the open land on which cattle are kept. This suggests that pastureland not woodland existed there when this name was formed.

Several names suggest that this *feld* land in the West Riding was often covered with scrub and bushes. On the low-lying lands north-east of Doncaster, among the many ditches that now drain what was once a wild fen, stand Hatfield and Thorne. In the eighth century Bede recorded the former as *Haethfelth* which had changed only to *Heathfeld* by the tenth century, both forms expressive of treeless fenland. Thorne has changed its name little since Domesday times, when it was recorded as *Torne*, from the Old English *thorn*. In the lower Calder valley south of Dewsbury there is a Thornhill – *Tornil* in Domesday Book – 'a hill overgrown with thornbushes'. Overlooking the Aire valley, now the north-eastern suburb of Bradford, Farsley preserves the Domesday rendering of *Fersellei*, from the Old English *fyrs*, furze, and *leah*, clearing. North of Otley, above the valley of the Wharfe, Farnley incorporates the Anglian word *fearn*, ferns, while north-west of Knaresborough, Farnham marks the homestead among the ferns. Brampton-en-le-Morthen draws the first part of its name from the Old English *brom* and *tun* – the farmstead where the broom grows. Brearton, near Harrogate, similarly originated as 'the farmstead where the briars grow'. From such place-names it would appear that the *feld* was often an expanse of heather, ferns, furze, broom, briars, hazel and thorn-bushes far different from the tamed and hedged pastures and arable plots of today.

On the other hand, many West Riding place-names indicate settlements established in forested country. Oakenshaw, between Bradford and Cleckheaton, derives its name from the Old English *acen*, of oaks, and *scaga* or *sceaga*, synonyms for wood. *Sceaga* frequently provides us with the modern suffix 'shaw' as in Birken-shaw and Oakenshaw. Beckwith has a name that goes back before Domesday times to the tenth century or further, when it was recorded as *Becwudu* – Old English for beech-wood. *Alor*, the Old English word for alder-tree, has given us the first element in Allerton, recorded in Domesday Book as *Alretun* – the *tun* or farmstead among among the alders. Woodhouse, near Sheffield, is another example of 'a house among the woods', suggesting again that the Pennine foothills were then forested. This conclusion is supported by the history of the name Lindley Green, a hamlet now situated beside the reservoir a mile or two north of Otley. As early as the tenth century it was written as *Lindeleh*, incorporating the Old English words *linde* and *leage*, the lime-wood. A few miles north of Penistone is a small village with the revealing name of Ingbirchworth, combining the Old English elements of *birce*, birch-tree, and *worth*, an enclosure. These last two examples are not at all confined to valley bottoms; they come from places high up on the Pennine moors. Such names in such locations pose the question – should we change our picture of the Pennines in the early Middle Ages into one in which at least the foothills were clothed in woodland, with trees climbing well above the 1,000ft contour ?

The case for this new picture is etched still more deeply by the evidence drawn from innumerable Yorkshire place-names ending in '-ley'. This element derives from the Anglo-Saxon term *leah*, which from an original meaning of grove or glade in a wood came to be applied to clearings deliberately made in the forest cover and even to the wood itself. *Leah* names abound in Yorkshire, especially in the West Riding. The list of them in A. H. Smith's book on that area occupies well over a page of close print. Map 6 locates the names in '-ley' still to be found in Airedale and Wharfedale. Such a cluster betokens extensive clearances and implies dense woodland in these valleys in Anglo-Saxon times. Frequently the *leah* element is compounded with a personal name. Keighley was recorded in Domesday Book as Chichelai, from 'the *leah* of *Cyhha*'. Ilkley has a similar history: a century before Domesday Book was compiled

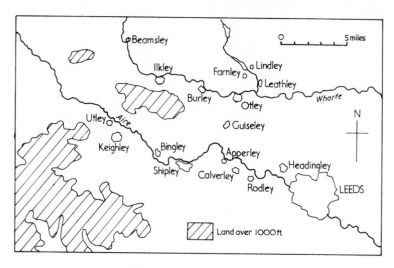

6 Place-names ending in 'ley'

it was written as *Hillicleg*, which had become *Yllic Leage* two generations later. The Domesday clerks wrote it as *Illicleia*, from the Old English personal name *Illica* – *Illica*'s clearing. Otley has similarly developed its name from '*Otta*'s *leah*'. Guiseley began as a clearing to which an Anglian farmer *Gislica* gave his name.

A similar development is revealed on the lowlands. The name Ripley, near Harrogate, recalls the early days of the tribal settlement – the *leah* of the *Hrype* – but is quoted here as evidence of the clearing of wooded country. Four miles to the west, Grantley has a name that appeared in Domesday Book as *Grentelai*, with an earlier recording as *Grantelege* – *Granta*'s clearing. Cantley, the eastern suburb of Doncaster, where once the Romano-Britons made pottery, draws its name from the Anglian personal name *Canta* – *Canta*'s *leah*. The first element in the name Wickersley, an eastern suburb of Rotherham, may well enshrine the Old English term *wicnere*, steward or bailiff, but an alternative explanation suggests that it was formed from a later Norse personal name *Vikarr*. In either case, the final *-ley* refers to a woodland in which a clearance has been made. Ardsley, now absorbed into the borough of Barnsley, originated from '*Eard*'s clearing'; Barnsley itself began as '*Beorn*'s *leah*'.

Not all names in '-ley', however, have preserved a personal name. Pateley Bridge in Nidderdale preserves the Old English word *paeth*, path – the clearing by the path. Wortley, near Barnsley, is shown as *Wirtleie* in Domesday Book, from the Old English word for plant, *wyrt*. Whether this indicated a clearing of scrubland or a clearing in which neglect had later allowed wild plants to shoot up none can tell. The name Morley suggests more definitely the clearing of scrubland or heathland – the *mor leah*. Burley in Wharfedale was first recorded as early as the tenth century as *Burhleg*, and later in Domesday Book as *Burghelai*; these names come from the Old English *burg* and *leah*, implying a *leah* belonging to a *burg* or borough – a derivation which suggests that corporate ownership or corporate establishment of a clearing was not unknown. It is surprising that the place-names do not show more evidence of this, for the task of felling the trees, clearing the site and removing the stumps was so arduous as to call for the joint efforts of all able-bodied villagers.

Frequently, in addition to indicating the existence of woodland the names reveal the purpose of the clearance. Wheatley Park, in the north-east corner of Doncaster, came originally from the Old English *hwaete* and *leah* – the clearing for wheat. Lindley, on the north-western fringe of Huddersfield, has a name that goes back to the Old English *lin* and *leah* – the *leah* where flax was grown. We still retain the Anglo-Saxon *lin* in our word linen, a cloth made from flax.

On the lowlands between Boroughbridge and Harrogate the village of Staveley preserves in its name the Old English words *staef* and *leah* – the clearing in the wood where staves are obtained. In an age in which wood was universally used, such sites were essential to village economy. Calverley, four miles north-east of Bradford, was 'a leah to provide pasture for calves'. Shipley was *Scipeleia* in Domesday Book and *Shepele* in the early thirteenth century from which it is recognisable as 'the clearance for sheep'. The need for forest clearance became increasingly more urgent as the rural population grew in numbers in late Saxon times—such clearances were made for both arable and pastoral purposes.

85

Such evidence for woodland clearance is not confined to the West Riding. A few miles south of Beverley in the East Riding, Bentley derives its name from the Anglian *beonet* and *leah* to indicate 'a clearing overgrown with coarse grass'. Farmers still speak of 'bent' as a type of grass. Sproatley in Holderness appears in Domesday Book as *Sprotele*, from the Old English *sprota*, a sprouting shoot or twig – the *leah* where the shoots are springing up. Also in Holderness the name Lelley was originally compounded of *leah* with the Old English word *laela*, which referred to twigs or brushwood in which presumably the clearing was made. The old word *laela* reappears in the name Lealholm in the North Riding. It belongs to a hamlet almost hidden among the trees on the bank of the River Esk, where scores of visitors gather every warm weekend to sit in the shade by the stream. The name was recorded in Domesday Book as *Lelun*, from the Old English *laelum*, dative plural of *lael* – among the twigs. No neater description of this wooded riverside scene today could be devised.

Many of the clearings in the North Riding either incorporate a personal name or indicate the purpose of the clearance. Helmsley was *Elmeslac* in Domesday Book – *Helm*'s forest clearing. On the coastal moors near Whitby the name Dunsley occurs, almost unchanged since Domesday times when it was known as *Dunesla* – *Dun*'s clearing. Near Helmsley, the name of Pockley marks the location of '*Poca*'s clearing'. Bickley, just off the road from Scarborough to Pickering, was first recorded as *Biggelea* – *Bigga*'s *leah*. Nearby is Stockland, a name interpreted by A. H. Smith as 'the wood from which the trees have been cut', the reference being to the stumps of trees or stocks that were left. A less arduous method of clearance was by burning, as suggested by the name Saintoft in the same area, from the Old English *sengan*, to burn.

Leah names are frequent among the Pennine foothills. Wensley, a flourishing settlement until the plague afflicted it in the sixteenth century, was recorded in Domesday Book as *Wendreslaga*, from the Old English personal name *Waendel* and *leah* – *Waendel*'s forest clearing. Brindley, a farm name in the same locality, supports the view that many clearings were made by burning the

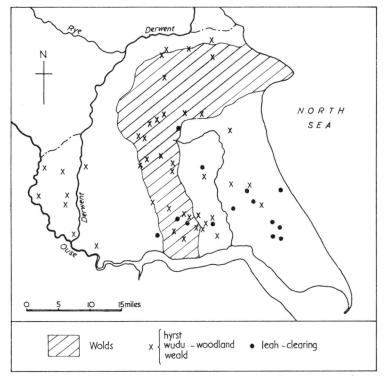

7 East Riding Anglian place-names indicating woodland (*after A.H. Smith*)

timber down, for the name stems from *leah* and *brende*, the latter an Old English word meaning fire.

To ascertain the extent of woodland in the Yorkshire of Anglo-Saxon times three maps have been included, one for each Riding, plotting the location of present-day place-names which include an Anglo-Saxon element indicative of a woodland neighbourhood at the time of formation. The names in -ley (from *leah*) have been distinguished by a special symbol to enable a further estimate to be made of the extent to which this woodland cover was cleared at the time. Map 7 shows the scatter of woodland names in the East Riding. There is some evidence that the damp lowlands between the rivers Derwent and Ouse and in Holderness supported some

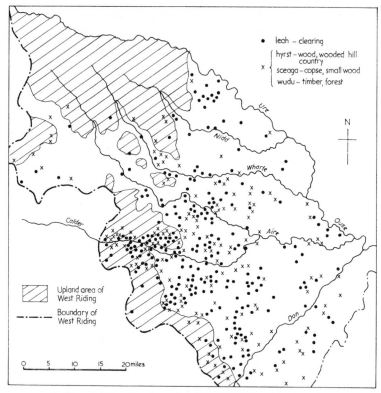

8 West Riding Anglian place-names indicating woodland

tree growth, though names like Sigglesthorne in Holderness and Thicket in the Derwent valley suggest that scrubland was prevalent. To those familiar with the rolling, grassy chalk downs of Sussex and Wiltshire, the scatter of woodland place-names on the chalk Wolds may come as a surprise, though north of the Thames the Chilterns carry a dense woodland growth, the beech-woods contributing largely to the scenic attractions of 'leafy Buckinghamshire'.

Map 8 shows how extensively the West Riding was forested when Anglo-Saxon place-names were being coined; it demonstrates more impressively than any list of quoted examples how widespread was this forest cover. The scatter of such woodland

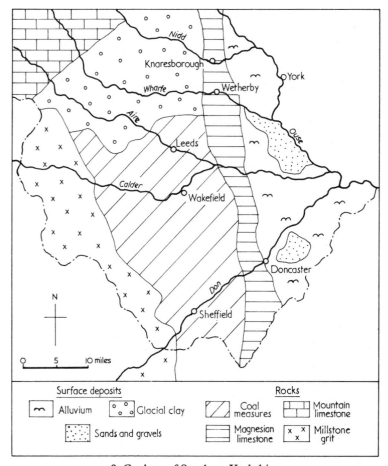

9 Geology of Southern Yorkshire

names, however, is uneven. The northern half of the Riding appears distinctly less wooded than the southern half, the eastern parts more open than the western. Altitude is clearly one factor influencing this distribution. There is little evidence for much tree growth on the high Pennine moors, but a dense forest is revealed clothing the Dales and spreading up the Pennine foothills. The two farms named Shaw and Hirst, north of Reeth on the side-slopes of Swaledale, give an idea of the altitude to which this woodland grew, for the names stem directly from the Anglian woodland terms *sceaga* and *hyrst*, and the farms stand at heights of 1,000 and 1,240ft respectively.

The scatter of woodland names in the Vale of York is much less compact. Here geological factors, illustrated in map 9, were influential. Comparison between Maps 8 and 9 shows that the woodland names cluster upon the outcrop of the coal measures, where the shales interbedded between the seams of coal weather into a clay favourable to tree growth. To the west the woodland can be seen thinning out against the outcrop of millstone-grit, the coarse, infertile sandstone of which the Pennine moors in south-western Yorkshire are composed. Even more abrupt is the manner in which the woodland names come to an end against the western escarpment of the belt of magnesian limestone.

Map 8 suggests that the low-lying and damp plains of the lower Ouse, Wharfe and Aire checked tree growth, for blank spaces appear between the place-names. Two localities, however, form distinct exceptions. The geological map shows two large patches of sand and gravel among the damp and heavy clays. Map 8 reveals that the areas of tree growth in this region coincide with these sandy patches. North of the Wharfe, however, the correlation between the two maps is less manifest. Here the irregular distribution of woodland names reflects the differing effects upon tree growth of the spreads of glacial clays and sands; this will be examined more closely later.

The scatter of woodland names of Anglo-Saxon origin in the North Riding, shown on map 10, confirms the evidence from other parts of Yorkshire. The scatter of such names in the Pennine valleys, especially in Swaledale and Wensleydale, suggests that the lower altitudes at least were still well forested. On the North York Moors in the east, the distribution of place-names indicates that woodland growth here was most developed on the limestone outcrop of the southern margin of the Moors, where fertile soil favoured tree-growth. But the absence of woodland place-names in the higher Pennines or on the sandstone Moors may not necessarily reflect a lack of woodland so much as a general absence

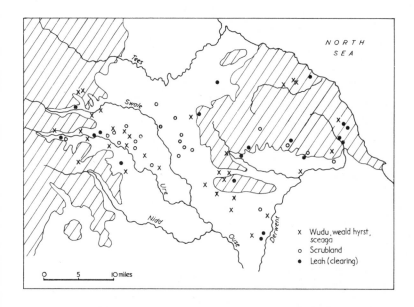

10 North Riding Anglian place-names indicating woodland

of settlement and therefore of place-names of any sort.

In the populated Vales of Mowbray, York and Pickering the place-names testify to a dispersed woodland, the irregular scatter of which reflects the distribution of glacial clays and sands. Such a wooded countryside, far from being a deterrent to settlement, offered many inducements. It provided ample supplies of timber for dwellings and outhouses, fencing and fuel. Wild fruit grew on the fringes; pigs fattened on the acorns and beech-nuts, while sheep and goats enjoyed the new shoots. But as the population increased, our ancestors set to work with fire and axe to clear this woodland and enlarge the local area of cultivation thereby adding their contribution to the clearance of the prevailing forest that their predecessors in the Iron and Bronze Ages had begun. The frequency with which the Anglian word *leah* has entered as 'ley' into the place-names of today reflects their success in the age-long task of transforming the landscape of the Yorkshire lowlands from forest to farmland.

91

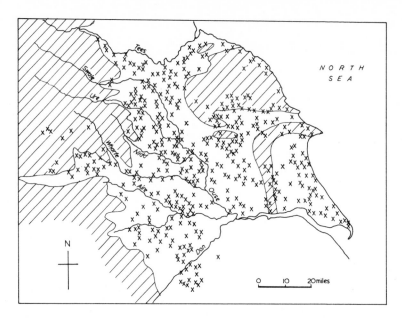

11 Anglian place-names with *ham, tun, inga, ingas, ingaham, ingtun* (*after G. F. Jensen*)

General Distribution of Anglian Place-Names in Yorkshire

Place-name formation continued throughout the period of Anglian settlement and long after, as the population grew in number by later arrivals and natural increase. In order to assess the eventual distribution of such settlements, map 11 plots the location of the Anglian place-names containing the elements *ham, tun, inga, ingas, ingaham* and *ingtun*. To have added other place-names of Old English derivation would have overcrowded so small a scale. Since the elements selected were in common use at the time and characteristic of the period, there is no reason to suppose that the distribution shown is unrepresentative. The most serious omission is that of the woodland names. But as that gap has already been filled by the maps of the previous section, it should be possible from map 11 to reach some general conclusions concerning the distribution of Old English place-names and therefore of Anglian settlement.

A glance will show that the distribution was uneven, following the pattern set by the first-comers. In the Pennine region to the west, Anglian place-names are confined to the Dales. The lack of such names above the 800ft contour line suggests that the Anglian immigrants had little taste for the high Pennine moors. Only in the Aire Gap did they spill over the watershed into the Ribble valley. The foothills and the interfluves were not bare of settlement, but the areas most favoured were the valleys of the Calder, Aire, Wharfe, Nidd, Ure, Swale and Tees.

A similar contrast is shown on the eastern side of the county in the North York Moors. An almost complete lack of Anglian settlement names on the sandstone moors suggests that this high plateau area was also avoided. Mostly over 800ft high, exposed to northerly gales, with long and hard winters, these Moors discouraged arable cultivation then as now. The sandy soil, thin and peat-covered, has remained infertile to this day, having received no admixture of more fertile glacial clay as the great ice-sheets of the ice ages were unable to override the high plateau. Only on the coastal moors, where the elevation is some 200–300ft lower, was the North Sea ice-sheet able to deposit its load of glacial clay, which has weathered into the relatively fertile Grade III soil of today. It is noticeable that the Anglian place-names on the Moors are largely confined to this coastal belt. In striking contrast to the lack of place-names on the northern sandstone moors is the spread of Anglian place-names along the fertile belt of corallian limestone in the south, extending from Sutton Bank, past Rievaulx and Pickering, to the coast near Filey.

The distribution of Anglian settlement names in the East Riding shows that the most favoured regions were the lowlands on each side of the Wolds. The pattern of settlement was most dense in Holderness, where in the neighbourhood of their first landfall, the Anglian immigrants found a damp, pastoral lowland resembling their homelands across the North Sea. Similar conditions explain the scatter of settlements in the Derwent valley. The most conspicuous topographical feature in the East Riding, the chalk uplands of the Wolds, was less populated. Here, as in all chalk-

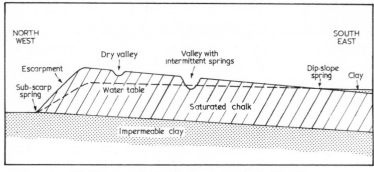

12 Factors affecting water supply in the Wolds

lands, the main factor influencing the choice of settlement was water-supply. Before the days of piped supplies to rural areas, no settlement, however insignificant, could succeed without ready access to some natural source of water. The factors determining this in the Wolds are illustrated in fig 12. The chalk strata are tilted, with the result that the Wolds present a steep escarpment edge to the west and north, but a gentle dip-slope to the east. Since the chalk is both fissured and permeable, rainwater has free

13 Anglian settlement along the northern Wolds

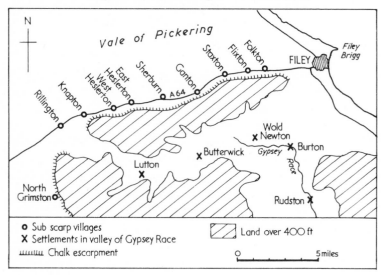

passage through the rock down to the clay bed below. This clay being impermeable throws out the chalk water in springs at the junction of the two rock strata. The diagram shows that these springs occur on both the east and west borders of the chalk, those emerging from the dip-slope tending to be more powerful than the ones at the base of the escarpment, since the former are served by a larger natural reservoir of underground water. But settlements located on either type of spring were assured of a natural and unfailing supply of water, cooled and filtered by its passage through the pores and fissures of the chalk.

The popularity of such sites is illustrated in map 13, which plots the location of the line of villages established along the spring-line at the foot of the northern escarpment of the Wolds. Within a distance of twelve miles the traveller along the A64

14 Ganton parish boundary

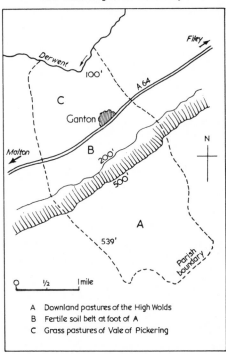

A   Downland pastures of the High Wolds
B   Fertile soil belt at foot of A
C   Grass pastures of Vale of Pickering

inland from Filey passes through no less than nine villages, each bearing a name containing an Old English element in -*tun*. Though some of these names were later modified under Scandinavian influence, these Old English elements show that all the sites were originally occupied by Anglian communities that settled at these springs gushing out at the foot of the chalk scarp. Similar Anglian place-names occur along the foot of the western scarp of the Wolds.

The parish boundaries of these sub-scarp villages throw an interesting light on other conditions of settlement. Map 14 shows that of Ganton as typical of the others. Like those of its neighbours, the parish boundary of Ganton run across the grain of the strata at right angles to the line of the escarpment. By this ancient device, each village received its fair share of the various types of soil in the locality – of the nutritious grassland on the top of the Wolds on which sheep could be reared; of the highly fertile belt that runs along the edge of the plain at the foot of the scarp, where an unfailing succession of arable crops is still reaped; and of the damp pastures of the Vale of Pickering lowlands, on which cattle could be raised. Such parish boundaries were not officially drawn until the very end of the Anglo-Saxon period, but they represented even then the age-old tradition of the inhabitants of the settlements concerned.

Compared with the dense groupings of place-names along the foot of the Wolds, the scatter of names in map 13 on the higher chalk downs is meagre. The explanation lies partly in the region's nature and partly in the difficulty of access to a reliable water-supply on these higher levels. In fig 12, farmsteads on the top of the Wolds can be seen to be far from a spring, and the upper level of the subterranean water in the chalk, commonly called the water-table, may lie far below the surface. Tapping it required the sinking of a well deep into the chalk, and though this was not wholly beyond the capacity of the Anglian settlers, it was difficult enough to send many an immigrant family searching for a valley that might contain a spring. One such valley, the Gypsey Race, appears in map 13 and is typical of these upland valleys in the high Wolds. It is deep enough to tap the underground water below the water-table (see fig 12), enabling springs to emerge from the valley sides and in the bed of the stream itself. This, however, does not ensure a permanent supply. In times of drought, when rain fails to replenish the subterranean reservoir, the water-table falls, the valley springs fail and the stream in the valley bottom dries up. Such intermittent streams are so common on chalk-lands that they are often known locally by special names. In the south they are called 'bournes', a term which often appears in place-names, as in Glyndebourne and Bournemouth. Map 13 clearly illustrates the contrast between the close alignment of sub-scarp villages, where the natural supply of water was perennial, and the thin and irregular scatter of the settlements in the Gypsey Race valley, where the water-supply was less assured.

In the Vale of Pickering the marshy nature of the lowland discouraged settlement, which tended to align along the north and south margins. The pattern is shown diagramatically below,

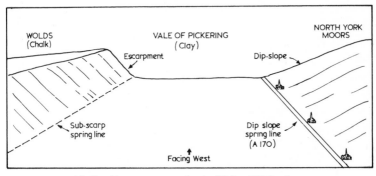

15 Settlement pattern in the Vale of Pickering

the row of sub-scarp villages at the foot of the Wolds being matched by a similar alignment on the north side of the Vale, where the dip-slope springs emerge at the junction of the limestone of the Moors and the clays of the Vale. The A170 between Scarborough and Helmsley follows this line of dip-slope springs. Map 16 shows that along its twenty-five miles no less than sixteen settlements are aligned, all bearing characteristic Anglian names -*ham*, -*ing* and -*ton*. In addition, access to the fertile soils of the limestone outcrop

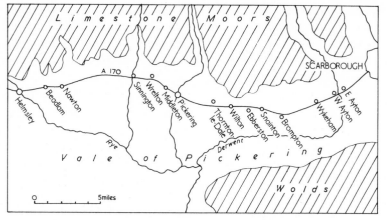

16 Old English place-names along the dip-slope springs

to the north and to the lush pastures of the Vale to the south encouraged settlement. It is significant that two of the earliest types of place-name in Anglo-Saxon Yorkshire – Pickering and Wykeham – occur on this line, which probably marks one of the early entry routes into the interior taken by the incoming Angles.

It is evident from map 11 that most of the Anglian settlement names of Yorkshire are to be found in the vales of Mowbray and York. Here, irregularly dispersed, are Anglian place-names of all types: habitative, topographical, descriptive and personal. In these lowlands the major factor affecting Anglian settlement was the contrast between clay and sandy soils. The area was covered by the ice-sheet of the last glaciation, which deeply buried the underlying bedrock beneath a thick cover of glacial clays, surmounted by patches of glacial sand and gravel. The clays weathered to a heavy, cold soil, which today yields good harvests and provides rich pastures. The sandy soils are lighter to work but less fertile, and they were valued for the dry sites they offered for settlement. Map 21 (see page 146) illustrates a not untypical part of the Vale of Mowbray, between Northallerton and Teesside. In the area mapped, ten settlements bear names of Anglian origin. Of these, three are sited on the glacial clays – Carlton and East and West Rounton – and one, Whorlton, on the glacial sands. The most sought-after sites were those at the junction of the clays and the sands. No less than seven of the ten settlements were sited at or very near such a location, which gave not only dry foundations for the farmstead but also access to both types of soil, a combination helpful to the mixed farming on which our Anglian ancestors depended for their living.

Abbreviated Etymologies

Pickering (NR, now North Yorks)

DB	1086	Pichering(a)
	1109	Pikeringes
	1119	Picaringes
	1157	Pikeringa(m)
	1579	Pekeryng

OE *Piceringas*: settlement of Picer and his dependants

Otley (WR, now West Yorks)

	972	Otton lege
DB	1086	Othelai, Othelei
	1198	Ottel(e), Otteleg, Ottelai
	1434	Otley

OE personal name *Otta*
OE *leah*: clearing or glade

Coxwold (NR, now North Yorks)

	757	Cuhu-walda
DB	1086	Cucualt
	1154	Cukewald
	1196	Cukwald
	1231	Cukewaud
	1308	Cucawald
	1545	Cookwald
	1577	Cuckwould

OE personal name *Cuha*
OE *weald*: wood
Cuha's wood

Howden (ER, now Humberside)

DB	1086	Hovedene
	1153	Ofendene
	1231	Houden
	1238	Howeden
	1402	Hawden
	1583	Howlden

OE *heafod*: valley-head
OE *denu*: valley

DB: Domesday Book   OE: Old English, Anglo-Saxon

5

The Scandinavian Place Names

By the end of the ninth century the Angles and Saxons were well on their way to establishing a distinctive culture in England. Their language had superseded both Celtic and Latin, and the Angles had given their name to the land. Their *hams, tuns, burhs, ings* and *leahs* lay widely scattered over the countryside from Northumbria to Sussex and from East Anglia to Offa's Dyke. The concept of a united England was not beyond the minds and ambitions of the more powerful of the Anglo-Saxon kings. They had evolved the title 'Bretwalda' to express such overlordship, and the rulers of Sussex, Kent, East Anglia, Northumbria and Wessex had in turn claimed it. As early as the eighth century Offa had broadened his title 'King of Mercia' to *Rex totius Anglorum patriae* – 'King of the whole realm of the English people'. By the ninth century these kingdoms had drawn up codes of laws, issued their own currencies and developed administrative machinery of varying degrees of efficiency. All had been converted to Christianity, the English Church achieving a European reputation for monastic learning. Bishoprics had been established in every realm, though the parish system was still in its infancy. Increasingly, the class structure of Anglo-Saxon society was becoming manifest, and most village settlements were dominated by a land-owning thegn to whom the

To avoid confusion in terminology, the use of the word *Danish* in this book is limited to the place-names of Danish origin as distinct from those of Norwegian origin, for which the terms *Norwegian* and *Norse* are reserved. Where such a distinction cannot or need not be made, the umbrella terms *Scandinavian* or *viking* are used to cover both elements. The term *Irish-Norwegian* is confined to place-names which indicate settlements of the Celtic Irishmen who accompanied the Norwegians on this migration, or which suggest the influence upon Norse names of the Irish-Celtic tongue.

local peasantry owed agricultural services in return for their holdings.

Then, when this English civilisation was on the verge of flowering, the Danish raids began. For reasons that are still obscure, but probably associated with a land-hunger that stemmed from an enlarging population, the vikings of Norway and Denmark began to embark on a series of voyages far and wide across the northern seas. They sailed eastwards to the White Sea, from which they penetrated into the heart of Russia, and westwards via the Shetlands, the Faroes, Iceland and Greenland to the coast of North America, five centuries before Columbus. Two thrusts involved England. The Norwegians followed the more northerly route, sailing round the north of Scotland to settle in Ireland, where they established a powerful and enduring Viking kingdom centred on Dublin. Meanwhile, the Danes were raiding more directly across the North Sea. Southampton was sacked in AD 842, and a few years later a king of Northumbria and one of his ealdormen were killed by them. In AD 865 a Danish army landed in East Anglia and occupied York the following year. By AD 871, the year of Alfred's accession to the throne of Wessex, every other English kingdom had succumbed to the invaders, and Wessex itself was under such severe pressure that the first half of Alfred's reign had to be devoted to withstanding it.

By the compromise agreed at the Treaty of Wedmore some time after AD 886, Alfred continued to rule over an intact Wessex. But Mercia was split down the middle by a boundary across the Midlands, roughly from London to Chester. To the north and east lay the Danelaw, where the Danes had established themselves with especial strength in the 'Five Boroughs' in the valley of the Trent, and at York in the valley of the Ouse. That Danish place-names abound today in the north of England is not therefore surprising – they might have been more prevalent had not the successors of Alfred of Wessex set themselves to recover the lost territories during the tenth century. From *burhs*, fortified posts and townships established at river crossings and at other strategic points along the frontier, they steadily pushed the border zone northwards until they had regained control over the whole of the Danelaw. For the first time a single united England became a reality.

Meanwhile, early in the tenth century, another influence was at work in the north which was to have a further effect upon place-names. The Norwegian settlements in Ireland became the base for a reverse migration across the Irish Sea into what are now the counties of Cumbria, Lancashire and Cheshire. A Norse kingdom was set up in the Isle of Man, where to this day the Manx Parliament bears the Scandinavian name of Tynwald. From the Lake District, where Norse names abound today, they spread across the Pennines into the north-western parts of Yorkshire, a trail of Norse place-names now marking their progress. By AD 919 a band of Norse invaders from Ireland had established a new Scandinavian kingdom at York.

Recent excavation of the Scandinavian settlement in York and the television series by Magnus Magnusson on the Scandinavian achievement in general have done much to modify our conception of viking life and influence in England. Brought up on a history based largely on the *Anglo-Saxon Chronicle* and other Anglo-Saxon records, whose biassed accounts have given the Danes an exceptionally bad press, we have tended to regard them as ruthless vikings determined on plunder at the sword's point. We are now rightly reminded that the vikings who came to this country included farmers as well as warriors, skilled shipwrights and craftsmen as well as destroyers of monasteries, and statesmen like Canute as well as ruffians like Eric Bloodaxe. It was fortunate for Yorkshire that the majority of the vikings who settled there came to farm or to trade, and that they took an active interest in the law and in the administration of their neighbourhood, for Scandinavian influences were paramount in northern England for over a century. During most of the period between AD 875–954 a Scandinavian kingdom was centred on York, first under Danish control and later under Irish-Norwegian vikings who maintained close connections with the kingdom of Dublin from whence they had come. Even after their eventual submission to Eadred of Wessex, the grandson of Alfred, the Scandinavian settlers in the north were allowed to retain their language, estates, laws and customs. It is not surprising, therefore, that two-fifths of the place-names of present-day Yorkshire are of Scandinavian origin. It has been claimed that many an old Yorkshire dialect word is still understood in Scandinavia.

The territorial divisions through which local government has operated in Yorkshire until 1974 date to this period of Scandinavian occupation. The term riding originated from an Old Norse term *Thrithiungr*, a third part. Equally Scandinavian in origin was the term wapentake, which replaced the former Anglo-Saxon hundred as the unit area of local government, at least in the north. The new term referred to the viking custom of flourishing weapons to mark the taking of a decision at the *Thing* – the public assembly where the freemen of the neighbourhood customarily met at frequent intervals to decide matters of local import.

Scandinavian Place-Names in -by and -thorpe in Yorkshire

As contemporary records of the Scandinavian period in the north of England are scanty, the main source of Scandinavian place-names in Yorkshire is Domesday Book. Compiled a little over fifty years after the death of Cnut, the Danish king of England, Domesday Book contains over 600 Scandinavian place-names in its Yorkshire folios, of which nearly 400 have survived with some modification to the present day. These names can generally be distinguished from the earlier Anglo-Saxon ones by their characteristic suffixes in *-by*, *-thorp*, *-thwaite*, *-gate*, *-garth*, *-scale*, *-gill* and *-how*. They are to be found in every part of the shire, and those pages of local newspapers that relate the events of the villages are full of them.

The most common ending is *by*, from the Scandinavian word *byr*. Of the 610 Scandinavian place-names examined by Dr Gillian F. Jensen in her detailed and scholarly study of the Scandinavian settlement names in Yorkshire, 214 – more than one-third – were

103

compounded with the element *by*. Though it distinguishes a Scandinavian settlement from an Anglian one, the term cannot be used to differentiate Danish from Norwegian sites, for it was used by both races to mean homestead, village or even township.

A large proportion of names in *-by* are compounded with Scandinavian personal names. Thornaby is today part of the Teesside conurbation, across the Tees from Stockton. Its name was written in Domesday Book as *Thormozbi*, which a century later had become *Thormodby*, from the Old Danish personal name *Thormoth* – *Thormoth*'s farmstead. Romanby, the name of a suburb of Northallerton, originated as '*Romund*'s farm' from the Old Scandinavian personal name *Hromundr*. Boulby, the village that has given its name to Boulby Cliff, the formidable headland north-west of Staithes, embodies the Scandinavian personal name *Bolli* – *Bolli*'s farmstead. A. H. Smith derives the name Whitby from the Old Scandinavian personal name *Hviti* – *Hviti*'s homestead. A few miles further along the coast a small hamlet bears the curious name of Ugglebarnby, preserving the viking nickname *Uglubarthi*, owl-beard. Visitors to the North York Moors will be familiar with the monument to Captain Cook on Easby Moor, if only as a distant landmark. The name of Easby hamlet has remained virtually unchanged since it was recorded in Domesday Book as *Esebi*, from the Old Scandinavian personal name *Esi* – *Esi*'s farm. In the heart of the North York Moors, not far from the ruins of Rievaulx Abbey, the scattered village of Hawnby began as 'the *by* of Halmi'. Travellers on the picturesque Esk valley railway between Middlesbrough and Whitby will recall Battersby Junction as the place where they caught their first close view of the moorland escarpment. The name was recorded in Domesday Book as *Badresbi*, combining the suffix *by* with the Scandinavian personal name *Bothvarr*. Ormsby, now a suburb of Middlesbrough, similarly derives its name from a viking settler named *Ormr*, as did Asselby near Howden from another viking, *Askell*.

In the West Riding the signposts in the neighbourhood of Roche Abbey near Rotherham bear the name of the small mining community of Maltby; this was originally '*Malti*'s farm'. In the East Riding the hamlet of Uncelby, tucked away at the foot of the chalk escarpment about six miles east of Stamford Bridge, was recorded in Domesday Book as *Unchelfsbi*, from the Scandinavian personal name *Hunkel* – *Hunkel*'s farmstead. Eight miles inland from Filey is the sub-scarp village of Willerby, originating from '*Wilheard*'s *by*'. Visitors to Bridlington may recall the neighbouring village of Sewerby. This is another name that has changed little through the ages, being entered in Domesday Book as *Siwardbi* – '*Siward*'s farm'. North-east of Selby, the hamlets of Barlby and Osgodby were once the farmsteads of *Bardulf* and *Asgaut* respectively.

Not all names in -*by*, however, include personal names; often they are topographical or descriptive of the type of farm. Wetherby, on the Great North Road, for instance, was recorded by the Domesday clerks as *Wedrebi*, from the Scandinavian word *vedr*, which meant a wether. It would seem that Wetherby entered history as 'a sheep farm'. There are several places in Yorkshire today that bear the name Sowerby – Sowerby Bridge, for instance, on the upper Calder, and Sowerby the suburb of Thirsk. In these names the first element derives from the Old Scandinavian word for mud or boggy land, *saurr*. Farmers still speak of undrained land as being 'sour'. Four miles north of Knaresborough the village of Ferrensby derives its name from the Scandinavian *faereyingr*, a word which denoted a man or men from the Faroe Islands. In the days of the sagas, participation in so long a voyage made a man nameworthy in rural Danelaw.

In the East Riding the hamlet of Burnby lies three miles southeast of Pocklington at the foot of the western scarp of the Wolds. It was recorded in Domesday Book as *Brunebi*, from the Scandinavian word for stream, *brunnr*; today the little stream is called the Bielby Beck. Another topographical place-name in -*by* is that of the lonely farm named Wauldby, on the top of the Wolds about two miles north-east of Brough-on-Humber. This appears in the Domesday record as *Walbi* – the farm on the Wold, still an apt description of this isolated site.

The North Riding provides many examples. A popular venue for an excursion is the attractive village of Thornton-le-Dale, near Pickering, where the Dalby Beck emerges on to the plain from the wooded gorge it has cut in the corallian limestone. Two farms, High and Low Dalby, today share the name with the stream. Even in Domesday times, when it was recorded as *Dalbi*, the name was topographically appropriate, for it included the Scandinavian word for dale, *dalr* – the valley farm. On the lowlands of the Vale of Mowbray, five miles north of Ripon, the village of Melmerby is situated on an extensive spread of glacial sands and gravels. The Scandinavian settlers may not have known much about glaciation in England, but they noted it with a farmer's eye, and referred to it when they coined the name of the settlement from their word *malmr*, a sandy field – the farmstead on the sandy soil.

Kirkby or Kirby is another place-name in -*by* that is common in Yorkshire. No less than sixteen places of that name were recorded in Domesday Book, eight from the North, six from the West and two from the East Riding. The name includes the Scandinavian word for church, *kirkja*, and can be translated as 'the church farm', 'the farm by the church' or 'the village with a church'. When these place-names were being coined only an occasional village had its own church. Even a wooden church was then a conspicuous feature and the use of the term *kirkja* as an element in a place-name helped greatly to identify a site.

Thorp is another Scandinavian element in common use in Yorkshire place-names, the Yorkshire folios in Domesday Book recording 156 *thorp* names, compared with the 214 in -*by*. The term was used by both Norwegians and Danes, generally to denote a relatively small outlying farm or hamlet, spreading out from and dependent upon an existing village. As the village population grew in number, individual families or groups tended to hive off to establish themselves in a fresh farm or hamlet in the neighbourhood.

In the East Riding, Northorpe and Southorpe arose as daughter settlements from Hornsea. At the southern tip of the Wolds a sub-scarp village settlement had already been endowed with the characteristically Anglian name of Brantingham. The Domesday clerks recorded an additional settlement or farm as *alia Bretingha*, the other Brantingham. This later became known as *Thorpe juxta Brantyngham* – the *thorp* next to Brantingham. The North Riding provides a similar example. Inland from Boulby Cliff near the moorland township of Loftus lie the twin settlements of Kilton and Kilton Thorpe. Both were there in Domesday times, for there is a record of *duas Chiltonas*, the two Kiltons. The Anglo-Saxon name Kilton, originally pronounced with the soft 'c' as in the Domesday entry, was the first; the other and later hamlet was entered as *Torp*, a Scandinavian addition. The process can be traced in operation in the records of the Fylingdales area above Robin Hood's Bay. Fylingdales has already been quoted in Chapter 4 as one of the early Anglian names dating probably from the sixth century, the element *ing* marking it as 'the settlement of the Fygelingas'. The Domesday clerks were still recording it in the eleventh century as *Figelinge*. But in the twelfth century another settlement appeared in the neighbourhood, recorded in a document of Whitby Abbey in 1133 as *aliam Fielingam* – the other Fyling. Today this daughter settlement is known as Fyling Thorpe.

A number of such subordinate hamlets or outlying farms are still known by the simple Scandinavian word *thorp*. There is, for instance, a Thorpe three miles north-west of Beverley, and another Thorpe in Wharfedale, once an offshoot from Burnsall. There is also a Thorpe-in-Balme near Doncaster. But fully half of the names in -*thorp* are compounded with Scandinavian personal names. Skelmanthorpe, between Huddersfield and Barnsley, was entered in Domesday Book as *Scelmertorp*, originally *Skialdmarr*'s *thorp*. Grimesthorpe, a colliery township well known today for its brass band, preserves the common viking personal name of *Grimr* or *Grim*. Despite the rural setting, the name of the little village of Cowthorpe on the banks of the Nidd north of Wetherby, has nothing to do with dairy-farming. In 1086 it was recorded as *Koletorp*, from the Old Scandinavian personal name *Koli* – *Koli*'s outlying farm. Hexthorpe, now part of Doncaster, began as '*Heggr*'s *thorp*. The hamlet of Carthorpe, just off the A1(M) two miles south of the Leeming Bar restaurant and filling station, similarly embodies an Scandinavian personal name, *Kari* – *Kari*'s *thorp*. Linthorpe, a suburb of Middlesbrough, was first recorded in the twelfth century as *Levingtorp*, which has been traced back to '*Leofa*'s *thorp*'. In the East Riding the sub-scarp village of Scagglethorpe, east of Malton, drew its name from the Old Scandinavian personal name *Skakel* – *Skakel*'s outlying farmstead.

Other names in -*thorp* include topographic or descriptive elements. Nunthorpe, an attractive hamlet now fast becoming engulfed in the expanding Teesside conurbation, is entered in Domesday Book as simply *Torp*. The name was recorded as *Nunnethorp* in 1240, after a nunnery had been established there. The picturesque road that runs along the foot of the moorland escarpment between Guisborough and Great Ayton passes through a small group of houses known today as Pinchinthorpe. The Domesday clerks returned it simply as *Oustorp*, from the Old Scandinavian word *austr*, east – the east *thorp*, a name which suggests it originated as an offshoot from the Anglian settlement of Great Ayton, four miles off to the west. Copmanthorpe, a few miles out from York on the road to Leeds, preserves in its first element the Old Scandinavian word *Kaupmanna* – the outlying settlement of the chapmen or wandering pedlars. At the eastern end of the Howardian Hills, four miles west of Malton, the hamlet of Coneysthorpe drew its distinguishing element from the Old Scandinavian *konungr*, the king's hamlet.

To this day, few settlements bearing names in -*thorp* are of a large size. From the start, most of these outlying farms and daughter hamlets lacked the resources of the old-established parent villages, and in the harsh conditions of the early Middle Ages many failed to survive. Of the Yorkshire settlements whose names contain the element *thorp* that are recorded in Domesday Book, eighty-eight no longer exist; all that is left of them today are their names and a few confused mounds and ditches. Some cannot be identified at all, and go to swell the numbers of 'lost villages', which are treated more fully in Chapter 9.

Until recently it was thought that the element *thorp* could be used as a test-word to distinguish Danish from Norwegian settlements, as the term was so rarely used in Norway in the tenth century. This view, however, has recently been challenged, since evidence has been found which suggests that the term was adopted in England by Norwegians entering from the north-west territory already colonised by Danish settlers. Though the evidence has not found universal acceptance, and most names in -*thorp* were Danish settlements, there remains a degree of uncertainty. Nor can the terms be used to discriminate between Scandinavian settlements and earlier English ones, for it has recently been found that the Anglo-Saxons had a similar term, which they spelt *throp*, with a somewhat similar meaning. Though this term *throp* is found mainly in southern England, its occasional use in the north raises the possibility that at least a few of the Yorkshire place-names which today contain *thorp* as an element had originated long before the viking invasions as Anglo-Saxon names in -*throp*. That the vikings would later change the English *throp* into their own more familiar cognate *thorp* was natural and inevitable.

Other Scandinavian Place-Names in Yorkshire

Few names illustrate more succinctly the effect of Scandinavian influence on English place-names than the two words in general use in England today for the round burial mounds of Bronze-Age times encountered on most of our downs and moors. Southerners refer to them as barrows, from the Anglo-Saxon *beorg*. Northerners speak of such tumuli as howes, from the Scandinavian *haugr*. Both terms were used to denote hills as well as burial mounds. The form in which the latter term howe has survived as an element in the place-names of modern Yorkshire varies greatly. It appears in Clitheroe, formerly *Cliderhou*, in which Ekwall says the element *haugr* is added as a suffix to the Old Scandinavian *klithra*, a song-thrush. It forms the suffix in the East Riding name Dringhoe. It is preserved in simple form in Howe, the name of a farm by Skipton-on-Swale. Between Saltburn and Loftus lies Carling Howe, a name which stems from the Old Norse *kerling*, an old woman – the old woman's mound.

109

Many Scandinavian elements in place-names referred to features of their homes or settlements. *Hus* was a word common to both Scandinavian and Anglo-Saxon tongues and meant house in both. Such names as Woodhouse, found near Sheffield and quite often elsewhere, therefore tell little of the origins of the settlements, though they remind us that dwellings for most families in the early Middle Ages were made of timber. But there is no ambiguity about such names as Lofthouse, examples of which can be found near Harewood House and on the road between Leeds and Wakefield, or Loftus, the busy little moorland town in East Cleveland. They originated from the Scandinavian word *lopthus*, denoting a house with a loft or upper floor. In a land where the peasantry everywhere lived in single-storeyed wood huts, a dwelling with a loft or upper storey was a conspicuous landmark and therefore likely to enter into any place-name coined in the neighbourhood. It is significant that no 'Stonehouse' was then recorded in the county; as a building material stone was expensive and used mainly for castles and the larger churches.

The word *toft* or *topt* also referred to dwellings. Originally denoting the site of a house and its outbuildings, the meaning broadened to cover the homestead itself. In general it conveyed what is meant today by a house-agent when he speaks of a curtilage. *Toft* names are fairly common in Yorkshire. The remote hamlet of Willitoft, on the lowlands of the lower Derwent five or six miles east of Selby, was entered in Domesday Book as *Wilgetot*, from the Scandinavian *welig*, willow-tree – the *toft* among the willows. Thrintoft, near Northallerton, developed its name from *thyrne*, the Scandinavian word for thornbush – the toft or house among the thornbushes.

The viking term for a rough wooden hut, or even a temporary shelter against the wind, was *skali*. The term has normally entered into the place-names of today as *scale* or more often in the plural as *scales*. Windscale in Cumbria, the site of the controversial nuclear establishment, is probably the most widely known example. The term has been preserved almost unchanged in the North Riding name of Scale Foot, a farm on the upper slopes of Commondale in the North York Moors west of Castleton. Not far away, on the slopes of the Moors north of Danby Beacon, there is a hamlet called Scaling, which has given its name to the reservoir and yachting marina by the moorland road between Whitby and Guisborough. This name is also derived from *skali*, a shieling. Such shielings were not confined to upland pastures. About three miles north of Rievaulx Abbey ruins, a small group of farm buildings is all that is left today of what was once a flourishing settlement named Laskill. This name originated in a combination of the two Norse words *lagr* and *skali* as 'the shieling on the low pastures', a reference to the water-meadows of the neighbouring River Seph.

The Norwegians introduced several words associated with their farming practices. Unlike the Danes, who came from a lowland region where arable farming was remunerative, their homeland was a land of mountains and valleys where pastoral farming predominated. The contrast between the high fjeld and the deeply cut fjords presented them with special problems. Accordingly, winter was spent by man and beast in permanent buildings down in the fjord valleys. But every spring as soon as the snows had melted they moved their flocks and herds up to the fresh upland pastures for grazing through the summer months, returning to their winter quarters only in autumn. Finding the landscapes in the Lake District not dissimilar from those of their homeland, the Norse settlers continued their practice of 'transhumance' and even extended it to their settlements on the Pennine moors. Their word *saetr* applied both to the upland pasture and to the huts built thereon in which the shepherds and herdsmen spent their summer supervising the sheep and cattle. The term has survived in many a north-country place-name as *sett* or *side*. In Yorkshire these names line the side-slopes of the Pennine valleys, and no one can cross from Yorkshire to Cumbria without seeing them on the signposts. In Wensleydale there are Appersett, Countersett, Burtersett and Sedbusk. Swaledale gives Gunnerside and Satron. Appersett was originally 'the *saetr* by the apple-tree', and Sedbusk 'the *saetr* by the bush'. The name Satron comes from the Norse words *saetr* and *rum*. The latter meant a clearing and the full name was 'the woodland cleared for an upland pasture'. The name Gunnerside combined the term *saetr* with a Norse personal name *Gunnarr* – *Gunnar*'s upland pasture. Wintersett in the West Riding was 'the winter *saetr* or shieling'. Another example of the survival of the term *saetr* in the modern form of *side* is given by the West Riding settlement of Selside in the Ribble valley between Horton-in-Ribblesdale and Ribblehead. The name appears in Domesday Book as *Selesat*, from the Old Norse words *seliu* and *saetr* – the shieling near the sallows or willows. Ekwall says it is a common place-name in Norway. More widely known is Ambleside in the Lake District, a name which denoted 'a *saetr* or shieling by a riverside sandbank'.

Another Norse term for these huts on the upland pastures has given us the present-day names of two places in the North Riding: Upsall, a hamlet at the very foot of the moorland escarpment four miles north-east of Thirsk, and another Upsall, a rural parish at the south-western end of the Eston Hills above Middlesbrough. Both names are derived from the Old Norse *up-salir* and referred to 'the high dwellings', an origin they shared with Upsala, the ancient capital of Sweden. The broad trail of names associated with transhumance from Cumbria eastwards suggests that not only did the Norse immigrants cross the Pennines by the northern dales to enter Yorkshire, but also that they found the high Pennine moorlands suitable for their pastoral farming and settled there to practise it by methods familiar to them.

So important was a natural water-supply to early settlers that many place-names incorporate the Old Scandinavian word for spring, *kelda*. There are about a score in the West Riding alone. Keld, the hamlet at the head of Swaledale, takes its name directly from this term, though in the fourteenth century it was known as *Appeltrekelde* – the spring by the apple-tree. Several place-names on the North York Moors illustrate this derivation. On the coastal moors between Skelton and Lingdale a spring named Cold Keld feeds the Boos Beck. There is a Potterkeld on the moors near Rievaulx. Still further south, just east of Kirkbymoorside, where the River Dove debouches upon the Vale of Pickering, one of the dip-slope springs has given a name to the hamlet of Keldholme, from the Old Scandinavian terms *kelda* and *holmr* – the water-meadow near the spring, or the spring in the water-meadow. In the East Riding several springs issuing from the Wolds have given names to settlements. One of the sub-scarp springs at the foot of the Wold escarpment east of Malton is called Roskell Spring, probably from the Old Scandinavian words *hross*, horse, and *kelda*. Two miles south of Driffield, two dip-slope springs from the chalk have given names to the small hamlets of Swinekeld and Cawkeld, respectively 'the pigs' spring' and 'the cold spring'.

To denote a road or street in the Danelaw the Scandinavian *gata* replaced the earlier Anglo-Saxon *straet*. The term is preserved intact in the name Gate Helmsley, half a mile west of Stamford Bridge in the East Riding. The reference is to the old Roman road from York to Malton beside which the settlement was sited. The old trackway over the North York Moors between Pickering and Whitby is still known as Saltergate – the salt way. Salt was conveyed by it to inland settlements from the evaporating pools on the coast. In Guisborough, Belmangate is the name of a street, and *gate* appears frequently in the street-names of York and many West Riding towns.

The Scandinavians also replaced the Anglo-Saxon word *ford* by their cognate word *vath*. As such river crossings were all-important in an age when even wooden bridges were none too common, it is not surprising that the term *vath* has entered into many place-names as wath. Several Yorkshire names are derived directly from it; there is Wath-on-Dearne near Mexborough and a Lambwath in Holderness. Two miles upstream from Pateley Bridge, on the outflow from the Gouthwaite Water reservoir, a hamlet called Wath marks the site of an old ford over the River Nidd. Even insignificant streams had to be forded: there is a Wath about five miles north of Ripon on the little Nunwick Beck, and another by a still smaller brook a mile east of Hovingham in the Howardian Hills. Many place-names of today combine the element with a descriptive comment. There is at least one Langwath and one

Broadwath within the county, and three settlements which bear the name Sandwath – the sandy ford. The moorland road to Whitby leaves Guisborough through the narrow gap of Slapwath, a name which incorporates the Old Scandinavian *sleipr* – the slippery ford. In contrast, one of the streams that flows off Fylingdales Moor into Robin Hood's Bay is called Helwath Beck, from the viking word *hella*, a flat stone – the ford made with flat stones.

The Old Scandinavian word *thveit* has entered into place-name formation in England through the dialect form *thwaite*. In this form it referred to a clearing, and the many place-names incorporating it show that the Danes and Norwegians continued the process of woodland clearance outlined in the previous chapter. On the rim of the valley of the Murk Esk near Goathland a farm bears the name Braithwaite, from the Old Scandinavian *breithr*, broad. There are three Braithwaites in the West Riding and another in the East Riding near Market Weighton, all denoting broad clearings. Midway along Arkengarthdale north-west of Reeth there is a hamlet called Langthwaite. The place-name Micklethwaite occurs three times in the West Riding, each originating from 'a large clearing'. Another West Riding settlement incorporating this term is Woolthwaite. It was recorded in the twelfth century as *Ulvathweit* – the wolves' thwaite, or the clearing infested by wolves – thus throwing a sinister light on living conditions in the early Middle Ages. Butterthwaite, also in the West Riding, derives its name from the Old Scandinavian *butere* and *thveit* – the clearing with the rich pasture.

Our present-day suffix 'garth' has come down to us virtually unchanged from the Old Scandinavian *garthr* and has retained the old meaning of an enclosed yard, or paddock. Many a village in the early Middle Ages consisted of a row of dwellings on opposite sides of the village street, each with its garth or yard opening out on to the road. Such a pattern can still be traced in villages like Cropton, near Lastingham, and in Cold Kirby, near Rievaulx. The term appears in many place-names in Danelaw, the garths now being utilised for garages and other small-scale village industries. Almost the last remaining garth in Marske-by-the-Sea was only recently built over by a supermarket. Hawsker, on the cliffs south of Whitby, was first recorded as *Houkesgarth*, incorporating the viking personal name or nickname *Haukr* to indicate '*Hawk*'s garth'. A lonely farm called Garfitt today stands on the southern slope of Hasty Bank, the high point in the moorland edge silhouetted against the skyline south of Stokesley, not far from the broken crags known as the Wainstones. In the fourteenth century the settlement here was recorded as *Garthwat*, combining the viking terms *garthr* and *thveit* – the clearing with the garth in it. The word is also found in Arkengarthdale, the name of the valley which branches off from Swaledale at Reeth. The dale element was not added till the time of Elizabeth I. In the twelfth century it was recorded as *Arkillesgarth*, incorporating the Old Scandinavian personal name *Arkil* – the valley of *Arkil*'s enclosure.

Other place-names indicated districts unfavourable for settlement. Both Danes and Norsemen had a variety of synonyms for marshy ground. A common one was *myrr*, still preserved in the final element of the Knavesmire at York, and in Gormire, the name of the lake seen by so many sightseers as they look down from the top of Sutton Bank near Thirsk. The term can be detected in the name Murk Esk, given to the tributary that flows into the River Esk at Grosmont, whose valley is followed by the popular and picturesque moorland railway line between Grosmont and Pickering. A variation of the term forms the final element of Ainderby Mires, the name of a parish north-west of the Leeming Bar motorway restaurant, denoting the original swampy nature of the ground. The first element of the name was derived from the viking personal name *Eindrithi* – *Eindrithi*'s farmstead in the marsh. Another synonym was *kjarr*, preserved in the name Redcar, a seaside resort near Middlesbrough. The derivation of this name – from the Old Scandinavian *read* and *kjarr*, the red marsh – compares with the derivation of the name of the neighbouring settlement of Marske from the Anglo-Saxon *mersc*, which also meant marsh and referred to the same damp coastal flats. The visitor to either of these resorts who cares to take an evening stroll in the fields behind them still comes across signs of the former boggy nature of the ground in the shallow pools and the remains of ditches dug in the eighteenth and nineteenth centuries to drain the land for cultivation. In the East Riding the term *kjarr* is preserved in the name 'carrs', given to the marshy lands on the southern border of the Vale of Pickering near the villages of Flixton and Folkton, and in the middle of the Vale around Seamer.

On the other hand, our viking ancestors with their interest in pastoral farming fully appreciated the value of the rich pasture afforded by the water-meadows that line the banks of the streams meandering slowly over the valley bottoms. Their word for these was *sletta*. The name appears today as Sleights, places of that name occurring in all three Ridings. Holidaymakers at Whitby will be acquainted with the neighbouring village of Sleights, where the houses climb steeply for nearly a mile up the southern side-slope of the Esk valley. But it was not the slope that impressed the Scandinavian settlers; their interest was caught by the flat water-meadows down on the valley bottom. They accordingly applied their term *sletta*, which has come down to us as Sleights through a thirteenth-century form *Slechetes*. A similar derivation applies to the name Sleightholme Dale, near Kirkbymoorside, which comes from a combination of *sletta* and another Old Scandinavian word *holmr*, meaning 'the flat ground of the water-meadows' in contrast to the moorland rising on either side.

Scandinavian Hybrid Place-Names in Yorkshire

The place-names so far treated in this chapter have in general been those of new settlements established by Danish and Norwegian immigrants. These people were not, however, settling in an uninhabited island – for four centuries the Angles and Saxons had been colonising the land, and the names of their towns, villages and farms had been well rooted in all parts of the country long before the Scandinavians arrived. In addition to adding new names required for the new settlements, the Scandinavian immigrants had a profound effect in other ways upon the existing Anglo-Saxon place-names.

The most dramatic consequence was the complete substitution, in some instances, of a new Scandinavian place-name quite different from the previous Anglo-Saxon one. The classic example of so complete a change comes from the Trent valley, where the Danes established their powerful kingdom of the Five Boroughs. One of these boroughs was Derby, a name which has come down to us from *Deorby*, the new name which the Danes substituted for the earlier Anglo-Saxon *Northworthig*. In Yorkshire, Whitby offers a less certain illustration. The name was established as *Witebi* by the time of the Domesday survey, with aspirated versions appearing later as *Whitby* and *Quiteby*. A mention in a Scandinavian saga as *Hvitabyr* confirms the origin from the Scandinavian personal name *Hviti* – *Hviti*'s settlement. But an early tradition has found general acceptance, by which the site has been identified as the *Streaneshalh* of Bede. If this identification is correct, the present-day name represents a complete, almost random, replacement of the Anglian name by a Scandinavian one.

Frequently, however, the newcomers replaced only a single element of an existing Anglo-Saxon village name by a cognate Scandinavian one, leaving the rest of the name unaltered. Such hybrid names are found in all parts of the Danelaw. In the West Riding, Mexborough derives its name from a combination of the Old English term *burh* with a viking personal name *Meoc* or *Miuk*. Silsden also bears a hybrid name, its first element probably representing a contracted form of the Scandinavian personal name *Sigulfr*, and its final element the persistence of the Old English word *denu*, a valley, the reference being to the valley of the River Aire.

In the area of the East Riding, Flamborough Head derives the first syllable of its name from *Fleinn*, and whether this represented a personal name or a noun meaning hook, its Scandinavian origin is beyond dispute. Equally certain is the Anglo-Saxon origin of the final element, *burh*. Another example of a hybrid name is Londesborough, given to a sub-scarp village about two miles north of Market Weighton. Again the final element is clearly derived from the Old English *burh*, indicative of some form of defensive work, ancient or contemporary. The first element comes from the Scandinavian personal name *Lothen* – *Lothen*'s *burh*.

In the lower Derwent valley there are several examples of such hybrid names in which the Anglo-Saxon word *wic*, indicative of a sheep-farm, was replaced by the Scandinavian *vithr*, a wood. Skipwith, for instance, was recorded by the Domesday Book clerks in Old English terms as *Schipewic*, the sheep-farm. By the thirteenth century this had become *Scipwid* and *Skypewith*, the final element being drawn from the Scandinavian *vithr*, a wood or copse. The alteration prevailed and the name has remained to this day as Skipwith. The neighbouring villages of Cottingwith and Bubwith obtained their final elements from the viking *vithr* by the same process. In the Vale of Pickering, the name Loft Marishes offers further illustration. The first element is the Scandinavian *lopt*, indicating a loft or upper storey; the second is from the Old English *mersc*, marsh. The complete hybrid name thus marked 'the house with a loft in the marsh'.

In the former North Riding, the name of the Halikeld Wapentake was a hybrid formation, combining the Old English term *halig*, holy, with the Scandinavian word *kelda*, spring. It is thought to have been the meeting-place of the *Thing* or public assembly of freeholders that played so important a part in local government in the Danelaw. Another example of a hybrid name is provided by the name Osmotherley, of a village that lies on the lower slopes of the moorland escarpment not far from the ruins of Mount Grace Priory just off the A19. The second element originated in the Old English word *leah*, a clearing. But the first came from the Scandinavian personal name *Asmundr*. Domesday Book recorded the name as *Asmundrelac* – *Asmund*'s clearing. Great Ayton, south of Middlesbrough, has already been quoted as having a name dating back to Anglian times, from *ea* and *tun* – the *tun* on the *ea* – *ea* being the Anglo-Saxon word for stream or river, in this case the Leven. The Scandinavian settlers subsequently converted the Anglian *ea* to simple *a*, their word for stream. Eton on the Thames has retained its Anglo-Saxon origin from *ea* and *tun*, but in Yorkshire the Scandinavian modification has prevailed.

Several of these hybrid place-names are to be found in the Pennines. Kettlewell, high up in Wharfedale under Great Whernside, derives its name from a combination of the Scandinavian *ketill*, a cauldron, with the Old English word *well*, a spring, the whole name picturesquely denoting 'the bubbling spring'. Austwick, between Settle and Ingleton in the Pennine uplands, is known to geologists for the many 'erratic blocks' or glacial boulders found in the neighbourhood. To place-name scholars it offers another example of the formation of hybrid names. The final element *wic* dates the origin of the name to Anglo-Saxon times, when it was probably known as *Eastwic* – the eastern dairy-farm. The Norse settlers replaced the Anglian *east* by their own familiar synonym *austr*, leaving both the *wic* syllable and the general meaning unaffected.

Further south, among the Pennine moors north-west of Otley, the name of the hamlet of Stainburn provides another illustration of the process. The Anglian settlers, impressed with the stony bed of the stream, coined the appropriate name *Stanburne* from their words *stan*, stone, and *burna*, stream – the stony brook. When the Scandinavians later settled in the district, they substituted their cognate word *steinn* for the Old English *stan*, leading to our present pronunciation of Stainburn. In upper Airedale, both the elements in the name Gargrave confirm the Anglian origin of the settlement. The first came from *gara*, the Old English word for a 'gore' – a triangular piece of land left after ploughing; the second came from *graf*, a copse or grove. The Scandinavian settlers in the locality retained the final element *graf*, which has come down to us as the suffix 'grave', but replaced the first with their cognate term *geiri*, thus changing the sound without altering the meaning.

One type of hybrid place-name is particularly common in the North – the type in which a viking personal name is combined with the Old English element *tun*. Dr G. F. Jensen has counted no less than thirty-three such names in the Domesday record for Yorkshire alone. In the East Riding area there are to this day three settlements named Grimston – one in Holderness, the others in the northern Wolds. The most attractive is North Grimston, at the

119

foot of the escarpment of the Wolds, where the road from Malton to Driffield swerves to take the steep wooded ascent at an angle. In all three names the final element is unquestionably the Old English *tun*. The first element is derived from the Scandinavian personal name *Grim* or *Grimr*, popular in the age of the vikings. So frequently does this particular combination occur that it has become the type-name for this kind of hybrid place-name. Another example of a Grimston hybrid name is to be found north of York in the name Wigginton, in which the Scandinavian personal name *Vikingr* prefixes the Anglo-Saxon *tun*. Similarly, in the name of the village of Nawton, three miles east of Helmsley along the road to Scarborough, the viking name *Nagli* was added to the Anglian settlement name *tun* – *Nagli*'s farmstead. Catton-on-Swale, a mile north of Topcliffe, combines the Scandinavian name *Kati* with the Anglian *tun* – *Kati*'s farm. The viking *Scurfa* substituted his name for one part of the Old English name, to give rise to the place-name Scruton, of a hamlet west of Northallerton. In Holderness, Rowlston combines the Scandinavian personal name *Hrolfr* with the English *tun*, to mark '*Rolf*'s farmstead'. By the same process, Towton, two miles south of Tadcaster and the site of a battle in the Wars of the Roses in 1461, combines the Danish name *Tovi* with the English *tun*.

Other Scandinavian Influences on Place-Names

The considerable Scandinavian influence on the pre-existing English place-names was greatly aided by the similarity between the languages. The language-barrier that had separated the Britons and the Angles in the sixth century, and which resulted in a thorough-going replacement of Celtic place-names by English ones, did not recur in the tenth century. Scandinavian and English languages had a common Germanic root. Many words were similar and some were identical. Reference has been made to *hus* as common to both tongues. There was little difference between the Old English word *cros* and the Scandinavian *kross* in pronunciation or meaning. *Land* appears in both tongues with the same connotation of estate or landed property. There was little to distinguish *micel* from *mikill*, the English and Scandinavian words respectively for great or large; nor the two words for valley – *dael* in Old English and *dalr* in Scandinavian. The English word for king, *cyning*, did not differ greatly from the Scandinavian *konungr*. The similarity between the Old English *stan* and the Scandinavian *steinn*, both meaning stone, has already been noted. Wolf was rendered as *wulf* in Old English and *ulfr* in Old Norse. This loss of the initial 'w' in the Scandinavian tongue was common and explains several of our place-names – for instance the name of Ulley, a small village and reservoir four miles south of Rotherham, which originated from the Anglo-Saxon *wulf* and *leah*, 'the wolf clearing', but which lost its initial 'w' under Scandinavian influence.

This linguistic similarity often makes it difficult to determine whether a place-name has an Anglian or a Scandinavian origin. For instance, did Drax, the name of a village between Selby and Goole, originate from the Old English word *draeg* or from the Scandinavian *drag*, both referring to a portage over the lower Ouse? We have no means of telling whether Hessay, a hamlet five miles west of York, was settled by the Angles with a name derived from the Old English *haesel* and *sae* to indicate 'a lake where hazels grow', or founded later by the Scandinavians as *hesli* and *saer*, with an identical meaning. Probably the modern name has descended from a replacement of the Anglian version by a later Scandinavian one.

But the similarity of the spoken word in the two tongues made for ease of communication between the two peoples. A. H. Smith quotes a story from the Scandinavian *Heimskringla* of a Norwegian viking who, fleeing from the defeat by Harold at the Battle of Stamford Bridge in 1066 and lacking warm clothing for so cold an evening, stole a fur-lined jacket from an East Riding farmer. Before eventually killing the farmer, they conversed. If the story is true, it would seem that Anglian speech was still intelligible to a Norwegian in the eleventh century. The basic similarity between the languages spoken by Angles, Danes and Norwegians during

121

the period of the Scandinavian immigration contributed to the eventual development of a joint Anglo-Scandinavian culture, especially in northern England. There was so often a convenient cognate word available for both races to use that linguistic fusion was facilitated.

The process was reflected in place-name formation. Conisbrough, between Sheffield and Doncaster and well known for its twelfth-century castle by the River Don, bears a name that originated from the Old English *cyning* – the king's *burh*. But by the time Domesday Book was compiled in the eleventh century it was written as *Cuningesburg*, the cognate Scandinavian *konungr* or *kunungr* having ousted the earlier English version. Similar replacements took place between the two words we translate as middle – the Old English *middel* and the Old Scandinavian *methal*. Methley lies in the coal-mining district south-east of Leeds. The Domesday Book clerks recorded it as *Medelai*, from the Old English terms *middel* and *leah* – the middle clearing. Under the influence of the cognate Scandinavian term *methal*, it became *Metheleia*, a change that has virtually persisted to this day.

Even more frequent than the substitution of cognate words or syllables were the changes in pronunciation that followed the Scandinavian settlement. The most common of these changes was that from the relatively soft sound of the Old English 'c' into the hard sound of the Old Scandinavian 'k'. Under such influence the Old English word for church, *cirice*, pronounced with a soft, palatalised sound, hardened into the Scandinavian pronunciation *kirkja*. The church dedicated to St Rumold in upper Teesdale was recorded in Domesday Book as *Rumoldescherce*, in its Old English form. A century later it had become Scandinavianised into *Rumbaldkirke*. Further south, on the southern fringe of the North York Moors near Ampleforth, a church was dedicated to St Oswald, probably the well-known Anglian Archbishop of York. The name of the village which had grown up around it was entered in Domesday Book in its Anglian form as *Oswaldescherca*. A century later, however, a document of Rievaulx Abbey recorded it as *Oswaldkirke*, in its Scandinavian pronunciation.

This change in pronunciation was widespread. It is reflected in the names of the hamlets Great and Little Kelk between Bridlington and Driffield. Domesday Book recorded them as *Chelche*, from an Old English word meaning chalk, which was appropriate to villages on the fringe of the northern Wolds. The name has since acquired the hard 'k' from the Old Scandinavian pronunciation. Birkin, a hamlet to the north-east of Knottingley, was similarly entered in Domesday Book as *Berchinge*, from the Old English *bircen*, birch-tree. Scandinavian influence has since substituted a medial hard 'k' for the softer and earlier Old English 'ch' sound, though we retain the latter in the tree name.

The two names Skipton, one of the busy market town in upper Airedale and the other of the smaller settlement Skipton-on-Swale, have also been modified. Both were recorded in Domesday Book as *Schipetune*, from the Old English words *sceap* and *tun*, sheep-farm. Under Scandinavian influence the softer 'sch' sound has hardened into the 'sk', a pronunciation retained to this day. This vocal change helps to explain the meaning of the place-name Skelton that is so frequently found in all parts of Yorkshire. A typical example is the Skelton that lies on the fringe of the North York Moors a mile or so inland from the seaside resort of Saltburn. Its church, solidly built of local sandstone, and the main street mark the original site of the settlement – on a natural terrace or shelf in the moorland slope as it falls away to the sea. The Domesday clerks recorded the name as *Schelton* – the *tun* on this natural shelf. A charter dated a century later, however, revealed the pronunciation to have become *Skelton*, to which we adhere today. A similar sound change is illustrated by the modification of the name Skirlaugh in Holderness from the early forms of *scir* and *leah*, the Old English for bright clearing, to its present form. Skipsea, on the coast of Holderness south of Bridlington, probably represents a Scandinavianised form of the Old English *Scip-sae*, a ship harbour. Skiplam, the name of a parish on the limestone moors above Kirkdale, carries the Scandinavian form of the Old English *scipen*, a shippon or cowshed. But perhaps the best known result of this sound change is to be found outside Yorkshire, in the place-name Keswick, though two hamlets in the area of the former West Riding, East Keswick and Dunkeswick, share the same derivation. All stem from the Old English *cese* and *wic* – the cheese farm. All three under Scandinavian influence lost their original soft Old English 'ch' sound for the hard 'k' of their present pronunciation.

Abbreviated Etymologies

Thornaby (NR, now Cleveland)

DB	1086	Turmozbi, Thormozbi
	1175	Thormodby
	1202	Thormodebi
	1279	Thormotebi
	1301	Thormotby
	1665	Thornaby

OSc personal name *Thormoth*
OSc *by*: farmstead or settlement

Gunnerside (NR, now North Yorks)

1301 Gunnersete
1655 Gonnerside
OSc personal name *Gunnarr*
OSc *saetr*: upland pasture

Osmotherley (NR, now North Yorks)

DB	1086	Asmundrelac
	1220	Osmundelai
	1398	Osmondirlay
	1536	Osmoderly

OSc personal name *Asmundr*
OE *leah*: clearing

Wetherby (WR, now West Yorks)

DB	1086	Wedrebi
	1190	Werebi
	1238	Wetherby

OSc *by*: farm
'farm where the wethers are kept'

Linthorpe (Middlesbrough)

1138 Levingtorp
1160 Levingthorp
1301 Leventhorp(e)
1614 Linthropp
OE personal name *Leofa*
OSc *thorp*, or *torp*: dependent settlement

Arkengarthdale (NR, now North Yorks)

1199 Arkillesgarth
1201 Arkillesgardh
1557 Arclegarthdaile
1671 Archengarthdale
OE *dael*: dale
OSc personal name *Arkil*
OSc *garthr*: enclosure

DB: Domesday Book   OE: Old English, Anglo Saxon
OSc: Old Scandinavian

6

The Scandinavian Settlement

For nearly a hundred years – from AD 867, when Halfdan first moved half the Danish host into Northumbria, until AD 954, when Eadred of Wessex recovered the territory for the English crown – Yorkshire had been subject to Scandinavian rule and settlement. Nevertheless, at the end of the eleventh century when Domesday Book came to be compiled, the proportion of place-names of English origin recorded in the Yorkshire folios (59 per cent) exceeded that of the Scandinavian, including the hybrid names (41 per cent). The ratio was not uniform over the whole county. The West Riding remained predominantly English, with 69 per cent of its eleventh-century place-names of Anglo-Saxon origin. In the East Riding the proportion was more evenly balanced, Scandinavian place-names forming only slightly less than half the total. The Norwegian settlement from Ireland via the Pennine passes helped to swell the Scandinavian ratio in the North Riding to 46 per cent.

Map 17 plots the general distribution of Scandinavian place-names in the county and so serves as a guide to the settlement pattern. It is a composite map, prepared from a number by Dr G. F. Jensen, and includes habitative types of name, such as those in -*by* and -*thorp*, as well as those descriptive of local topography. Hybrid names and names incorporating Scandinavian elements have been included, for such place-names indicate the presence of powerful viking influences that should not be overlooked.

The dispersal of place-names in map 17 shows that the pattern of Scandinavian settlement repeated in general that of Anglian times. The Pennine uplands and the North York Moors remained negative areas, for the perennial reasons. Settlement was as much confined to Airedale and Wharfedale as before. The overspill through the Aire Gap into Ribblesdale continued from Anglian times, and the place-names point to some Scandinavian penetration into Wensleydale and Swaledale. In the North York Moors the only parts that attracted settlement remained the glacial clay belt of the coastal moors and the fertile outcrop of corallian limestone in the south. The high sandstone moors to the north made no greater appeal to the Danes and Norwegians than they had to the Angles.

The Scandinavian place-names, like the Anglian names before them, are largely confined to the lowlands. Here the soil factors that had so much influenced the location of Anglian settlements in the vales of York and Mowbray continued to control the siting of the subsequent Scandinavian ones. Sites on sub-scarp and dip-slope springs appear to have been developed both in the Yorkshire Wolds and along the magnesian limestone belt of the West Riding. To the line of Anglian settlements whose Old English place-names have been plotted on map 13, the Scandinavians added at least two fresh names: Hunmanby, 'the *by* of the *Hundamanna*, the keepers of the hounds'; and Willerby, '*Wilheard*'s *by*'. A third name, Flotmanby, incorporates the Anglo-Saxon word for viking – *flotman* – marking the site of a viking settlement and offering a further example of a place-name coined not by its inhabitants but by the neighbours. A similar development can be traced along the line of dip-slope springs on the northern margin of the Vale of Pickering, where the vikings added three new names to the line of Anglian place-names plotted in map 16: Scalby, Aislaby and Kirkby.

Map 17 further shows a spread of Scandinavian place-names along the lower Derwent between Malton and its confluence with the Ouse. Kirkham and Scrayingham both show Scandinavian influence in the hard 'k' sound. High and Low Catton incorporate the viking personal name *Kati or Catta* in hybrid names meaning *Kati*'s or *Catta*'s *tun*. Thorganby derives its name from either the Old Danish personal name *Thorgrim* or the Norwegian *Thorngrimr*, as a hybrid denoting '*Thorgrim*'s farmstead'. The vikings *Askell*

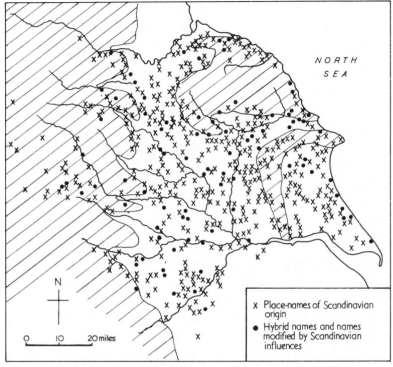

17 Distribution of Scandinavian place-names (*after G. F. Jensen*)

and *Biarni* gave their names to Asselby and Barmby, now villages in the lowland around the confluence of the Derwent with the Ouse.

The close scatter of Scandinavian place-names in map 17 suggests that the numbers of vikings involved were considerable. In view of the large number of Scandinavian and Scandinavianised place-names in northern England Stenton saw no reason to distrust the estimates of the great size of the viking armies as reported in the contemporary *Anglo-Saxon Chronicle*. Recently, however, following the work of P. Sawyer, historians have tended to regard these counts as exaggerations by a defeated party, and to attribute the success of the Danes to their mobile tactics. To account for the undoubted large number of Scandinavian place-names, K.

Cameron suggests a later secondary immigration of Danes – farmers rather than warriors – into the Midlands, arriving via the Wash and settling down under the protection of the Danish armies fifty years or so after the initial invasion. G. F. Fellowes has suggested that a similar development occurred in Yorkshire, presumably via the Humber. The frequent appearance of female names among the Scandinavian place-names, to which reference is more fully made in the final chapter of this book, suggests that the womenfolk were brought over in this later migration – a development that would have been unlikely until the initial period of fighting had yielded to a later one of settlement.

A Chronology of the Scandinavian Settlement of Yorkshire as Suggested by the Place-Names

The obscurity that surrounds the general history of northern England in the ninth and tenth centuries is especially dark concerning the manner in which the Scandinavian settlement was effected. We know from the written records that the composite Danish host split apart in AD 874. Guthrum with half the army remained in the Midlands to threaten Wessex. His fellow leader Halfdan moved his followers northwards against Northumbria, and two years later carried out a great partition of land in Yorkshire. This event is recorded in a brief but illuminating note in the contemporary *Anglo-Saxon Chronicle*, which recorded that in the year AD 876 'Halfdan divided out the land of the Northumbrians, and they [ie the Danes] proceeded to plough it and to support themselves . . .' Tantalisingly short though the statement is, its language suggests that the division of the land was done in an orderly and unhurried fashion. It also indicates a date when, after nine years of constant warfare ranging from the Tees to the Thames, at least part of the Danish host was beginning to think in terms of farming rather than of fighting, and that the rank-and-file of the viking army was realising that more profit was obtainable from settled agriculture than from further plundering of an impoverished countryside. Beyond this the written record fails.

No contemporary account has come down to us, assuming one was ever written, of what exactly occurred when a viking leader divided out a province. We are left to make what we can of the place-name evidence.

It is likely that the upper ranks of Anglo-Saxon society were the first to be adversely affected. A viking of high rank may well have been awarded a large tract of land, comprising the estates of several Anglian thegns. There is written evidence that something of this sort happened. A generation later, when the viking Raegnald established himself in the kingdom of York and seized the estates of the Bishop of Durham, he gave much of south Durham 'to one mighty warrior' and an equally large territory to another. Such beneficiaries would have lesser leaders to reward, and so down through the military grades, until the rank-and-file warriors were established on sites where they could either live on the rents of their newly-acquired estates, or occupy farmsteads whereon they could maintain themselves and their families, as described in the *Chronicle* extract quoted above.

Such dispossession of Anglian landowners may not have been so extensive as might be thought, for in the course of the Danish war many such Anglian thegns would have perished, leaving their estates for the taking. Nor is such a process inconsistent with the place-name evidence. Many a hybrid name, especially those of the Grimston type in which a viking personal name was added to the Old English term *tun*, could have been formed in this way. Community life had to continue in spite of military vicissitudes. This would account for the retention of the Anglian term *tun* as the second and original element in the place-name, while the name of the new Danish occupant or landlord was added or inserted to distinguish the estate from its neighbours. If the vikings Flikkr and Folki acquired their lands in two of the sub-scarp villages on the southern fringe of the Vale of Pickering by such a grant, their own interests would have induced them to encourage rural life to continue much as before. That being so, it is not inconceivable that the people of the neighbourhood, Angles and Scandinavians alike, would soon come to attach the names of the new landowners to the former place-names ending in -*tun*. In such a manner the names Flixton and Folkton, and many other typical Grimston hybrid names, could have originated.

To account for the hundred or more purely Scandinavian place-names included in the Yorkshire folios of Domesday Book in which a viking personal name is combined with a Scandinavian term such as *by*, other explanations may be possible. These names may indicate a general establishment of the rank-and-file of the Danish armies on farms in the north. The more peaceful settlement of the Norwegian immigrants from Ireland, and a later, unrecorded immigration of farming communities from Denmark as has been suggested, may have contributed. Such men would not become landlords of sizeable estates, but cultivators of small farms, possibly seized from the previous Anglian occupier, or more probably carved out of the uncultivated wastelands that separated the villages. The inclusion of their names in local nomenclature did not indicate any seigniorial status. One need not assume that the viking *Esi* whose name appears in our Easby Moor, marked for us by its monument to Captain Cook, was the owner of a large estate there. Even if he had been no more than an ordinary Danish farmer of his day, his neighbours would naturally have named the farmstead after him as '*Esi*'s *by*', either because he was the first viking occupant or because for some other reason unknown to us he was a noteworthy member of the village community in which he played a part.

Such peasants, holding their farms by tenures that rendered them largely if not wholly independent of any jarl or lord of the manor, formed a distinctive feature of northern England in the tenth and eleventh centuries. Southern England could offer no parallel to the large class of dependent or semi-dependent peasants who fitted so inconveniently into the developing manorial system. The Domesday Book clerks classified them as *freemen* or *socmen*, and the frequent use of such terms indicates the presence in Yorkshire of large numbers of such privileged peasants. This documentary evidence is supported by the frequent occurrence of nicknames in place-name formation. The hamlet near Whitby called Ugglebarnby has already been quoted as originating from the Scandinavian nickname *Uglubarthi*, Owl-beard. Faceby, a hamlet at the foot of the western escarpment of the North York Moors not far from the well-known inn on the A19, the Cleveland Tontine, similarly bears a name derived from *feitr* and *by* – the '*by* of the fat man'. Cadeby in the West Riding bears a name embodying the Scandinavian nickname *Kati*, the cheerful one. In the East Riding, Nafferton is a hybrid name stemming from the Scandinavian nickname *Nattfari*, the tun of the 'night wanderer'. Not only do such names remind us that they were coined by neighbours rather than by the owner of a property, but they also suggest that the original owners were men of no higher status than that of ordinary villagers.

Yorkshire place-names throw a helpful light upon the relationship between the established Angles and the incoming Scandinavians. A comparison between the distribution of Anglian place-names in map 11 with that of the Scandinavian place-names in map 17 has shown that the Danes and Norwegians settled in the same lowland areas previously favoured by the Angles, and avoided the same uplands which the Angles had found unattractive. Nowhere in Yorkshire are Scandinavian place-names to be found isolated in separate enclaves; Anglian and Scandinavian place-names are intermingled everywhere. It is manifest that in tenth-century Yorkshire there was no major expulsion of the native English. Scandinavian settlements were juxtaposed with, rather than superimposed upon, the existing Anglian ones.

The signposts in the rural lanes of most parts of Yorkshire, with their admixture of Scandinavian and Anglian names, testify to this racial co-existence. Map 21 (see page 146) conforms this mingling of names in the area south-west of Stokesley and Middlesbrough. But the most striking evidence comes from the name Hutton Rudby, borne by an attractive village marked in map 21 on the River Leven. The river cuts a deep cleft; on one side of this is the settlement called Rudby with its old church, and on the other, Hutton, a dignified village of stone houses built around a large green, shaded with ancient trees. Both settlements were well established by the eleventh century, for both are recorded in Domesday Book. Hutton was the *Hoton* in 1086 – from the Old English *hoh*, meaning high, 'the high *tun* or settlement', standing high above the stream on the southern bank. Rudby was recorded as *Rodebi*, a purely Scandinavian place-name, from the viking personal name *Rudi* and the Scandinavian *by* – *Rudi*'s farmstead or settlement. It is inconceivable that two settlements so closely situated could have survived to the end of the eleventh century and beyond if Yorkshire had been torn asunder by bitter racial rivalry between Englishman and Dane.

The traditional picture of the fierce and ruthless viking requires modification. The place-names offer no evidence that the native Anglian population of Yorkshire was driven off its fields, still less exterminated, even in areas where Scandinavian place-names are most frequent. The many hybrid names and the still greater number of Old English place-names that were modified under the influence of Scandinavian speech suggest that the immigrant farmers settled down in a neighbourly relationship with the existing Anglian farmers. There was no shortage of land in the tenth century. The numerous place-names in *-thorp* – 155 in Yorkshire alone – show that the Scandinavian immigrants had no difficulty in finding unoccupied or undeveloped sites for their outlying farms and daughter settlements. A common racial stock, a not dissimilar language, and above all a common interest as farmers facing the perennial threat of famine were powerful factors in bringing the incoming Scandinavians rapidly into economic and social touch with the Anglian population. Vikings and Angles began to merge their cultures. The amalgamation was marked by an interchange of personal names, Scandinavian settlers adopting Anglian Christian names and vice versa in the eleventh and twelfth centuries. The coining of hybrid place-names was a significant aspect of this cultural and social fusion, and continued until as late as the thirteenth century. This may have rendered it impossible for us today to affix a certain date for the formation of any particular hybrid name, but it is evidence that the development of an interracial Anglo-Scandinavian culture had gone far by the time of the Norman Conquest.

Though Scandinavian and Anglian settlements were in general intermingled, the scatter of Scandinavian place-names was still uneven. We have seen that there were areas where, by sheer numbers or by social power, the Danes were able to replace an existing Anglian place-name by a fresh one of their own. Derby and Whitby have been quoted in illustration. But these towns were important enough for their Old English names to have been preserved in the urban records. If this happened to a small and insignificant Anglian village or hamlet, the change might go unrecorded and the old name pass into oblivion. In such a case we would have no inkling today that the Danish settlement had been preceded by an Anglian one.

G. F. Jensen has suggested that this happened more frequently than we realise. In support, she calls attention to settlements like Easby on the North York Moors and Melsonby and Kirby Hill near Richmond. These today bear such undoubtedly Scandinavian names, combining the viking *by* with Scandinavian personal names and the Scandinavian *kirkja*, that we could be forgiven for assuming that they were Scandinavian foundations – but for one thing. The church in each of the villages contains a stone cross carved by Anglian sculptors in a style that was essentially English, without a trace of Scandinavian influence. From this it is reasonable to conclude that these Scandinavian settlement names had been preceded by Anglian ones. Further evidence comes from the discovery of traces of pre-viking churches there, confirming the existence of these settlements in Anglian times. G. F. Jensen has listed no less than forty-eight places in Yorkshire with such Scandinavian names for which there is independent evidence for an original Anglian settlement – eighteen in the West Riding, seven in the East Riding and twenty-three in the North Riding. It is evident that the complete substitution of a new Scandinavian name for the previous Anglian one was by no means uncommon.

On the other hand, the survival of an Old English place-name is no guarantee that the Scandinavians were successfully excluded from an exisiting Anglian settlement. It appears that not infrequently the Scandinavians retained the Anglian place-name virtually unaltered. G. F. Jensen reminds us that in Yorkshire today there are nearly a hundred towns and villages, every one bearing an unquestionably Old English place-name, where the visitor can see a massive stone sculpture, carved in Scandinavian style and decorated with Scandinavian motifs, obviously designed to suit viking taste. Examples are to be found in all parts of the county. They include well-known towns like Aberford, Bingley, Dewsbury, Ilkley and Otley in the West Riding; and Bedale, Helmsley, Hovingham, Lastingham, Northallerton, Ripon, Wensley and Yarm in the North Riding. She concludes that despite the Anglian origin of the place-names, the erection of such massive Scandinavian sculptures, too heavy for anything but permanent siting, suggests the presence in each settlement of a powerful, wealthy and influential viking who was content to leave unaltered the existing Anglian place-name.

In view of the lack of recorded details of the Scandinavian settlement, attempts have been made in recent years to trace the stages of the Scandinavian migration into England through place-names. From the researches of P. Sawyer, K. Cameron and G. F. Jensen a tentative chronology has been evolved. Sites now bearing hybrid names, especially of the Grimston type, are thought to have been among the first to have been taken over. The retention of the Old English element *tun* in hybrid names of the Grimston type, and of *ham* or other Old English terms in other hybrid types, suggests that most English inhabitants of such settlements continued to live on largely undisturbed. Such a conclusion presupposes that these hybrid names date to an early stage in the migration, when a relatively small number of viking warriors of high rank were taking over Anglian estates where Old English place-names were still in general use by a predominantly Anglian population. During this stage, nothing could have been more natural than for the people of a neighbourhood, still mostly English, to continue their customary reference to the estate by its traditional name in -*ham* or -*tun*, while prefixing it with the name of the new viking overlord.

Most Scandinavian place-names in *-by* are thought to belong to a later, second stage in the settlement, when the bulk of the rank-and-file warriors of the Danish host were disbanded and established on farms 'to support themselves', as the *Anglo-Saxon Chronicle* expressed it in the passage quoted at the beginning of this section. There is nothing intrinsically unlikely about such a suggestion – as already mentioned, the vikings were as much farmers and colonisers as sailors and fighters, and plenty of productive but unused land was available in the England of the tenth century. It explains the high proportion of personal names that enter into the Scandinavian place-names, and the many small but independent farmers in Yorkshire recorded later in Domesday Book. It covers the settlement of those farming families who are thought to have come over from Denmark in that second migration mentioned above. It accounts for the intermingling of Scandinavian and Anglian settlements.

Thereafter began the long and later period of colonisation. Place-names in *-thorp* are generally regarded as dating from this third period. They were mostly secondary settlements, outlying farms on the fringe of a village, or daughter hamlets stemming from and dependent upon an established village, like Kilton and Kilton Thorpe in the North Riding. More than half the *thorp* names in Yorkshire are compounded with personal names, of which 85 per cent are Scandinavian. Such figures support the view that the majority of settlements with names in *-thorp* were established by colonising farmers after the disbanded Danish host had firmly established their villages and farms. Even today, the *thorp* names that have survived refer mostly to insignificant sites – hamlets or isolated farms – though there are marked exceptions, such as Cleethorpes in Lincolnshire.

Of these three phases the last was the most prolonged. This process of infilling those parts of lowland England that had hither-to not been cultivated continued far beyond strictly Scandinavian times, as shown in Chapter 9. Sawyer sums the matter up in these words: 'The extension of Scandinavian settlement in the *by* areas of England is in large measure a continuation of that movement of expansion that began in Scandinavia and itself led to the migration overseas, and this expanding Scandinavian settlement in England was the beginning of the process of internal colonisation that was to reach its greatest extent in the thirteenth century.

Norse and Irish Place-Names in Yorkshire

Map 17 has plotted the general distribution of Scandinavian place-names in Yorkshire without making any distinction between those of Danish, Norwegian and Irish origin. The similarity between the languages makes such a distinction well-nigh impossible. To denote, for instance, an island or a relatively dry patch in a fen the Danes used the term *holm*. The corresponding Norwegian term was *holmr*. Equally close were the Danish and Norse versions of the Scandinavian word for king – *konung* in Old Danish, *konungr* in Old Norse. Such terms as *thveit*, a clearing, now preserved as *thwaite*; *kelda*, a spring; *vithr*, wood or forest; *skogr*, a wood; and *myrr*, mire or bog, were in common use by both communities. It is virtually impossible therefore to distinguish between Danish and Norwegian origins of place-names recorded in Domesday Book, compiled more than a century after the initial Scandinavian settlement in northern England.

We can no longer assume, as once was thought possible, that a place-name in *thorp* indicated a settlement of Danes as distinct from one of Norwegians. It is true that the term was as common in Denmark as it was rare in Norway, and that most *thorp* names in Yorkshire indicate Danish colonisation. But evidence has come to light which suggests that after the Norwegians had settled in England some of them encountered Danish settlers and borrowed the term, adopting it into their own tongue. In the case of any particular *thorp* name we can rarely be sure that this has not happened.

Occasionally, however, the incorporation of a personal name into a Scandinavian place-name may reveal the racial origin. Gunnerside, the name of the picturesque village in upper Swaledale, has already been traced to a viking named *Gunnarr* –

Gunnarr's *saetr*. Since this personal name is known to have been very popular in Norway at the time of the migration, it is reasonable to conclude that Gunnerside began as a Norse rather than a Danish settlement. Another example of similar confirmatory evidence comes from Scarborough. A saga of the period relates how a Norseman known by his nickname *Skarthi*, 'hare-lip', after 'harrying in Ireland, Wales, England and Scotland . . . set up the stronghold which is called Scarborough' – Skarthi's *burh*. Such voyaging around the Irish Sea was more characteristic of Norse vikings than Danish. But such exceptions only prove the general rule.

Nevertheless, some agricultural terms may be found helpful as a general guide. Transhumance terms such as *saetr* and *up-salir* were so characteristic of Norse pastoral farming that it is tempting to use them to distinguish Norse from Danish settlements. But since some Danish immigrants penetrated into the Pennine valleys, settled there, copied the farming practices of their Norwegian neighbours and adopted their terminology, these words cannot today be used as distinguishing type-words. Nor, for similar reasons can the Old Norse word *thveit*. We can only surmise in general that if such place-names occur frequently in a district, Norse settlers predominated there.

Some topographical terms may prove helpful, though only as a general guide. *Gill* and *force* are both derived from Norwegian words that have entered into many place-names in the high uplands of north-west Yorkshire. The element *force*, found in many Pennine place-names, came from the Norwegian word *foss* or *fors* denoting a waterfall. It survives in Hardraw Force, the well-known cataract near Hawes in Wensleydale. Presumably the fall impressed the Scandinavians who first settled in the locality, as well it might, for the term also appears as an element in the name of Fossdale Farm on the neighbouring fell. On the opposite side of Wensleydale, its waters tumbling into Semer Water, is Yorkshire's High Force, sharing with its famous namesake in Teesdale the same etymological origin. A few miles north-east of Scotch Corner on the A1.M is the hamlet of Forcett. Its name is derived from the Norwegian words *fors* and *saetr*, giving the attractive meaning of 'the shieling, or upland pasture by the waterfall'.

The present-day word 'gill' comes from the Norse *geil* or *gil*, which originally denoted a ravine rather than the stream itself, as today. Walkers in all parts of the Pennines will be familiar with the term, and numerous place-names incorporating the element occur in the county. Gayles, on the road between Richmond and Barnard Castle, derives its name from this Old Norse word *geil*, applicable to several ravines in the vicinity. There is a village of Gayle in Wensleydale, immediately south of Hawes, where the name originally referred to the ravine of Sleddale Beck, which formerly turned the village mill. This village name was recorded in the thirteenth century as *Sleddalgayle*, combining the Old English word *slaed* with the Norse *dalr* and *geil*. The first two elements both meant valley, and the final one a ravine – an example of triple tautology. In the same neighbourhood High Gill and Low Gill are names of farms near the well-known Aysgarth Falls on the northern slope of Wensleydale. The many examples of such place-names derived from these Old Norse terms which visitors to Swaledale and Wensleydale see on the local signposts can be accepted as reasonable evidence that the early Norse settlers in Yorkshire crossed the Pennines by these dales as they entered the county from Cumbria.

One type of Yorkshire place-name, however, suggests with some degree of certainty a distinctively Danish settlement. Readers of Canon Atkinson's classic *Forty Years in a Moorland Parish* will be familiar with the scattered village of Danby in the Esk valley described in that book. The name is not uncommon, and is found in all parts of the county. Passengers on the inter-city trains pass the hamlet of Danby Wiske just north of Northallerton. There is also a Danby-on-Ure. In Holderness, five miles east of Hull, Danthorpe Hall today marks the site of the Domesday hamlet of *Danetorp*. Near Penistone are Denby and Denby Dale. All these names indicate a '*by* or village of the Danes'. It is reasonable to conclude that such a name would have been given either to distinguish a Danish settlement in a mainly Anglian district, or to differentiate a settlement of Danes from one of Norwegians.

Norwegian settlements can often be recognised by an element in a place-name that refers to Normans or Northmen. In the area of the North Riding alone there are three examples. Normanby today forms a suburb of Middlesbrough at the foot of the Eston Hills. Another Normanby is to be found in the Vale of Pickering, a few miles north-west of Malton. A third is a hamlet near Hawsker just off the A171 from Whitby to Scarborough. All these names appear in Domesday Book as *Normannebi* – the *by* of the Northmen. In the West Riding there is Normanton, just west of Castleford — the *tun* of the North men. The Northmen referred to in all these cases were probably Norwegians rather than Danes.

Sometimes it was an English village that was conspicuous in an area of predominantly Scandinavian settlement. South of Stokesley the hamlet of Ingleby Arncliff lies near the foot of the scarp of the North York Moors. There is an Ingleby Barwick and an Ingleby Greenhow near Middlesbrough. The Ingleby part of these names comes from the Old English *Engle*, a reference to the Angles, or English. The final element *by* suggests that the name was coined by Scandinavian immigrants to mark an Anglian village in a neighbourhood where Scandinavians had settled in numbers large enough to render a village of English folk unusual.

Settlements of Irish-Norse immigrants from Ireland can similarly be traced by specific elements in place-names. In the lowlands between Northallerton and the Tees, Irby Manor marks the site of a '*by* of the Irish'. *Airgh* is an Old Irish word from the Celtic that has entered into Yorkshire place-names through the speech of the Scandinavian settlers who came across the Irish Sea. It indicated an upland pasture or a shieling used in the summer – clearly a transhumance term. One such name is Airyholme, of a village in the Howardian Hills near Hovingham. It was first recorded in the twelfth century as *Erghum*, from the Old Irish *airgh*. On Great Ayton Moor, just south of Roseberry Topping, there is a farm called Airy Holme, the original element *airgh* having shrunk to *Ergun* by Domesday Book times to give the element 'airy' of our day. The same element appears in a slightly distorted form in Arrathorne and Eryholme. Arrathorne lies three miles north of Patrick Brompton at the entrance to Wensleydale. The name was first recorded as *Ergthorn* – the shieling by the thorn-bush. Eryholme, the name of a hamlet south of Darlington, shares the derivation.

Personal names sometimes reveal a settlement by Celtic Irish-men who joined the Norse immigration. In upper Wharfedale there is a hamlet called Yockenthwaite. The thirteenth-century form, *Yoghannesthweit*, combined the Scandinavian term *thveit* with the Irish name *Eogan*, to give *Eogan*'s clearing. Carberby, a hamlet on the side-slope of Wensleydale opposite Aysgarth, was recorded in Domesday Book as *Chirprebi*, a name which Ekwall derives from the Old Irish personal name *Cairpre*. The place-name Lackenby, now of an outer suburb of Middlesbrough, probably combined the Old Irish personal name *Lochan* with the Scandina-vian settlement term *by*. The gorge which the River Dove has cut in the limestone as it emerges from Farndale to enter the Vale of Pickering bears the name Douthwaite. A twelfth-century docu-ment of Rievaulx Abbey reveals this as *Duvanesthwat* – *Duvan*'s *thwaite* or clearing – from the Old Irish personal name *Duvan*. Still more disguised is Commondale, the name of a small hamlet in the steeply entrenched valley of that name in the North York Moors that carries the Esk Valley railway line as it leaves the lowlands of the lower Tees to enter the moorland. The earliest recording of the name, in the thirteenth century, significantly gave it as *Colemandale* – *Colman*'s *dael* or valley. The name *Colman* is of Irish origin, being a shortened form of the Irish name of *Columban*. Irish personal names are found as elements even in the East Riding. Just over the crest of the chalk escarpment south-east of Malton lies the hamlet of Duggleby. Domesday Book gives it as *Difgelibi* – *Dufgall*'s *by*. *Dufgall* is a Norse personal name which was borrowed from the Old Irish *Dubhghall*. This Irish-Celtic name meant black foreigner, a term commonly applied in Ireland to the Norwegian raiders whose black sails struck terror into the coastlands.

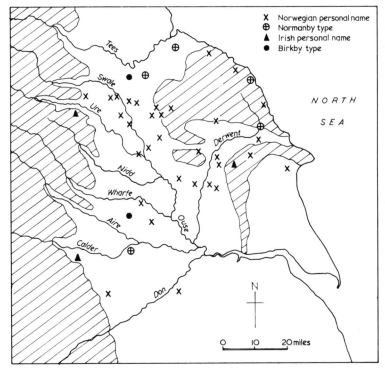

18 Distribution of Norse and Irish place-names

Reference is occasionally made in place-name elements to 'the Britons'. Five miles north of Northallerton stands the village of Birkby, a name recorded in Domesday Book as *Bretebi* – the Britons' village – from the Old Norse *breta* and *byr*. It is unlikely that the Britons referred to in such names were descendants of the sixth-century Celts of Cumbria; they are almost certain to have been Irish Celts who migrated with the Norse settlers, first to Cumbria and later over the Pennines into Yorkshire.

Map 18 plots the distribution of the place-names suggestive of Norse and Irish settlements in Yorkshire. The Norwegian place-names used are confined solely to those in which their Norse origin is attested by a Norse personal name forming an element. Such topographical elements as force and gill, and terms associated

141

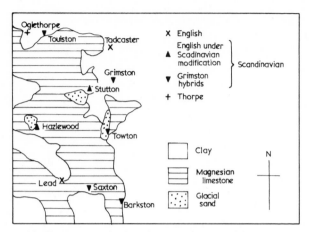

19 Place-names and geology south-west of Tadcaster

with transhumance have been excluded on the grounds of a measure of uncertainty. As a result, the map fails to reveal the considerable scatter of Norse place-names in the dales in the north-west of the county. But it does illustrate the spread of Norse settlements across Yorkshire from the Pennine crossings to the eastern seaboard, thinning out with the distance eastward.

Scandinavian Place-Names and Geology in Yorkshire

Of the recent developments in the study of place-names, one of the more interesting has been the examination of their distribution in relation to local geological features. The technique, developed by K. Cameron and G. F. Jensen, has passed beyond correlating settlement sites with geological outcrops; attempts are now being made to use such correlations to contribute to a solution of the problems of settlement chronology.

Map 19 reproduces in simplified form a map by G. F. Jensen of that part of the Vale of York south and west of Tadcaster. The main geological feature is the belt of magnesian limestone about four miles wide which crosses the region from south to north – part of the limestone outcrop from Nottinghamshire to the Durham coast. This stone was quarried at Tadcaster for the Roman legionary fort at *Eboracum* and, in medieval times, for

142

York Minster. The strata dip gently down towards the east, forming a low escarpment facing west, just off the map. Within the region mapped this limestone outcrop is flanked largely by deposits of glacial clay. The main geological control over settlement has been the contrast between the permeable limestone belt, with its naturally drained and fertile soil, and the heavy, impermeable boulder clay on each flank.

Only two place-names directly testify to Anglian settlement: Tadcaster and the hamlet called Lead. It does not follow, however, that these were the only Anglian settlements in the region. There are no less than five Grimston hybrid names – Barkston, Grimston, Saxton, Toulston and Towton. The preservation of *tun* as the second element of each name bears witness to their English origin. The vikings whose names form the first element presumably took over established Anglian villages. Two other names, Hazelwood and Stutton, also of English origin, were modified under later Scandinavian influence. G. F. Jensen reasonably concluded that it was likely that the whole area mapped was fully occupied by the English long before the coming of the Danes. When the Danes did arrive it seems likely that they took over the majority of the settlements the old names of which were then gradually changed to incorporate the names of the new viking masters or were modified in other ways. Such a large proportion of hybrid and Scandinavian-ised place-names suggests an early stage in the migration, and could denote part of the settlement of Halfdan's warriors in the partition of AD 876 or of a subsequent partition.

Map 20 draws upon another map by G. F. Jensen, which takes us back to the region of the northern Wolds. The major geological factors in the early Anglian settlement of this region were outlined in Chapter 4 as the clay plain in the north, the steep chalk escarpment with the line of sub-scarp springs at its foot, and the higher levels of the Wolds to the south, with their characteristic dry valleys, including the Gypsey Race. The Anglian settlements were shown in map 13, in which the line of villages on the spring-line contrasted with the few and widely dispersed settlements in the Gypsey Race valley. Map 20 shows the effects of the Scandinavian

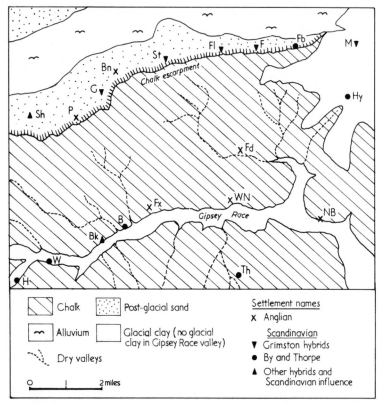

20 Place-names and geology in the northern Wolds (after *G. F. Jensen*)
Key: B Baythorpe; Bk Butterwick; Bn Binnington; F Folkton;
Fb Flotmanby; Fd Fordon; Fl Flixton; Fx Foxholes; G Ganton;
H Helperthorpe; Hy Hunmanby; M Muston; NB Burton Fleming;
P Potter Brompton; Sh Sherburn; St Staxton; Th Thwing; W
Weaverthorpe; WN Wold Newton.

Within the legend:

Chalk

Post-glacial sand

Alluvium

Glacial clay (no glacial clay in Gipsey Race valley)

Dry valleys

0   1   2 miles

Settlement names
x Anglian

Scandinavian
▼ Grimston hybrids
● By and Thorpe
▲ Other hybrids and Scandinavian influence

immigration into the same area. The contrast between the line of
spring-line villages and the dispersed settlements on the Wolds
remains. But of the nine Anglian place-names of the former period
located along the spring-line only two have survived unchanged –
Binnington and Potter Brompton. Six others still proclaim their
Anglian origin by their final element *ton*. From west to east five
are recognisable as Grimston hybrid names – Ganton, Staxton,

144

Flixton, Folkton and Muston – each compounding a viking name with the Anglian *tun*. The most westerly, Sherburn, is another form of hybrid name. It is highly likely that all these survived from Anglian times, each village being taken over by vikings as their allocation in the early stage of the viking settlement.

Later Danish settlement is reflected in the place-names Hunmanby and Flotmanby. We have already encountered Hunmanby as a completely Scandinavian name *Hundemanebi* in Domesday Book, meaning 'the by of the houndsmen'. Flotmanby is a hybrid place-name, but it differs from other hybrid names quoted in the previous paragraph in that its Anglian element *flotman* was commonly used to refer to the vikings, giving a meaning to the whole name as 'the *by* where the vikings live.' If the hybrid place-names of the previous paragraph reflected the parcelling out of the Anglian estates among the leaders of the viking host in the initial stage of the settlement, Flotmanby and Hunmanby illustrate a subsequent stage when the rank and file were settled on hitherto unoccupied land. The siting of the *by* names only on the less fertile glacial clays or at the narrowing end of the fertile sub-scarp belt is in keeping with the theory of such a general settlement in a later phase, after the better sites had been taken.

The situation was different upon the high Wolds. Here, some eight miles inland from Bridlington, lies the small hamlet of Thwing. The name comes from the Scandinavian word *thvengr*, meaning a thong, strap or shoe-lace, probably a reference to the long and winding chalk ridge on which the settlement stands at an approximate height of 400ft. Fig 12 (page 94) illustrates the difficulty of obtaining a permanent water supply in such locations, and it is not surprising that Thwing is the only hamlet at this altitude in this part of the northern Wolds. The larger hamlets – Rudston, Burton Fleming, Wold Newton and Foxholes – were confined to the Gypsey Race valley, where access to underground supplies of water was easier. Here there are no Grimston hybrid names to suggest viking take-overs in the early stage of the migration. The contrast in location is significant – the Anglian sites in the lower and more accessible end of the valley, the Scandinavian settle-

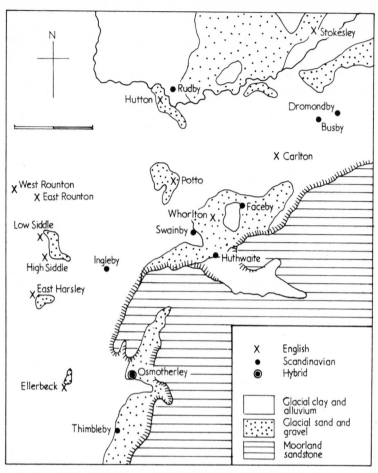

21 Place-names and geology south-west of Stokesley

ments further up the vale – suggesting a later Scandinavian colonisation of unoccupied territory. This impression of later Scandinavian settlement is borne out by the place-names themselves – Baythorpe, Helperthorpe and Weaverthorpe. In each case the *thorp* element indicates a daughter hamlet of a later phase of the settlement, possibly in connection with Danish development of sheep-farming on the Wolds.

Map 21 plots the Anglian and Scandinavian settlements in their geological setting within the enclave of lowland in the moorland escarpment south-west of Stokesley. The south-eastern portion of the area is occupied by the fringes of the North York Moors, which here form a sandstone plateau over 1,000ft in altitude. In a spectacular escarpment over 800ft high, the Moors overlook the lowlands of the lower Tees and the Vale of Mowbray. These lowlands, which occupy the north-western half of the area mapped, undulate gently around the 200ft contour – an extensive plain of glacial drift left by the ice-sheet of the last glaciation. It is mostly composed of boulder-clay, which has weathered into a heavy, tenacious soil yielding good harvests of grain and root crops while affording rich pasture for cattle. Upon it lie irregular patches of glacial sands and gravels which give lighter and more easily worked soils, and drier sites for settlement.

In the area mapped, twenty-one settlements of various sizes and ages can be found, eleven bearing names of English origin and nine with viking antecedents. Their distribution confirms the conclusions previously reached – that the settlements of the two races intermingled. Nowhere in the area can any enclave be found where the place-names of either English or Scandinavian origin cluster to the exclusion of the other. The evidence of the map strongly suggests that the farming instincts of both groups of immigrants sent them to the same kind of site. Both avoided the high moors, where in the area of the map no name of any settlement appears. On the lowlands, the boulder-clay attracted only six settlements. Of these, three bear place-names of Old English origin: the village of Carlton and the hamlets of East and West Rounton. Three have Scandinavian names – Dromonby, now surviving only as an isolated hall, and the villages of Busby and Ingleby. Of these, the latter (the *by* of the English) testified to an Anglian survival. On the much smaller area of glacial gravels and sands three settlements are located: Hutton, Whorlton and Faceby. Hutton still flourishes, but Whorlton is today a decayed village, marked only by a few undulations in the fields and its ruined castle. The only Scandinavian settlement on the glacial sands is Faceby, and that only marginally.

There can be no question as to the kind of site most favoured by both races. No less than eleven settlements are located at the junction where the glacial sands and gravels overlie the boulder clay. The advantages of such a site have already been commented upon. Of these eleven 'junction' settlements, seven bear names of Old English origin: Stokesley, the largest, now a flourishing market town; the villages of Potto, Ellerbeck and East Harlsey; and the hamlets of High and Low Siddle. To these seven Anglian settlements Osmotherley might be added, for the preservation in its name of the final element *ley*, from the Old English *leah*, a clearing, is evidence of its Anglian origin. This leaves just four names of Scandinavian origin: Thimbleby, Swainby, Rudby and Huthwaite. The disproportion suggests a prior occupation by Anglian settlers of most of the more favoured sites, a view that would be supported by the likelihood that in order to secure one of them Asmundr had to take over an already established Anglian village.

As for the manner in which the Scandinavian newcomers imposed themselves upon the native Anglian villagers, the distribution of place-names at least in this area provides no evidence of inter-racial hostility. Bitter or sustained inter-racial feeling would have rendered most unlikely the development of English and Scandinavian settlements so close together as Potto and Swainby or Whorlton and Faceby in the centre of the area mapped, and particularly Hutton and Rudby in the north.

Abbreviated Etymologies

Danby (NR, now North Yorks)
DB 1086 Danebi, Daneby
    1285 Danby
The *byr* or village
  of the Danes

Commondale (NR, now North Yorks)
1273 Colemandale
1539 Colmandale
1573 Colmendall
OE *dael:* valley
Ir-N personal name, *Colman*,
  shortened form of OI *Columban*
Colman's valley

Irton (NR, now North Yorks)
DB 1086 Iretun
    1223 Irton, Yrton
    1572 Urton
The Irishman's *tun* or farm

Eryholme, near Croft (NR, now North Yorks)
DB 1086 Argun
    1285 Eryom
    1665 Eriholme
OSc *holmr:* water-meadow
Ir-N *erg*, from OI *airgh*:
  upland summer pasture

Hutton Rudby (NR, now North Yorks)
          Hutton
DB 1086 Hotun
    1204 Hottona juxta Rodeby
    1582 Hooton Rudbye

          Rudby
DB 1086 Rodebi
    1150 Rudebi
    1190 Ruddeby
    1285 Rudby
OE *hoh*: high
OE *tun*: settlement or farm
OSc personal name *Rudi*

Grimston (ER, now Humberside)
DB 1086 Grimestun
    1219 Grimiston
    1265 Grimston
OE *tun*: farmstead, settlement
OSc personal name *Grimr*

DB: Domesday Book   OE: Old English, Anglo-Saxon
OSc: Old Scandinavian   Ir-N: Irish-Norse   OI: Old Irish

7
The Norman-French Place Names

The events of 1066 revealed the basic insecurity of the later Anglo-Saxon state. Only fifty years previously England had been conquered by a viking leader, and had Cnut not died young, leaving a disputed succession, he might have founded a ruling Scandinavian dynasty in England. The death of Edward the Confessor in 1066 revived the possibility that England might still be drawn into the ambit of a Scandinavian empire. Harold of Wessex and William of Normandy were not the only claimants to the vacant throne at Westminster – Harold Hardrada, King of Norway, was also in the field and a month before William's landing in Sussex had brought a viking army into Yorkshire to support his claim. Had he won the Battle of Stamford Bridge, near York, England might have become a province of a Norwegian empire ranging from the Baltic to Iceland and Greenland. The resounding victory of Harold of Wessex in Yorkshire ended a threat that had hung over England for more than a century.

Hopes of the survival of Anglo-Saxon England as an independent state, however, were shortlived, ending a few weeks later with the victory of William of Normandy and the death of Harold of Wessex at the Battle of Hastings. Normandy was already a highly organised feudal state, with close connections with the Papacy, and William's victory turned the face of England southwards to continental feudalism and the Church of Rome.

This Norman invasion of the eleventh century was no folk-migration like that of the Anglo-Saxon and Scandinavian peoples of earlier times. It was the result of one man's ambition, and was essentially a military operation in which far fewer forces than had fought at Stamford Bridge were engaged. The hilltop at Senlac on which Harold made his last stand was too small to accommodate a large army. Less than 3,000 men is the generally accepted estimate of the numbers involved. The decisive battle was over in the course of a single day, and though William adopted a scorched earth policy in his slow and circuitous march on London to reduce resistance, he was crowned king at Westminster within three months of his landing.

Nor had William much more in mind at first than a dynastic change. He opened his reign with a policy of continuity and for three years made a serious attempt to govern through the administrative machinery of the later Saxon monarchy, directed by men who had held high office under his predecessor. Only after the revolt of the northern earls in 1069 did he change this policy, and with ruthless determination imposed a Norman rule in England. Royal castles, strongly built of stone, arose in London, York and other strategic centres. Norman barons were planted in the estates of dispossessed Englishmen to such an extent that when Domesday Book was completed only two English landowners of large estates remained in possession. Throughout England he combined several thousands of small estates, previously held by Anglo-Saxon thegns or Scandinavian 'holds', to form some two hundred 'honours' – large feudal estates – held by Norman barons. By the end of his reign, the jarls or earls, the highest grade of Anglo-Scandinavian society, had been superseded by this new Norman aristocracy. The alien élite established in tenurial power, however, was very few in number. Domesday Book recorded only 180 tenants-in-chief – the great Norman barons and the higher ecclesiastics. Even if the lesser knights are added, the total did not exceed 6,000.

In Yorkshire the number of tenants-in-chief barely exceeded ten. The ruins of their castles lie scattered over the county – at Wakefield, Pontefract and Knaresborough in the West Riding, and Skipton, Middleham, Bolton, Pickering, Helmsley and Scarborough in the North Riding, to mention only the better known. The Norman tenants-in-chief established few new settlements. Even their castles were built in established locations, and the towns that so often grew under the protection of the castle walls developed from villages that had already been in existence for centuries and which were known by long-established names. Though their aristocratic names adorn many a Yorkshire settlement, the family names are almost always attached to these Anglian or Scandinavian place-names that long preceded them, as in Wharram Percy, Percy Rigg, Carlton Miniott and Thorpe Bassett.

To the mass of the peasantry, the coming of the Normans meant little more than a new landlord in the old village and all the social consequences that followed from that, but it resulted in no widespread addition to the number of place-names. Manorial discipline hardened, marked by an increase in the labour services and rents in kind exacted by the new masters. Many a small freeholder now found himself reduced to the semi-servile status of a villein, doing compulsory service on the lord's farm and unable to leave the village without the lord's permission. But such a lowering of status was due as much to economic as to political causes. Field-names reflected the slow change in village communal farming from a two-field to a three-field system. The clearances in the prevailing woodland continued throughout the Norman period, leaving their mark on local nomenclature. However, such changes came less from Norman rule than from within the agrarian system itself, in which the Normans had no new techniques to offer.

It is not surprising, therefore, that Norman-French words do not contribute largely to the place-names of Yorkshire. French was the language of fashion, learning and officialdom, and its use was largely confined to castles, manor houses, schools and universities, the law-courts, the exchequer and other centres of royal administration. To this day we are ruled by a *parlement*, literally the 'talking place', and no Bill can become law until the monarch has endorsed it by the old Norman-French words *le roi* [or *la reine*] *le vault*. In course of time, ambitious burghers found it advisable to learn and speak French, but the bulk of the population continued to speak its traditional Old English tongue, modified in the North by Scandinavian influences. The effect of the Norman Conquest on place-names was minimal.

Rarely did the Normans completely replace an existing Old English place-name with a fresh one of their own as the Scandinavians had done. Castle Howard, the stately home near Malton in the East Riding, scarcely qualifies as an example, for though this name replaced the former *Hinderskelfe*, the change did not occur until the eighteenth century, when the Howard family built the present mansion there. A better example in Yorkshire is that of Richmond. The site was recorded in Domesday Book as *Hindrelac*, a name which continued in use well into the following century as *Hindeslak*. Early in the twelfth century Count Alan of Brittany, realising the strategic importance of commanding the entrance to Swaledale, built himself a castle there, renaming the town *Richemund*, after many similar sites in France where the name was popular. It came from the two Old French words, *riche*, strong, and *mont*, hill. Anyone who has seen the castle on its precipitous crag overlooking the rapids of the Swale will realise how appropriate the name was. The title to the earldom later passed to the Tudor family, and when Henry Tudor came to the throne as Henry VII he transferred the name of his northern manor to one he held in Surrey, hitherto known as Sheen. No one, therefore, can say for certain whether the folk-song 'The Lass of Richmond Hill' refers to Count Alan's Richmond in Yorkshire or to Henry Tudor's Richmond, now a suburb of London.

The Norman Conquest encouraged many French monasteries to seek additional sites in England, and some of these offshoots from famous French foundations introduced French place-names into this country. The best known in Yorkshire are probably Fountains Abbey near Ripon and Rievaulx Abbey near Helmsley, both founded in the twelfth century. If the medieval chronicler Matthew Paris is to be believed, the former took its name from local springs, known by the French word *fontaines*. Rievaulx was built within seventy years of the Conquest as a daughter house of the famous Abbey of Citeaux, the foundation house of the Cistercian order. The name, first recorded in the twelfth century as

Rievalle, was from the start a direct translation into Norman-French of the English name Rye Valley in which it was built. Jervaulx Abbey was similarly named from the River Ure on the banks of which it was built, between Masham and Leyburn. The name was recorded as *Jorvalle* in the twelfth century – the Ure vale. This old name is still preserved in the geological term 'Yoredale', given to the series of alternating beds of limestone and shale in Wensleydale. Roche Abbey, some six miles south of Doncaster, is another Cistercian abbey, built in a thickly wooded valley like so many of its sister houses. It took its name from the crags of magnesian limestone that overlooked the abbey – Old French *roche*, rock or crag.

Grosmont, the village in the Esk valley with a station on the railway line between Middlesbrough and Whitby, copied the name of another French religious house, that of the mother priory near Limoges in southern France. Though all traces of the priory in the Esk valley have vanished, the name has remained, for the French name *Grosmont* – the large hill – was readily applicable to the Yorkshire settlement whose main street still climbs steeply up the side-slope of the valley. One priory founded at this time adds to the rare examples of the complete replacement of an Old English place-name by a Norman-French one. This is Mount Grace Priory, the best preserved ruin in England of a Carthusian house. Motorists on the A19 pass within sight of the ruins at the foot of the moorland escarpment near Osmotherley. The Domesday clerks recorded the site as *Bordlebi*, a hybrid name combining the Anglian personal name *Bordel* and the Scandinavian *by* – '*Bordel*'s farmstead'. The change to the French *Monte Grace* was not recorded until 1413, a date which shows how late into the Middle Ages French influence on the formation of place-names continued. Another fourteenth-century religious house has left an unusual name near Hull. After establishing a priory at Cottingham, the Augustinian canons moved it a year or so later to a neighbouring site. This removal was their 'great enterprise', which inspired the place-name recorded in the Norman-French of the time as *Haute Emprise*, a name which has come down to us as Haltemprice.

The regular clergy find their place in the place-names of the period. Bishop Wilton, some six miles north of Pocklington, had been plain *Wilton* – the wild, uncultivated *tun* – in Domesday times, although the manor had been held by the Archbishop of York since the days of Edward the Confessor. The addition of the prefix 'Bishop' in the fourteenth century was a belated recognition of this ecclesiastical link. The archbishop similarly held a manor at Bishop Burton some twenty miles further south, and had a palace there. Today the archbishop's palace is at Bishopsthorpe, on the Ouse a few miles below York. The western suburb of the cathedral city of Ripon still retains its ancient name of Bishopton.

The practice whereby the name of a Norman-French family was added to that of an existing Anglian or Scandinavian village was not confined to the castles of the great barons. It extended to the names of numerous manor houses of lesser knights and land-holders. Five miles or so to the south-west of Bridlington is the attractive village of Burton Agnes, where the Department of the Environment still preserves the ruins of the Norman manor house built at the end of the twelfth century. The name was recorded in Domesday Book as plain *Bortona*, from the Old English *burh* and *tun* – the fortified farmstead or manor house. So it remained until the thirteenth century, when the name Agnes, in various spellings, was added to the earlier name Burton. The Agnes who had become associated with the village was a member of the powerful Percy family who held extensive estates in all parts of the north at that time. It has given the family name to hamlets as widely scattered as Wharram Percy in the northern Wolds and Kilnwick Percy further south, about a mile east of Pocklington. In the North Riding the name still appears in Percy Rigg and Percy Cross in the neighbourhood of Guisborough, where the family had another large estate.

Another such Norman-French family were the Buscells, whose name was added to the Hutton near Pickering to distinguish it, as Hutton Bushell, from the many other Huttons in the North Riding. A little north of Ripon, the name of Conyers was added to another Hutton when that family acquired land in the neighbourhood during the twelfth century. North of Northallerton the name Hutton Bonville refers to the Boneville family who acquired the manor in the reign of Henry III. Carlton Miniott, a single-street hamlet west of Thirsk, was recorded in Domesday Book as simply *Carletun*. Not till the time of Elizabeth I does Carlton Miniott appear in the records, though the Miniott family had held land there since the fourteenth century.

The introduction of the French definite article *le* into several Yorkshire place-names dates from this period. Hutton-le-Hole, the charming village in the North York Moors, was plain *Hotun* in Domesday Book, a name derived from the Old English words *hoh* and *tun* – the high farm. The addition of 'le Hole' presumably referred to the hollow in which the modern village is situated. Facing each other diagonally across the Vale of Pickering are the villages of Appleton-le-Moors and Appleton-le-Street. Each was recorded by the Domesday scribes as simply *Apeltun*, from the Old English *aeppel* and *tun* – the farm by the apple-tree. The addition of 'le Moors' fitted the topography of a settlement on the fringe of the North York Moors, and that of 'le Street' referred to a location on the old Roman road between Malton and Hovingham.

The examples of Norman-French influence upon place-names so far quoted have involved mainly Old English names, but this influence applied equally to place-names of Scandinavian origin. In the East Riding is Thorpe-le-Street, the name of which was entered in Domesday Book as plain *Torp*, from the Scandinavian *thorp* or *torp*, an outlying hamlet. The full name, *Thorp in Strata*, first appears in a document of York Minster in the fourteenth century, the 'street' being the ancient Roman road linking *Eboracum* with the Humber ferry at *Petuaria*. Reference has previously been made to the hamlet of Countersett near Bainbridge in Wensleydale as a name derived from the Old Norse *saetr*, upland pasture. The first element, derived from the Old French personal name *Constance*, was added later, to give the thirteenth-century version *Constansate*. Today, Pinchinthorpe comprises nothing more than a few cottages and a farmhouse scarcely noticeable to the motorist as he passes along the road between Guisborough and Great Ayton at the foot of the moorland escarpment. The Domesday clerks recorded it simply as *Oustorp* – the eastern *thorp* or daughter hamlet. By about the year 1200 this had been enlarged to *Pinzunthorp* and *Pynchunthorpe*, a name which it has retained to this day. The added prefix referred to the Pinchun family, Norman-French landowners who held an estate there during the twelfth and thirteenth centuries.

It was the practice for the great landowners to move around their estates from manor to manor, leaving manorial officials to supervise in their absence. Some of these servants were men of considerable standing – for instance, the constable and steward of Richmond Castle. Both these titles have frequently entered into the place-names of Yorkshire. The village of Constable Burton lies some four miles east of Leyburn at the entrance to Wensleydale. Its earliest record gives the name as plain *Burton*, from *burh* and *tun* – fortified farmstead, but after Stephen, Earl of Richmond, granted the manor to his chief officer in about the year 1100, the Norman title 'constable' was added. A similar addition of the Norman word 'steward' is illustrated in the name of the hamlet Thornton Steward, a few miles further south. Before the Norman Conquest this settlement, under the simple name *Tornentone*, was held by an Anglo-Scandinavian named *Gospatric*. When later the Norman Earl of Richmond gave the manor to his steward, the village was distinguished from the many others of the same name as Thornton Steward.

Many French names introduced into place-names after the Conquest were descriptive. Beachy Head, for instance, became known as *Beau Chef* – the beautiful headland. The Vale of Belvoir in Nottinghamshire literally denoted a vale 'beautiful to view'. Guisborough, at the foot of the North York Moors, has its 'Belmont', the beautiful hill, which it is allowing to be disfigured today by housing development. The Norman aristocracy was more famous for its fighting capacity than for an aesthetic appreciation of the beauties of nature, so it is more likely that such names reflect the influence of new fashions among the upper classes of Norman England. As the new baronage settled down on its newly-acquired estates and grew rich from the labours of the peasantry on its manors, the more socially ambitious were particularly open to the blandishments of the speculative builders of their day, who spoke in beguiling terms of the splendid manor houses they could build for them, worthy of their new dignity. And so in the East Riding we have the name Bellasize, of a manor house on the lowland of the lower Ouse east of Goole, a name which has come down to us from the Norman-French *La Belle Assise* – the beautiful seat or country-house.

Abbreviated Etymologies

Richmond (NR, now North Yorks)

DB   1086 Hindrelac
        1108 Richemund
        1176 Richemunt
N-Fr *mont*: hill, crag
N-Fr *riche*: strong
Name popular in France

Hutton Conyers (NR, now North Yorks)

DB   1086 Hoton, Hotune
        1198 Hotonconyers
        1530 Howton Coniers
OE *hoh*: high
OE *tun*: farmstead
'farmstead on spur of land'
Conyers family held land here in early twelfth century

Burton Agnes (ER, now Humberside)

DB   1086 Bortona, Burtun(a)
        1234 Anneis Burton
        1255 Burton Agnetis
        1271 Burton Anneys
OE *burgh*, *tun*: fortified farmstead
N-Fr Agnes, from Agnes de Percy, twelfth-century landowning family

Mount Grace (NR, now North Yorks)

DB   1086 Bordlebi, Bordelbia
        1243 Bordelby
        1297 Bordilbi
        1301 Borthelby
        1413 Monte Grace
        1414 Mountgrace
OE personal name *Bordel*
OSc *by*: farmstead
N-Fr name of priory

Thorpe-Le-Street (ER, now Humberside)

DB   1086 Torp, Rudtorp
        1301 Thorp in Strata
        1413 Thorp in le Strete
OSc *thorp* or *torp:* outlying hamlet
Situated on Roman road

DB: Domesday Book
OE: Old English, Anglo-Saxon
OSc: Old Scandinavian
N-Fr: Norman-French

8

The Street Names of York

The street-names of York take one back through history even more than the old houses, if only because a greater proportion of them have survived. Having been the centre of military, civil or ecclesiastical administration since the first century AD, the city furnishes examples of names dating from every period of English history; though as the Danes occupied and ruled the town in the ninth century and the Irish Norwegians in the tenth, it is not surprising that Scandinavian names predominate.

The earliest names are those of the two rivers, the Ouse and its tributary the Foss. The latter name dates back to the Romano-British period and stems from a British loan-word from the Latin *fossa*. Originally this word denoted a ditch, but it came to be applied to any embanked or deepened stream. The Fosse Way, the name of the Roman road across the Midlands from Lincoln to Bath, is thought to have been derived from the drainage ditch dug alongside it throughout much of its length. A tributary of the River Wharfe near Tadcaster is called the Foss, and the word has already been encountered in several place-names in the East Riding – Catfoss, Fangoss, Fosham and Wilberfoss. In all four instances the name is compatible with the construction of drainage works in marshy areas.

The name of the River Ouse is much older. The name first appears as *Use* and *Usa* in written records of the eighth century, but philologists have traced the name still further back, to a Celtic river name *Use* or *Usa*. Its origin may have been even older. W. H. F. Nicolaisen, who has made a special study of early river-names, has come to the conclusion that the Ouse is one of several British rivers whose names represent survivals from the language

159

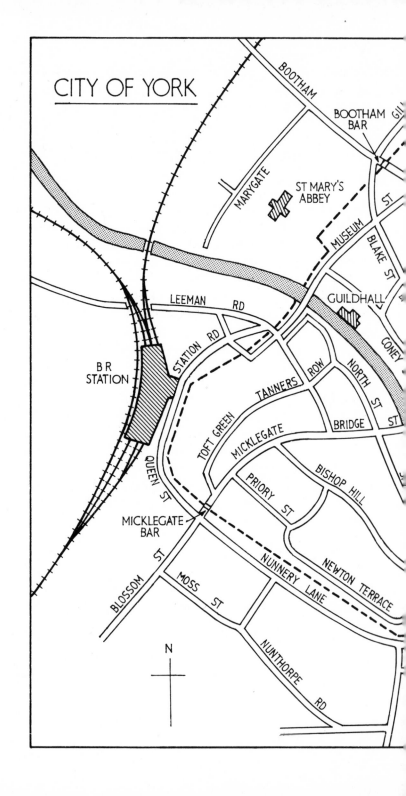

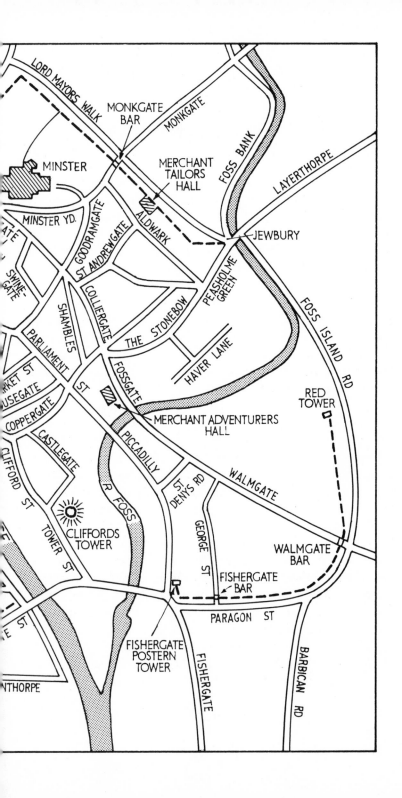

that preceded Celtic. Ekwall lends his authority to this view, linking the name Ouse with the Sanskrit *udan*, water, and found in the Sanskrit word for well, *utsa*.

The origins and development of the city name have already been traced in some detail in Chapter 1, at the end of which there is a simplified etymology. Of the street-names, probably the oldest remaining in existence today is Aldwark, borne by the street which runs parallel to the city wall east of the minster, between the Merchant Taylors' Hall and the Black Swan Inn. The name comes from the Old English *ald* and *weorc*, the old fortification. The final element is still retained in our word bulwark. The reference was probably to the old Roman wall, the line of which is followed at this point by the Aldwark.

Among the street-names of York few have survived with such completely Anglian origins as Aldwark. Scandinavian influences were too strong, and most of the street-names are either hybrids or have survived in a form modified by Scandinavian influences. The element *gate*, which occurs so frequently in the street-names of present-day York, is derived from the Scandinavian *gata*, which meant a road or street. The road leading down to the river was called the Ousegate. The Fossgate led to the River Foss, and Castlegate to the castle, now marked by Clifford's Tower. Micklegate was the 'great street', a hybrid name formed by a combination of the Scandinavian *gata* with the Old English *mycel*, large, great; it might be rendered as the High Road, or by the Americans, as Main Street. Monkgate was recorded in 1070 as *Munecagate* – the street of the monks – from the Old English *munuc*, monks, and the Scandinavian *gata*. Petergate indicated the street leading to the minster, dedicated to St Peter. Visitors passing down Stonegate, which links York Minster with the Guildhall and the Mansion House, are rightly impressed by the old timbered houses dating from the fifteenth and sixteenth centuries. But the street-name is much older, incorporating two Scandinavian words, *steinn*, stone, and *gata*. It has been suggested that the name referred to the loads of stone carted along the street to be used in the building of the minster. But the building of the present minster in stone was

162

begun in the thirteenth century, and the street-name was in existence long before that. A. H. Smith explains the name as 'the stone-paved street'. At a time when most streets, even in flourishing towns, were of pounded earth, a paved road would certainly have been distinctive enough to enter into local nomenclature. Goodramgate, joining Monks Bar to Petergate, was first recorded in the mid-twelfth century as *Gutherungata*, and later in the same century as *Guthrumgate*. The first element of this name stemmed from the Old Scandinavian personal name *Guthormr*, anglicised to *Guthrum* – *Guthrum*'s street. The reference need not necessarily have been to the Danish leader who came to terms with Alfred in the Treaty of Wedmore, for the name was a popular one and could have been proudly held in later periods by any man of viking descent.

The four Bars of York guarded the principal entries into the city, and took their name from the streets they protected. The term was the chief Norman-French contribution to the local nomenclature. It came from the Old French *barre*, to bar the way. Walmgate Bar guarded the entry to Walmgate, a hybrid name incorporating the Old English personal name *Walba*, shortened from *Wealhbeort* – *Walba*'s street. Bootham Bar derived its name from the Norse *buthum*, the dative plural of *buth*, and meant 'at the booths'. The abbot and monks of the neighbouring St Mary's Abbey held a weekly market there, which suggests that the street-name must have arisen after 1089 when the abbey was founded.

On the whole, Norman-French influences have left few traces on the street-names of York, though they enlarged its size. The Normans built two castles in York, one on each side of the Ouse. Of that on the west bank near Skeldergate Bridge nothing remains but a tree-shaded hillock, formerly the motte of the castle. This mound still retains its Norman-French name – Baile Hill – from the French word *baille*, the bailey or court-yard of the castle. The site of the castle built on the east side of the Ouse is, as already mentioned, marked today by Clifford's Tower near the Castle Museum. The name perpetuates that of its first governor. The neighbouring bridge over the River Foss is called Castle Mills

163

Bridge, recalling the water-mills along the river at this point.

Ecclesiastical influences have left their mark – as may be expected in a city that not only housed the archiepiscopal cathedral of the North, but also contained within its walls no less than forty churches, nine wayside chapels, four monasteries, four friaries and seven hospitals under monastic service, one specially devoted to the care of lepers. The Bedern, the street joining Goodramgate with Aldwark, bears a name that goes back to early Anglian days. It meant 'the house of prayer', from the Old English words *gebed*, prayer, and *aern*. Streets of the same name are to be found in Ripon and Beverley. Bishophill, in the south-western corner of York, marks an area formerly within the jurisdiction of the archbishop. Gilligate – the street of St Giles – running parallel to the city wall north-eastwards from Bootham Bar, preserves the name of a church that has long since vanished. St Andrewsgate and St Saviourgate also refer to medieval churches that no longer exist.

Royal interests are not without representation among the street-names of York. Leading from the Mansion House to the Ouse Bridge and following the line of the south-western wall of the Roman legionary fort is Coney Street. It was known in the twelfth century as *Cuningestreta*, a hybrid name combining the Scandinavian word for king, *kunung*, with the Old English *straet* – the king's road. King's Square or King's Court at the northern end of the Shambles was recorded in the thirteenth century as *Kuningesgard* – the king's residence – from the Old Scandinavian *Konungsgarthr*. A. H. Smith suggested that the name could have marked the residence of the viking kings of York. Near the site of the old railway station is Toft Green which leads to Micklegate Bar. In the thirteenth century this was recorded as *Kingestoft* – the king's *toft*. *Toft* or *topt* was an Old Scandinavian word applied to the wite of a house and its outbuildings, and its use here indicated a royal messuage within an area under the general jurisdiction of the archbishop.

By present-day standards all medieval towns were extremely small in size and rural in outlook. Though medieval York was then by far the largest town in northern England, its walls enclosed an area scarcely three-quarters of a mile in diameter, and many of its street-names bear testimony to its rural interests. The butchers plied their trade in the very centre of the city, in the Shambles. The name was recorded in the early fourteenth century as the *Marketskire alias Flesshamelles* – the market place, otherwise the meat stalls. Nearby was Swinegate, now Little Stonegate – the street where pigs were kept. Leading out of Market Street is Feasegate, a name drawn from the Old Scandinavian word *fe-hus*, the cattle sheds, and originally denoting a Cow House Lane. Collectively these indicated a rural precinct in the very heart of the city. Within the bend of the River Foss lies Hungate, recorded in the twelfth century as *Hundegate* – the street where the dogs were kennelled. Leading out of Hungate is Haver Lane, taking its name from either the Old English *haefer* or the cognate Old Scandinavian *hafr*, both terms meaning goat – the street of the goats. Outside the walls the road from Tadcaster approaches Micklegate Bar today as Blossom Street. Its name in the thirteenth century was *Ploxhsuaingate*, modified a little later into *Plouswayngate*. It came from two Old Scandinavian words, *plogr* and *sveinn* – the street of the ploughman.

Two streets survive to remind us how narrow and crooked many of the city lanes could be. Finkle Street was recorded in the late fourteenth century as *Fynkullstrete*, probably from a common northern dialect word *fenkl*, bend, corner or elbow. It is a singularly narrow and crooked lane. Grape Lane, which has been so called since the fourteenth century, derived its name from the Old English word *grapian*, meaning to grope – highly suggestive of the unlit, dark alleys of medieval York.

The urban crafts of medieval York have left their memorials in the city of today. The Guildhall, built in 1448 on the north bank of the River Ouse by Lendal Bridge, marks the site of the common hall of the many craft-guilds of the medieval city. These guilds were organisations of the master-craftsmen of the various crafts. They had considerable powers, regulating the practice of their respective trades in the town. They fixed prices and wages; they maintained standards of workmanship, prohibiting night-work since quality deteriorated under the poor light from the candles and rush-lights which were then the main sources of illumination; and they controlled admission to the crafts by a system of compulsory apprenticeship that normally extended over seven years. Many of the leaders became civic dignitaries and played an active part in the administration of the city. The more prosperous of these craft-guilds could afford to build their own guildhall. The Merchant Taylors' Hall, built towards the end of the fourteenth century, still stands in Aldwark, where it has been restored to its original appearance. The Merchant Adventurers, a commercial guild, built a sumptuous half-timbered hall in Fossgate in 1356, which is now open to the public. They made their profits from shipping cloth in the raw state, undyed and unfinished, to be worked up in Germany and the Low Countries. In Tudor times they were the virtual rulers of the city.

The memory of many of these craft-guilds has been preserved among the street-names. The name Tanner Row, of a street by the old railway station, is self-explanatory. Skeldergate, running parallel to the Ouse on the west bank, was frequently mentioned in the records of the twelfth century as *Skeldergate*, from the Old Scandinavian *skjaldari*, the makers of shields. Coppergate, the name of the road parallel to High Ousegate, originated from the Old Scandinavian word *koppari* – the street of the joiners or turners. Blake Street, now a turning out of Duncombe Place, was recorded in the twelfth century as *Blaicastret*. This name may have preserved an Old Scandinavian nickname *Bleiki*, but it was more probably derived from the Norwegian word *bleik*, bleaching – the bleaching place or the street of the bleachers. Felter Lane was originally recorded as *Feltergayl(e)*, from the Old English *felter*, a felt-maker, and the Old Scandinavian *geil*, a narrow passage.

Many of the street-names so far quoted were first recorded in the twelfth and thirteenth centuries, but many more date from the fourteenth century and after. Spurriergate was not mentioned in the records till the early seventeenth century, when it was written as *Litle Conystrete alias Spurryergate*. The later version incorporates the medieval word *sporier*, a spur – the street of the spur-makers. Colliergate was *Colyergate* at the beginning of the four-teenth century and *Colliergate* at the end. Both names incorporated the medieval word *coliere* and indicated 'the street of the charcoal-burner'. Church Street of modern times was known in the four-teenth century as *Gyrdlargate* – the street of the girdle-makers – from the medieval word *girdelere*, a girdle.

King's Staith and Marygate Landing remind us that medieval York had a busy commercial life. Ships had no difficulty in sailing up the Ouse to unload their cargoes at the two wharves or staithes by Lendal Bridge; *staeth* was the Old English word for a landing place. A twelfth-century record refers to a *Sancti Martini Lending* – the landing-place near St Martini's church – in Coney Street. An unidentified *Fysshlendyng* is recorded in the fifteenth century. The major exports were wool and woollen cloth and vessels from York sailed to the Baltic to challenge the trade of the powerful Hanseatic League of North Germany. To supply the raw material, trains of pack-horses descended Holgate Hill (the Old English *hol*, hollow, and the Scandinavian *gata*), bringing fleeces from the Pennine farmsteads. Those from the Wolds en-tered via Layerthorpe and Walmgate. Sheepskins were in demand for the manufacture of parchment, while the mutton found a ready sale in the Shambles. Cattle were driven to York 'on the hoof' from the Vale of York to provide for the needs of the leather-workers and butchers of the city.

A few miscellaneous local names are left for consideration. Knavesmire was first recorded in the fourteenth century as *Guaresmire*, from a combination of the Scandinavian *myrr*, mire, and the personal name *Knorr* – *Knorr*'s marsh. But it had become the recognised place of execution by the early fourteenth century, and this may have influenced the change of the first element into its present form. Many have puzzled, too, over the curious name Whip-Ma-Whop-Ma-Gate, the meaning of which is as obscure as its origin. Some suggest that it referred to a local custom of dog-whipping on St Luke's Day; others claim it alludes to the pillory and whipping-post that stood at one end of the site. Jubbergate has a still more intricate history, which is reflected in the etymology

167

at the end of this chapter. It was first recorded in the middle of the twelfth century as *Brettegata*, from the Scandinavian word *Bretar* – the street of the Britons. That an enclave of Celts descended from Britons of the fifth century could have survived in York to Norman times is inconceivable. It is more likely that the term referred to the Irish Celts who accompanied the Norse vikings in the tenth century. The *Bretar* element can be seen persisting in the etymology unchanged for two centuries. Then in the fourteenth century Edward I expelled the Jews from the city, and the area became a Jewish ghetto outside the wall. This event is noted in the etymology by the addition of the prefix *Ju* to form *Jubretegate*. Thereafter it is interesting to trace the slow vanishing of all reference to Britons in the middle syllable till it has completely gone by the sixteenth century.

Though names like Aldwark and Goodramgate take us back to Anglo-Saxon and Scandinavian times respectively, a great number of the local names in York were formed too late to be recorded in Domesday Book. Many, such as the names of the guildhalls and the streets in which the craftsmen lived and worked, were essentially medieval in date, representing organisations and crafts that belonged to the Middle Ages. But the formation of local names did not cease when the Middle Ages passed into the modern period. The eighteenth and nineteenth centuries have made their contribution. In 1725 the Mansion House appeared, built as a residence for the lord mayor. Shortly afterwards the fashionable citizens of York were flocking to the new Assembly Rooms, built in 1736 by the Earl of Burlington to rival those of Bath. At about the same time, a York physician of repute built himself a house in Lendal. After 1806 it was used as a lodging for the justices on circuit and was known as The Judges' Lodging. Both name and function survive to this day. Station Road and George Hudson Street date to the nineteenth century and the Railway Age. Hudson was the 'railway king' of the North and did more than any other man to make York a railway centre. The old railway station was built in 1841, just inside the walls, to be replaced outside them by the present-day one in 1877. All who visit York by rail know

Station Road, for they use it to set foot in the city as they emerge from the station and see the city wall rising opposite.

The twentieth century has seen the growth of new suburbs, but not of new place-names. The Chalfont Estate on the Tadcaster Road, the Garden Village at New Earswick and the university campus at Heslington have made their mark in the architectural world; but their contribution to developments in local nomenclature has been uninspired, for each of the three has been content to adopt an already established local name.

Abbreviated Etymologies

Bootham
1145 Bouthum
1150 Buthum, Budum
1449 Bothom
1498 Bowdom
ON *buthum*: at the booths

Micklegate
1161 Myglagata
1189 Mykelgate
1206 Miclegate
13th cent Mekilgate
OE *mycel*: great
OSc *gata*: street

Goodramgate
1154 Gutherungata
1240 Goth(e)rumgate
1293 Godromgate
1581 Gooderamgate
OSc personal name *Guthormr*,
  Anglicised to *Guthrum*
OSc *gata*: street

Blossom Street
13th century Ploxhsuaingate
            Ploxwangate
            Plouswayngate
       1421 Plughswayngate
OSc *plogr-sveinn*: ploughswain
'street of the ploughman'
OSc *gata*: street

Jubbergate
1145 Brettegata
1180 Bretegate
1256 Bretgate
1356 Jubretegate
1443 Jubergate
1459 Jubertgate
1550 Joopergayte
1575 Jupergate
OSc *gata*: street
OSc *Bretar*: Britons
Med *Jewe*: Jew

OE: Old English, Anglo-Saxon   OSc: Old Scandinavian
ON: Old Norse   N-Fr: Norman-French
Med: medieval, Middle English

9

The Place Names of Domesday Book and Later

Having emerged from the first twenty years of his rule triumphant over all rebellions, William of Normandy found the time ripe for stocktaking. After the 'exhaustive discussion' with the Great Council at Gloucester, referred to in Chapter 3, the inquiry was set in motion which resulted in the compilation in 1086 of the Domesday Book, so called, according to a writer of the following century, because it became the final source of appeal in subsequent questions of tenure.

The inquiry extended into every corner of the realm. Commissioners were sent round the shires to collect local information concerning the properties of every landowner, to estimate the taxable value. The details were gathered from local juries composed in general of the village middle class – the freeholders, smaller farmers, reeve and priest. It was then the business of the Exchequer clerks at Winchester to rearrange this mass of material, transferring it from the geographical basis on which it had been collected into a manorial order, arranged to group together the various holdings of each magnate within each county. The speed with which the operation was conducted was remarkable. The investigation itself was carried out within eight months, half of which were in winter. The final survey seems to have been available before the end of 1088, or even, as some think, by the end of 1087. As an administrative achievement this would have been impressive in any age. No other kingdom of contemporary Europe achieved anything of the sort. Even in England no comparable survey of the details of rural economy, recorded uniformly over the whole land, was available until shortly before World War II, when the Ordnance Survey Department and L. Dudley

Stamp published the Land Utilisation Maps.

The Yorkshire folios begin with the City of York, followed by the Honours or estates of the tenants-in-chief – magnates who held their lands directly from the king. The holdings of lesser tenants follow, until all the land in the county has been accounted for. The detail recorded is surprising, as may be seen from the translations at the end of this chapter, selected as representing contrasting types of settlement. The extract concerning Huddersfield shows that that settlement, then known as *Oderesfelt* (*Huder*'s *feld*), was then no more than an insignificant hamlet, valued at only 100s. Wilton, now the administrative headquarters of the ICI complex, was even smaller and was valued at only 36s. Ripon was then, as now, an ancient cathedral and market town. The extracts illustrate the form in which the eleventh-century manors were described by the Domesday clerks. The place-name is stated first, followed by the name of the landowners involved. Any change of ownership since 1066 is recorded. Then follows the assessment for taxation or 'geld' of each holding. Two values of the manor are entered: that at the time of the inquiry, and that *Tempore Regis Edwardi*, a phrase abbreviated to 'T.R.E.' and referring to the time of King Edward the Confessor, the last Saxon king of England recognised by William I.

The number of ploughs working on an estate was recorded as indicative of the degree to which the land was being cultivated or neglected. The population of each manor was entered, according to the social classes of the time – the freeholders listed as *liberi homines* (freemen) or socmen, and the unfree tenants classified as villeins, bordars or cottars according to the size of their holdings. The entry normally concluded with a summary of the natural resources of each manor – its woodland, meadowland, any watermill or fishery and the like. It is obvious that the record is a rich quarry for the names of settlements existing towards the end of the eleventh century, even though the names of innumerable natural and other features found no mention, since the Domesday clerks were little concerned with hills, streams, fens, tumuli, etc, and did not record them.

Domesday Book Place-Names and the Population of Yorkshire

There are 1,830 place-names recorded in the Yorkshire folios of Domesday Book, and their distribution among the three Ridings, and other associated detail, is tabulated below. The actual number of place-names was probably greater than that listed, for often the names of inhabited settlements were omitted if they were subordinate to a large estate, the clerks including them under the single name of the chief manorial centre. The extract for Ripon, for instance, lists no less than fourteen outlying berewicks, situated on the fringes of the chief manor, which extended 'around the church'. This case is exceptional in that the names of these fourteen berewicks were given, and the details of several of them recorded separately. The more normal procedure would have been to include such details in the single total for the manor, and had this practice been followed, these additional names would have been lost to us.

Map 24 plots the place-names recorded in Domesday Book for Yorkshire. It has been compiled from the separate maps for each Riding printed in *The Domesday Geography of Northern England* by H. C. Darby and I. S. Maxwell, and shows in general the distribution of settlements in 1086 over the whole county. If this map is compared with Maps 11 and 17, which show distributions for Anglian and Scandinavian times, it will be found to repeat the same pattern. On the west, the Pennines were still largely uninhabited, most place-names being confined, as in earlier times, to the Dales. The concentration in upper Wharfedale and Airedale, where settlement spilled over the watershed into the Ribble valley, continued the trend already established in previous periods.

In the North York Moors, the high sandstone plateau still remained uninhabited, as in earlier times, though a thin scatter of place-names marked the beginning of settlement in the Esk valley. The boulder-clay belt along the coastal fringe of the Moors between Saltburn and Whitby continued to attract settlers. The spread of place-names on the belt of corallian limestone along the

172

Riding	Number of place-names recorded in Text	Total population recorded in Text	Freemen and Socmen	Unfree: Villeins and Bordars	Percentage of unfree elements in total recorded population
West	719	3,192	406	2,786	87%
North	639	2,014	100	1,914	95%
East	424	2,363	208	2,155	98%
Shire Total	1,782	7,569	714	6,853	90%

23 Domesday population

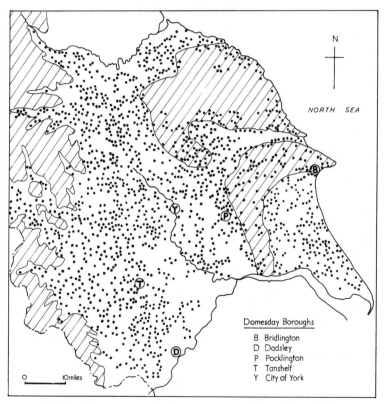

24 Domesday place-names (*after H. C. Darby and I. S. Maxwell*)

southern borders of the Moors maintained the earlier contrast with the absence of settlement on the high sandstone moors to the north. The relatively few place-names on the Wolds suggests that these chalk uplands were no more favoured in Norman times than in earlier days, for reasons already discussed.

As in Anglian and Scandinavian times, the place-names of the Norman period were most densely distributed on the lowlands. In Holderness the distance between settlements appears very close. On the lowlands of the lower Tees the place-names were distributed slightly less densely than in the Vale of Mowbray, though both lowlands display concentrations along the base of the escarpment of the North York Moors. In the Vale of York the spread of Domesday place-names was relatively dense, except for the marshy alluvial tracts in the neighbourhood of the lower Ouse and Humber confluence. The outcrop of the coal-measure shales and sandstones was still well populated, and an increased number of place-names on the magnesian limestone belt suggests that this was being settled.

Any imaginative restoration of eleventh-century settlements, however, must make due allowance for their small size. London, the largest, richest and busiest of all the towns at that time, covered only a single square mile. No other town approached this size. The Domesday count gives the total number of houses in York as well under 2,000, of which about half were uninhabited or unoccupied at the time of the inquiry. The city population can therefore be reasonably estimated at between 5,000 and 6,000, according to the estimate of the number of persons inhabiting each dwelling. This total is roughly no more than that of the present-day population of Filey – and York was then by far the largest town in northern England, defended by the city wall and two castles, a busy mercantile centre, and the seat of an arch-bishopric. Less important settlements were proportionately smaller in both size and population. In the extract from the Domesday account of Wilton given at the end of this chapter, only two bordars are recorded on Nigel's estate and no more than ten bordars with eight villeins on Maldred's, totalling no more than twenty.

The tabulated synopsis of information relating to population recorded in Domesday Book (page 173) shows that the total population for the whole county numbered about 7,500, spread among slightly less than 2,000 settlements – an average of only four persons per settlement. The Wilton total and the county averages, however, do not give a reliable picture. The Domesday clerks were mainly concerned with heads of families, men who could carry on the heavy and unceasing daily work on the land. The place of most women in eleventh-century Yorkshire was in the home, possibly in a nunnery, but not in Domesday Book records. To obtain the real totals of village populations, it is therefore necessary to multiply the Domesday totals by whatever factor is thought to represent the size of an average family in those days. H. C. Darby suggests four or five. The latter figure brings the total population for the shire to scarcely 40,000 – less than one-sixtieth of the $2\frac{1}{2}$ million that live within its boundaries today. This ratio probably applies to most of the individual settlements in the county.

Of this population, unfree elements vastly outnumbered the free. Of a total recorded peasant population of about 7,500 in the county, nearly 7,000 were unfree. This represents a proportion of 90 per cent, which rose in the East Riding to an incredible 98 per cent (see fig 23). The conclusion is not to be drawn from this that slavery was widespread. No slaves were recorded for Yorkshire in Domesday Book. The villeins, bordars and cottars who constituted the unfree tenantry were neither destitute nor wholly lacking in rights, and the prosperous villein was by no means an unusual member of a village community. The normal villein holding was some 30 acres, an acreage upon which it is still possible to maintain a livelihood. Some villeins worked much larger holdings and were eventually able to buy their freedom by a payment to the lord of the manor. But however large or small his holding, the villein shared this lack of freedom with the bordars and cottars, who had to manage on much less land, with such supplementary work as could be got from their more prosperous neighbours. Every such unfree peasant held his lands only at the will of the lord of the

175

manor, to whom he owed unpaid, weekly services, cultivating the lord's demesne throughout the year. At busy times, such as the spring sowing and the autumn harvesting, 'boon-work' was required in addition to the regular 'week-work'. Nor could he buy or sell a horse or an ox, still less his holding, without the permission of the lord, whose sanction was also required before his daughter could marry or the family could move to another district. He was, as the twelfth-century lawyers picturesquely expressed it: *adscriptus glebae* – 'tied to the soil'. But within such limits he could live his own life. For half the week he was free to work on his own land, aided by his sons; and in the course of time the 'custom of the manor' hardened to protect him from excessive demands by the lord. Such were the people who occupied the settlements plotted in map 24, and who shaped the place-names of fully two-thirds of the villages and hamlets of today.

Not only were the eleventh-century settlements extremely small by the standards of today, they were essentially rural. York was the only really urban centre in the county, yet we have seen that cattle and pigs were normally kept in its very heart. No boroughs were recorded for the North Riding. Northallerton, known then as *Aluretune*, was entered as a rural manor with 66 villeins and 35 plough-teams. Within its jurisdiction were 11 outlying farms and 21 other settlements in which 45 plough-teams and 116 socmen were registered. No trace of urban life is suggested by this record. For the rest of the shire only four settlements were classified as boroughs – Dadsley and Tanshelf in the West Riding and Pocklington and Bridlington in the East Riding. Dadsley, now on the outskirts of Tickhill, then had a recorded population of only 98, of whom 54 were villeins and 12 bordars or cottars. The rest was made up of a priest and 31 burgesses. Even assuming that the latter represented tradesmen or craftsmen, two-thirds of the townsfolk relied upon farming for their living. Tanshelf, now part of Pontefract, had a recorded population of only 101, including the priest. After due allowances are made, a possible population of between 400 and 600 men, women and children is not impressive by modern standards. Again, most of the interests were rural.

176

Pocklington was recorded with a population as low as 38, of whom 15 were described as burgesses, representing burghal interests, and 22 as villeins and bordars, concerned with rural affairs. In Bridlington only 4 burgesses were noted. Leeds, Sheffield, Bradford, Halifax and the other industrial towns that today form the nuclei of the conurbations of West Yorkshire were then insignificant rural hamlets, unconscious of their future.

Place-Names Recorded After the Compilation of Domesday Book

Place-name formation did not cease with the compilation of Domesday Book. The names of the Norman-French families were obviously added to village names after 1066, some not until the thirteenth and fourteenth centuries. It has been observed that many of the street-names of York and of other ancient boroughs were named from craft-guilds that were not formed till late in the Middle Ages. Though the tides of Anglian and Scandinavian immigration had largely ceased to flow, the national population continued to grow by natural increase from an estimated 1 million in 1086 to approximately 3 million by 1349, when the Black Death and other plagues brought this increase to an end. Yorkshire shared in this development, which stimulated the foundation of new settlements and the formation of new place-names. The original small village from which Middlesbrough, for example, has descended was not in existence in 1086, though its present-day outer suburbs of Acklam, Hemlington, Coulby and Ingleby Barwick had all been recorded in Domesday Book. The name did not appear in the records till the twelfth century, when it was entered as *Midlesburc,* which Ekwall renders as 'the middlemost *burg*'. Though mentioned in Domesday Book, Driffield and Market Weighton did not develop into thriving market centres, nor did Kingston-upon-Hull grow rich on the Baltic trade, until long after the compilation of Domesday Book. The industrial expansion of the West Riding did not come until the eighteenth and nineteenth centuries.

177

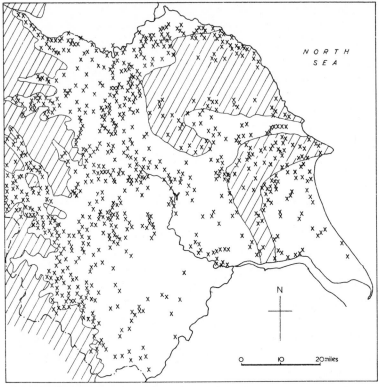

25 Uninhabited settlements in Yorkshire in 1086 (*after H. C. Darby and I. S. Maxwell*)

By contrast, many villages declined in importance to such an extent that their names on the maps of today represent only hamlets or even just farmhouses. Some do not appear on present-day maps at all, having long since been abandoned by their inhabitants in the intervening centuries and left to decay. All that remains to mark their original sites are a few grass-covered undulations in the ground. Sometimes the place-name has lingered on, preserved in parish records or in the oral tradition of the neighbourhood. But frequently even this has gone, and every trace of what was once a living settlement has utterly vanished – a 'lost village' indeed.

One terrible feature of the Yorkshire folios of Domesday Book is the occurrence of the words *Wasta est* – 'It is waste' – in the record of manor after manor. The extract for Huddersfield at the end of this chapter, for instance, contains an example, but the extent of the desolation is more vividly revealed by map 25. Even if allowance is made for the Domesday clerks' habit of registering many villages as 'waste' despite the fact that a few inhabitants survived to eke out a meagre existence, the map is a witness to widespread disaster. Only Holderness and the lowlands of the lower Ouse in the extreme south of the county seem to have escaped.

This devastation is usually attributed to the 'harrying of the north' by William I in the course of his suppression of the rebellion of the northern earls in 1069–70. There is no doubt that William was responsible for much of it, for he ruthlessly adopted a scorched earth policy to show his strength and to make an English recovery impossible. But both the Danish army that landed at this time to take advantage of the rebellion and later raiding by the Scots contributed greatly to the damage. T. A. M. Bishop has observed that the destruction among settlements in the Pennine uplands was even greater than upon the lowlands; he commented that 'it must appear remarkable that William's army should have indulged in no more than sporadic devastation of large parts of the plain, while carrying fire and sword to remote upland settlements'. He suggests that the decay of the Pennine villages was due not so much to ravaging armies as to a deliberate policy of the landlords to move their tenants from settlements on such unrewarding, upland areas in order to restock their ravaged manors on the more fertile lowlands.

Other causes of village decay were operating slowly but inexorably throughout the Middle Ages. Coastal settlements were exposed to sea erosion, which has completely engulfed the Roman signal station that once stood on Huntcliff above Saltburn. This site was on a high and resistant sandstone cliff; settlements on the low shore of Holderness, formed of soft clay, were still more exposed. Here, many coastal villages recorded in Domesday Book

179

have since been washed away by the encroaching sea. The erosive process continued throughout the Middle Ages – the village of Ravenspur on the Holderness coast, where Henry of Lancaster landed in 1399 to make his bid for the throne, has long vanished beneath the waves. Even today, coastal protection forms a major concern of many Yorkshire seaside resorts.

Plagues have been suggested as another cause of village decay during medieval times. It has been calculated that the Black Death of 1349 carried off one-third of the medieval population. But though there are authentic instances of villages rendered uninhabited at this time, when W. C. Hoskins came to study the population changes in medieval Leicestershire he could ascribe the depopulation of no more than eight villages in that county to this cause. Many settlements were already decaying and their populations declining long before the advent of the Black Death. And well-documented examples of villages totally abandoned long after 1349 show that the process continued well beyond the end of the pestilence.

A further cause of village depopulation from the fourteenth century onwards was the practice of enclosing the arable fields for sheep-rearing, a process encouraged by the increasing demand for English wool to supply the looms of the Low Countries and later of our own towns. A flock of sheep could graze under the eye of a single shepherd on lands that had formerly occupied a whole village community in arable farming. 'When men have gotten many houses and tenements into their hands,' wrote a fifteenth-century pamphleteer, 'yes, whole townships, they suffer the houses to fall into utter ruin and decay; so that by this means whole townships are become desolate and like unto a wilderness, no man dwelling there, except it be the shepherd and his dog.' A contemporary poet expressed the process more succinctly in the following couplet:

Sheep have eaten up our meadows and our downs,
Our corn, our wood, whole villages and towns.

180

The site, size and age of a settlement were factors that often affected its fate. Hamlets on marginal soils that were dependent on arable farming tended to decline as the climate of western Europe gradually became more rainy during and after the thirteenth century. A large village, long-established on fertile soil with associated woods and meadows, was better able to withstand or recover from adverse circumstances than was an impoverished hamlet. In her study of the Scandinavian place-names of Yorkshire, G. F. Jensen found that whereas only 12 per cent of the villages bearing place-names of the Grimston hybrid type eventually became 'deserted or decayed villages', no less than 57 per cent of the daughter hamlets bearing names in -thorp failed to survive. Well over 100 deserted sites have been located in the East Riding, of which Wharram Percy in the northern Wolds is the best known. Nearly 200 are known in the area of the North Riding. Local earthworks recognisable as a decayed settlement can still be seen at Stainton near Thornaby and at Newton Mulgrave two miles from Runswick Bay.

As the population trebled between the eleventh and the fourteenth centuries, however, the toll of decayed villages was far outnumbered by the enlargement of many settlements and the formation of new ones. As families grew in size, younger members tended to branch off in search of new holdings, carved out of the extensive uncultivated territory between the existing settlements. Such land was known as 'the waste'; but this is a deceptive term, for such land provided rushes for thatching, rabbits and hares for the pot, fruits, nuts and timber, as well as extra pasture for the village herd. Often the lord of the manor, hoping to bring this waste land into the cultivated area of his estate, would establish a tenant thereon, granting him several acres and setting him up with seed and cattle, in return for the usual villein services.

Place-names in all parts of Yorkshire reflect these colonising trends. Some three miles south of Whitby stands the small village of Sneaton. The name has remained almost unchanged since it was recorded in Domesday Book as *Snetune*. This hybrid name, combining the viking personal name *Snjo* with the English *tun* –

181

Snjo's farmstead – was the only place-name recorded there in 1086. It had changed only to *Snetton* by the twelfth century. But the Yorkshire Assize Rolls for 1231 mention an *Ouersneyton*. The addition of the prefix 'Over' signalises the growth of a subordinate hamlet on the lower ground nearby. A hundred years later a document of Whitby Abbey named the two settlements without ambiguity as *Snetun et Thorp*.

In the Vale of Pickering, in the lowlands around the confluence of the rivers Rye and Derwent, stand the two settlements known today as Great and Little Habton. Only one existed in 1086, named in Domesday Book as *Habetun* – *Habba*'s *tun*. But within a century another settlement was mentioned in a charter as *parva Habeton*, clearly a daughter hamlet. The two were still in existence in the fourteenth century when they were still being referred to as *Great* and *parva Habton*. Today both are small hamlets, but it is Great Habton that possesses the church. The neighbouring hamlets of Great and Little Barugh developed in a similar manner, though somewhat earlier. Domesday Book mentions only a single settlement, *Berga*, from the Old English word for hill, *beorg*. By about the year 1200, however, *magna* and *parva Berch* appear in the records. The hill is scarcely noticeable, but in this low and marshy terrain the most gentle rise is significant, especially when a daughter hamlet has to be distinguished from the established village.

Some ten miles to the south-east, in a dry valley of the northern Wolds to the west of Weaverthorpe, are the hamlets of East and West Lutton. Again the process of duplication can be followed from a study of the place-names. Domesday Book recorded only a single settlement *Ludton* – *Luda*'s farmstead. Within a generation the contemporary documents were referring to two settlements, recorded as *duabus Luttunis* – at the two Luttons. In the thirteenth century they were distinguished as *Estlutton* and *Westlutton*, or sometimes *altera Lutton* – the other Lutton. The joint township was still officially termed *Luttons Ambo* – Both Luttons – as late as the nineteenth century.

Visitors to Middlesbrough will be familiar with Roseberry

Topping, the conspicuous peak in the escarpment of the North York Moors, which looks down upon two settlements today named Ayton. The larger is Great Ayton, a thriving village with two village greens on the banks of the Leven, a well-known Quaker boarding school and a memorial to Captain Cook who spent part of his early life there. A mile or so away a small collection of farm buildings constitutes Little Ayton. Only one place-name – *Atuna*, the farm by the river – was entered in Domesday Book. But the reference to *Parva Hatona*, Little Ayton, in a document of Whitby Abbey shows that a daughter settlement appeared a century later.

The development of the two Otteringtons south of Northallerton can be similarly traced from place-names. Today they are distinguished by their geographical location along the A167. Domesday Book mentions only one *Otrin(c)tun(e)* in 1086. But a Durham manuscript as early as 1088 records a *Sonotrinctune* – South Otterington – from the Old Scandinavian *sunnr*, south. *Northoterington* does not appear in the records until the thirteenth century.

Near Brough on the Humber lowlands the hamlets of Brantingham and Brantingham Thorpe are still to be found. The entry in Domesday Book of a *Brentingeham* and an *alia Brentingeham* shows that the daughter hamlet was already in existence by 1086. Like so many such offshoots the 'other Brantingham' did not prosper, for its inferior status was still implied in a reference in a fourteenth-century document to *Thorpe juxta Brantyngham* – the hamlet near Brantingham. Not till the sixteenth century did it acquire some independent identity as *Thorpe Brantingham*. Today Brantingham Thorpe is too insignificant to be marked on any maps except the 6in OS sheets. Early colonisation did not necessarily presage a successful or permanent one.

Most of the formations of new place-names so far quoted occurred during the eleventh and twelfth centuries. Others suggest that the coining of new place-names continued for another century or more. Motorists on the moorland road from Whitby to Guisborough will be familiar with the two reservoirs of Scaling and Lockwood. Between them a side road opposite Freebrough Hill leads off to Great and Little Moorsholm. Great Moorsholm is a single-street village fully half a mile long, while the memory of Little Moorsholm is preserved in the name of a farm two miles further north. In 1086 there was only one settlement there, entered in Domesday Book as *Morehusum* – the houses on the moor. So it stayed till the thirteenth century, when a distinction appeared in the records between *magna* and *parva Morsum*. The two settlements continued as Great and Little Moorsholm until the beginning of the fifteenth century, at which point the records reverted to a plain *Muressom*, reflecting the declining fortunes of the lesser settlement in the later Middle Ages.

New place-names were similarly formed in the East Riding. Today Great Driffield is the rural centre of the boulder-clay lowlands east of the Wolds between Bridlington and Beverley. In Domesday times it was known simply as *Drifelt* or *Drifeld*, from the Old English *drif*, stubble, and *feld*, open country. At the end of the thirteenth century a new settlement appeared in the records, named *Parva Driffeld* – Little Driffield. But it never achieved equal status, remaining today only as the small offshoot of the larger town.

East of Malton the escarpment of the northern Wolds is dissected by a broad combe, on the floor of which lie the two villages of Thorpe Bassett and Wintringham. If any priority can be given to either today, it must go to Wintringham as it is slightly larger and possesses the church. The Domesday clerks had no doubts. They entered *Wentrigha* as the major settlement and the other as plain *Torp* – an outlying dependent hamlet. By the end of the twelfth century the former had become *Winteringeheim*, the Old English *ham* having been replaced by the cognate Scandinavian *heim*. The name reached its present form early in the fourteenth century. The daughter settlement remained a humble *thorp* until the thirteenth century, when it passed into the possession of the Bassett family. Under their influence it achieved an independent identity as Thorpe Bassett, which it has maintained to this day. Some five miles north of Hull the adjoining hamlets of North and South Skirlaugh developed along similar lines. In 1086 there was only one settlement – *Schireslai*, the bright clearing. The name was modified to *Scirlaga* in the twelfth century. Then in the thirteenth century *Suthskirlaghe* appeared in the records, and in the fourteenth *Northkirlagh*. Since then they have remained North and South Skirlaugh.

Although the general increase in population came to an end in the fourteenth century, new place-names still continued to make their appearance in the later records, as colonisation of the uncultivated waste around the villages was carried on in favoured localities. Reference has already been made to the twin villages bearing the name Ayton on opposite sides of the River Derwent as it emerges from the picturesque and wooded Forge Valley near Scarborough. The Domesday clerks found only a single village which they recorded as *Atun*, from the Anglian *ea*, stream or river, and *tun*, the *tun* on the river. With minor modification into Atone this single name persisted for the following 300 years. Then at the very end of the fourteenth century, a new name appeared, *Vestheton*, indicative of a late hiving off of an additional settlement across the river.

Translations of Selected Extracts from Domesday Book
HUDDERSFIELD – ODERESFELT (Former WR, now West Yorkshire)
In ODERESFELT, Goduin [Godwin] had 6 carucates of land for geld, where 8 ploughs can be. Now the same [Goduin] has [it] of Ilbert, but it is waste. Pasturable woodland 1 league in length and 1 in breadth. T.R.E. it was worth 100s.

RIPON – RIPUN (Formerly NR, now North Yorkshire)
In RIPUN there can be 10 ploughs. Archbishop Eldred held this manor. Now Archbishop Thomas has on the demesne 2 ploughs and 1 mill of 10s. [annual value] and 1 fishery of 3s. and 8 villeins and 10 bordars having 6 ploughs. 10 acres of meadow. Underwood. Of this land the canons have 14 bovates. The whole [extends] around the church.

[Here follows a list of 14 berewicks, some of which are quoted below.]

Together there are 43 carucates for geld and 30 ploughs can be [there]. All this land is waste, except that in MERCHINGTON [Markington]. There is on the demesne 1 plough and 2 villeins and 3 bordars with one plough, and 1 socman with 1 plough. In MONUCHETON [Bishop Monkton] 1 thegn has 5 villeins and 5 bordars with 4 ploughs. In ERLESHOLT [Herleshow] there are 3 villeins and 3 bordars, with 2 ploughs. There are 75 acres of meadow. Pasturable woodland belonging to these lands contain 1 league. The whole [has] 6 leagues in length and 6 in breadth.

In ALDEFELD [Aldfield] 2 bovates for geld. It belongs to Ripun and is waste.

To Ripun belongs the soc of these lands: ESTANLAI [Stainley] and SUDTUN [Sutton], ESTOLLAIA [Studley], NORDSTAN-LAIA [North Stainley], SCLENEFORDE [Sleningford], SUTHEWIC [Hewick].

In all there are 21½ carucates for geld and 15 ploughs can be there. 5 villeins and 3 bordars are there now, having 3 ploughs. 2 acres of meadow in Suthewic. Underwood 1½ leagues in length and 1 league in breadth.

T.R.E. RIPUN was worth £32; now it is worth £7.10s.

WILTON – WIDTUNE (Formerly NR, now Cleveland)
In WIDTUNE 4 carucates for geld and 2 ploughs can be there. Norman had 1 manor there. Now Nigel has it of the Count [of Mortain]. 2 bordars are there; and 6 acres of meadow. T.R.E. it was worth 16s; now 16d. In the same town there are 4 bovates for geld, the soc belonging to the land of Nigel.

[Later, under the heading LAND OF THE KING'S THEGNS the following is added.]

In WILTUNE Altor had 3 carucates and 6 bovates of land for geld. Land for 2 ploughs, Maldred has 1 plough there and 8 villeins and 10 bordars with 3 ploughs and 6 acres of meadow. T.R.E. it was worth 20s; now the same.

In WILTUNE and LESIGBI [Lazenby], 1 carucate of land for geld. Land for half a plough, the soc belongs to Wiltune.

10

Medieval Life

During the course of the Middle Ages the place-names of old foundations and of new settlements alike settled down into their Middle English forms, and in doing so preserved many a reference to the features of the social and economic life of early England. Some of these features and their associated place-names have already been discussed in the chapters on the Anglo-Saxon period. This chapter adds to this and extends the review to include those of Anglo-Scandinavian, Norman and medieval times.

Place-Names and Social Classes

Upon the already hierarchical structure of society in the late Anglo-Saxon period the Normans imposed a feudal pyramid, and the place-names of Yorkshire contain many references to the various social classes of feudal England. The biggest landowner was the king, and both the Old English term *cyning* and the Scandinavian equivalent *konungr* have frequently entered into local nomenclature. Conisbrough, between Doncaster and Rotherham, was recorded as *Cuningesburg* in Domesday Book – the king's *burh*. A similar development explains the names of settlements so widely scattered as Conistone in upper Wharfedale, Cold Coniston in upper Airedale, Coneysthorpe in the Howardian Hills near Hovingham, and Coniston north-east of Hull. Less frequently a place-name preserves the royal title of *Aetheling*, given in Anglo-Saxon times to the king's eldest son and heir-apparent. Today Ellenthorpe is the name of a parish east of Boroughbridge at the confluence of the Swale and the Ure; in Domesday Book it appears as *Adelingestorp* – the *thorp* of the *Aetheling*. The title is more closely preserved in the name of Adlingfleet, a hamlet in the Humber lowland east of Goole – the *fleot* or stream of the *Aetheling*.

Baronial names appear frequently in the place-names of Yorkshire and several examples have already been quoted. Hooton – from the Old English *hoh* and *tun*, the high farmstead – was such a common place-name that the addition of the baronial name was a convenient way of distinguishing one from the others. Hooton Levett, Hooton Pagnell and Hooton Roberts are examples. The Norman-French family name Tyas occurs in Middleton Tyas, a village near Scotch Corner, and in Farnley Tyas south-west of Huddersfield. The Aldelin family, who held estates in the West Riding in the twelfth century, has given its name to Thorpe Audlin near Ackworth, as the Salvein family gave its to Thorpe Salvin. High on the southern flank of Wensleydale between Aysgarth and Bainbridge lies the hamlet of Thornton Rust. The Thornton was from the Old English for 'the farmstead among the thorn-bushes.' The additional Rust is probably an abbreviated form of *Hrosskell*, the name of an Anglo-Scandinavian landowner who later came into possession of the manor.

The class who in more modern times was called yeomen, holding land in free tenure and independent of any overlord save the king, is well attested in the medieval place-names of Yorkshire. For such small freeholders the Anglo-Saxon word was *ceorl* and the Scandinavian equivalent *karl*. Neither term then carried overtones of the later association with the word 'churl.' Normally a *ceorl* or *karl* was the responsible head of a peasant household, farming 30 or more acres. The term appears in the place-names of today in the form of Charlton or Carlton – the *tun* of the *ceorl* or *ceorls*. Examples abound: the North Riding alone has eight such names, and others are to be found in the area of the former West Riding.

The vikings had other words to denote various social ranks among peasant proprietors. One was *drengr*, the Scandinavian version of the Anglo-Saxon *dreng*. First applied to a young man or servant, it later developed the meaning of a privileged peasant holding his land by an ancient, pre-Conquest tenure. The term is preserved in Dringhouses, the name of a suburb of York, first recorded in the thirteenth century as *Drengus* and *Drenghous*. A mile west of Skipsea in Holderness, the hamlet of Dringhoe was known in the twelfth century as *Drenghou*, from *dreng* or *drengr* and *haugr* – the hill or mound of the *dreng*. The name Holderness itself incorporates as its first element a word of Scandinavian origin. The term *hold* was applied in the Danelaw to men of high rank – military leaders and great landowners. The *hold* whose rank is commemorated in the name Holderness must have been a powerful figure in the East Riding.

It was possible for a person of unfree status to obtain his freedom, either by purchase or by a grant of manumission from a generous overlord. For such men the Danes had a special word, *leysingi*. The term is preserved in the name Lazenby, a small village at the foot of the Eston Hills, now dwarfed by the huge ICI works near Redcar. The Domesday version was *Lesingebi* – the *by* of the freed men. The Lazenby near Northallerton has a similar history.

The humblest members of medieval society, the cottars, are remembered in place-names mainly by the mean and impoverished huts in which they eked out an existence. The Anglian word for such a dwelling was *cot*, a term which often entered into place-names in the plural *cotes* or dative plural form *cotum*, at the cottages. Coatham, the western suburb of Redcar, has previously been quoted. Cottam, a small hamlet between Bridlington and Sledmere, was recorded in Domesday Book as *Cottun* – at the cottages. Near Hull there is a hamlet known today as Southcoates, developed perhaps surprisingly from the Old Scandinavian personal name *Soti* – *Soti*'s cottages. In the Vale of Pickering, near the confluence of the rivers Riccal and Rye, a farm named Muscoates preserves virtually unchanged the twelfth-century name *Muscotes* – *Musi*'s cottages.

The Position of Women in Medieval Society

Several women of royal rank distinguished themselves in Anglo-

Saxon history. Hild, the kinswoman of Oswiu, King of Northumbria, achieved a European reputation in the seventh century as Abbess of Whitby. In the tenth century, Aethelflaeda, the daughter of Alfred the Great, ruled Mercia as 'Lady of the Mercians', and was closely associated with her brother, Edward of Wessex, in organising the series of successful campaigns that laid the foundations for the eventual reconquest of the Danelaw. Cnut appointed his Saxon wife, Aelfgifu, as Regent of Norway while he was engaged in England; and though her rule turned out to be unpopular, this was because of her severity and not from any feminine weakness.

There is documentary evidence that women could hold and inherit land even before the Norman Conquest. Stenton has quoted a pre-conquest narrative in which one lady expressed some very clear views on the subject to a deputation from the local shire court. 'Here sits Leoflaed, my kinswoman,' she declared, 'to whom after my death I grant my land and my gold, my robes and my raiment, and all that I have. Behave like thegns, and give my message to the good men in the court, and tell them to whom I have given my land and my property – and to my son, nothing!'

At the end of the Yorkshire folios of Domesday Book, reference is made to the landed estate of a woman named Asa, who, we are informed, 'had her land separate and free from the lordship and power of Bernulf her husband, even when they were living together. Moreover, after their separation, she withdrew with all her land and possessed it as lady'.

Women's names frequently enter into the place-names of Yorkshire. As might be expected, the name *Hild* is well represented in the North Riding. It appears in the first element of Hinderwell near Runswick Bay – *Hild's* well (DB: *Hildrewelle*) – and in the small inland hamlet of Hinderskelf. On the left bank of the Swale two miles from its confluence with the Ure, stands the small village of Helperby. This name perpetuates that of a Scandinavian woman, *Hjalp* – *Hjalp's* farmstead. This was included in a list of properties acquired by Oakatel, Archbishop of York. As Oakatel died in AD 971, it follows that the ownership of a farm by a woman was

191

not unknown as early as the tenth century. Another Helperthorpe, a village on the northern Wolds midway between Bridlington and Malton, adds to the evidence.

In the Humber flats between Hull and Spurn Head is the hamlet of Winestead. The Domesday Book versions included *Wifestede*, from the Old English *wifa*, meaning 'of the women', and *stede*, which had a meaning in the north of farm – the farmstead of the women. A little further north, on the road from Hull to Aldbrough, Wyton also derives its name from the Old English *wifa* and *tun* – the women's tun. The small hamlet of Gunby, on the lower Derwent six miles east of Selby, was first recorded in the eleventh century. It was then known as *Gunelby*, embodying another Scandinavian feminine name, *Gunnhildr* – *Gunhild*'s farmstead. Wilberfoss, five miles out from York on the road to Market Weighton, derives the first element of its name from the Old English feminine name *Wilburg*.

In the West Riding, Hubberholme was recorded in Domesday Book as *Huburgheham*, from another feminine name, *Hunburg* – the woman *Hunburg*'s farmstead. Scandinavian feminine names form the first elements in Ingerthorpe in the West Riding and in Whenby on the southern fringe of the Howardian Hills, a few miles west of Malton. The former was recorded nearly a century after Domesday Book as *Ingeridtorp*, from the Scandinavian feminine name *Ingirithr*, denoting 'Ingrid's outlying farm'. Whenby appears in Domesday Book as *Quennebi*, of which the first element came from the Old Scandinavian *kvenna*, of the women – the women's *by*. A Norman example comes from Burton Agnes near Bridlington, previously quoted.

Stenton's conclusions are summed up in the following passage:

The place-names into which the names of women enter form a minute proportion of the place-names of all England. It would be easy to exaggerate their significance. Nevertheless, there are enough of them to carry a few modest generalisations. They show that before the Norman Conquest it was not unusual for women, like men, to give their names to villages, hamlets and parcels of land brought into cultivation from brushwood and forest. They imply that a considerable number of women possessed estates which can properly, if untechnically, be described as manors. Regarded as a whole, they give the impression that women were associated with men on terms of rough equality in the common life of the countryside.

The Place-Names of Paganism and Christianity

The sight of the spire or tower of the village church rising above the cottage roofs or emerging from the surrounding trees is so familiar a feature of the rural landscape today that it is often difficult to realise that in Anglo-Scandinavian times, and even in the early Middle Ages, it was exceptional. The parish system was still incomplete in England at the time of the Norman Conquest. Even when a parish was eventually established, the building of the village church often had to wait until the local lord of the manor was moved by piety or by a desire for social approbation to pay the cost. Services were commonly held in the open, where an air of sanctity was given to the proceedings by the raising of a wooden cross. In the course of time this would be replaced in many instances by a stone cross, examples of which can still be seen in Yorkshire villages. Stone crosses were often erected to mark ecclesiastical boundaries. Three parish boundaries meet at Ralph's Cross on the watershed of the North York Moors at a high point over 1,400ft. Others seem to have marked trackways across the lonely moors.

Most of the crosses have gone, but the element *cros* frequently persists in local place-names. Buckrose, the name of a wapentake in the East Riding, thus emerged from the *Buccros* of the twelfth century – *Bukki*'s cross. In the North Riding, between Barnard Castle and Middleton-in-Teesdale, a *Crosthwaite* was recorded in the thirteenth century – a clearing by the cross or in which the cross stands. Cross Sike, near Scarborough, was known in the same century as *Crossik* – the cross by the stream. A contemporary document from Guisborough Priory referred to a *Cruce de Bothine* from the Old Scandinavian term *botn* – the cross at the valley-head. The cross has vanished, but the term *botn* survives in Botton Hall, the village settlement at the head of Danby Dale that today thrives under the auspices of the Camphill Village Trust.

Little is known of the conversion of the vikings, but they seem to have been much less tenacious of their paganism than the Angles and Saxons had been. Guthrum and his followers readily accepted baptism as a condition of their treaty with Alfred; and the first Danish King of Northumbria had already embraced Christianity before his accession. The Norwegians had encounted the faith in Ireland, where it had been established since the time of St Patrick. Many of the Irishmen who accompanied the Norwegians in their settlement of Yorkshire were probably already Christians. The Scandinavian word for church, *kirkja*, has entered into so many place-names of Yorkshire, as either kirk, kirkby or kirby, as to suggest that the conversion of the Scandinavian population was both unresisted and widespread.

These forms give Kirby in Cleveland, Kirby Wiske, Kirby Sigston and Kirby Misperton. In the West Riding there are Kirkby Malham, Kirkby Malzeard, Kirkby Wharfe and South Kirk. Kirkby Overblow relates to thirteenth-century iron-smelting. Kirkstall Abbey near Leeds was first recorded as *Kirkstal* – the church site. Woodland clearances were often associated with a church, as in the place-names Kirkless and Kirkley, from the Old English word for a clearing, *leah*. Near Redcar, Kirkleatham was recorded in Domesday Book as *Westlidun*, a reference not to any church but to the settlement's situation beneath the western slope of the Upleatham Hills, from the Old English *hlith*, hill-slope. The 'kirk' was added in the following century after a church had been built there. This etymology is paralleled by that of Kirkburn, a village in the East Riding four miles south-west of Driffield – the church by the stream.

Churches were rarer in the earlier Anglo-Saxon period, but place-name evidence for their existence is not wholly lacking. The ruins of Kirkham Priory stand beside the Derwent, just before the river enters its gorge. The 'ch' sound of the first element and the *ham* in the final syllable of the Domesday Book name *Chercham* confirm the Anglian origin. The hard 'k' sound of the present-day name is the result of later Scandinavian influence. Kirkdale, three miles west of Pickering, is famous for the 'hyena' cave that attracted the attention of archaeologists at the beginning of this century. The name is a hybrid, combining the Scandinavian *kirkja* with the Old English *dael*, valley. The pre-Norman date for a church here is further confirmed by an inscription on an ancient sundial preserved on the site. Translated it reads: 'Orm, Gamel's son, bought St Gregory's Minster when it was all ruined and fallen down, and he caused it to be built new from the ground in the days of Edward and in the days of Tosti the Earl.' The personal names Orm, Gamel and Tosti are Scandinavian, and mention of King Edward the Confessor ties the date to between 1055 and 1064. The ruined minster must have dated from Anglian times.

The clergy, as distinct from the buildings, are frequently re-represented in Yorkshire place-names. Prissick Farm, on the outskirts of Middlesbrough, was known as *Prestsic* in about the year 1200 – the priest's stream. The name Preston, of a hamlet in Holderness, has a similar history – the *tun* of the priest. Nun-thorpe, an attractive village now rapidly being absorbed into the suburbs of Middlesbrough, was recorded in Domesday Book as plain *Torp* – an outlying hamlet – and so it remained throughout the subsequent century. In a document dated 1301, however, the name is enlarged to *Nunnethorpe*, as a result of the establishment there of the Nunnery of St James.

Yorkshire provides few examples of names of pagan origin. The most widely known, especially in the neighbourhood of Teesside, is Roseberry Topping, which forms so conspicuous a landmark on the moorland escarpment to the south. It is not recorded in Domesday Book, and is first mentioned in a twelfth-century document as *Othenesberg*, from the Anglian *beorg* – the hill of *Othin*. Othin was the Scandinavian equivalent of the Anglo-Saxon god Woden. The peak retained this name, with its hint of pagan worship, for centuries. Even as late as the seventeenth century it was still known as *Ounsbery*, though the present version was then coming into use.

Another old name for Woden was *Grim*, which appears in

195

Grim's Dyke in the West Riding. Goblins were known by the Old English words *grima* and *hob*. There is a Hob Hill just beyond Saltburn, where an early Anglian pagan burial site has been excavated. Grimshaw and Grimescar preserve the synonym in the West Riding. Scratters, a hamlet of the East Riding, derives its name from the Scandinavian *scrathou* which combines the elements *haugr*, a mound, and *skratti*, wizard or goblin. Scratch Lane in the West Riding has a similar origin. Dragons still survive, somewhat tamed, in a few place-names, the Old English term *dracan* still appearing in such West Riding names as Drake Hill and Hell Drake Woods.

Later Woodland Clearance as Shown in Place-Names

The considerable place-name evidence for the woodland cover of much of Yorkshire and for the clearance therein during Anglo-Saxon times has been discussed in Chapter 4. The story is now taken up for the Scandinavian and subsequent periods.

The Scandinavian words for woodland – *skogr*, *vithr* and *lundr* – are found in profusion in all parts of the county. *Skogr* has given us the element *skew* that appears in many place-names of today. Passengers on the Esk Valley railway pass a farm and a moor near Commondale station named *Skelderskew*, derived from an Old Scandinavian personal name *Skjoldr* and *skogr* – *Skjoldr*'s wood. On the southern flank of the Howardian Hills the small hamlet of Skewsby was known in Domesday times as *Scoxebi* – the *by* in or beside the wood. Near the rim of the limestone scarp between Gillamoor and Fadmoor, Loskay House began as 'the house in the wood', from a combination of the Old Scandinavian words *loft* and *skogr*. In the East Riding, six miles north of Beverley, Scorborough Hall is all that survives today from a settlement recorded in Domesday Book as *Scogerbud*, from the Old Scandinavian words *skogr* and *buth* – the booth or hut in the wood. The same element appears in Hessleskew, near Sancton – the hazel wood – from the Old Scandinavian *hesli*, hazel, and *skogr*. Nor are examples confined to the lowlands. In Wensleydale, two miles east of the well-known Hardraw Force, stands a farm named Litherskew. The first element is from the old word for slope, *hlith*. The description is still applicable, for the farm is situated at a height of nearly 1,000ft up the steep northern flank of the dale. The combination of the viking terms *hlith* hill-slope, and *skogr*, wood, suggests that when Scandinavian-speaking settlers coined this name the slopes of Wensleydale were wooded to a considerable height.

The Scandinavian synonym for forest or woodland, *vithr*, often appears in the place-names of today as the suffix *with*. Hartwith, high on the Pennine moors not far from the popular Brimham Rocks, was originally 'the wood of the harts or stags'. The name confirms the wooded nature of at least the lower Pennine slopes when this settlement was named. A viking named *Bubba* gave his name to a wood in the lower Derwent valley that has survived today as Bubwith. Rookwith, the name of a parish and a farm north of Masham, originated from the Old English *hroc*, rook and the Scandinavian *vithr* – the rook wood. To the south Nutwith Common derived its name from *hnutu* and *vithr* – the nut wood. The third Scandinavian synonym, *lundr*, was normally applied to a grove or copse. The name still survives in two hamlets, each named Lund, one near Beverley and the other near Lastingham. The name is also found in the North York Moors, in Wensleydale near the Litherskew mentioned above, and in the Vale of York near Easingwold.

Many woodland names of Scandinavian origin indicate the predominant species of tree. In Wharfedale, between Ilkley and Otley, the hamlet of Askwith denoted 'the ash-wood', from the Old Scandinavian *ask*, ash-tree. In upper Ribblesdale there is the hamlet of Selside, named from the Old Scandinavian *seliu*, willow-trees, and *saetr*, a shieling or an upper pasture. Briscoe in the upper Tees valley was originally 'the birch-wood', from the Old Scandinavian *birki* and *skogr*. Aiskew, at the approaches to Wensleydale, derives its name from the Scandinavian *eiki*, oak, and *skogr*, wood. The widespread distribution of such woodland names indicates how extensive the forest cover still was at the time

197

of the Scandinavian settlement, despite the clearances of the previous Anglian age.

Equally widespread are place-names of Scandinavian origin indicative of Danish and Norwegian efforts to extend the clearances of earlier times. The Old Scandinavian term for such a woodland clearing was *thveit*, which has entered into the place-names of today as thwaite. Over fifty such names have survived within the area of the former West Riding alone. To the examples already quoted in Chapter 5 can be added Langthwaite – the long clearing, and Slaithwaite, south-west of Huddersfield – the clearing where the sloes grow. In the North Riding the gorge cut across the limestone belt by the River Dove as it approaches the Vale of Pickering is called Douthwaite Dale – *Duvan*'s clearing. On the plain overlooked by the Kilburn 'white horse' stands a village named Husthwaite, from the Old Scandinavian *hus* and *thveit* – the clearing with the house on it. The village of Thwaite in upper Swaledale and two farms of the same name in Wensleydale between Hawes and the Moorcock Inn mark clearings in a woodland that seems originally to have extended up both these Pennine valleys.

Some place-names throw light upon the purpose for which the woodland was cleared. High up Swaledale, near Muker, lies the hamlet of Satron, the name of which was first recorded about AD 1300 as *Saterom*. The first element is clearly from the transhumance term *saetr*, an upper pasture. The second was from another Scandinavian synonym for a woodland clearance, *rum*. The full name indicated 'a forest clearing for upland grazing'. Boldron, near Barnard Castle, began as 'a forest clearing for keeping steers', from a combination of *rum* with the Old Scandinavian *boli*, a bull.

In view of the many place-names of Scandinavian origin denoting woodland and clearances, it is difficult to avoid two conclusions. The first is that the Danes and Norsemen arrived to find much of Yorkshire, including the Dales and the lower slopes of the Pennines, still forested, despite the clearances of earlier ages. The second is that the process of woodland clearance that had been going on from Bronze-Age to Anglo-Saxon times was still vigorously continued during the subsequent Scandinavian, Norman and early medieval periods.

The Domesday survey enables an assessment to be made of the extent to which those clearances had reduced the woodland cover by the end of the eleventh century. The Domesday clerks, not unmindful of their royal master's love of hunting and fully aware how valuable an asset woodland was to a manor, took pains to include it in their reports. May 26 has been prepared for Yorkshire from maps by H. C. Darby and I. S. Maxwell in their massive and detailed study of *The Domesday Geography of Northern England*. The Domesday clerks rarely gave the area but indicated the extent of a woodland by noting its length and breadth. Since this practice makes calculation of areas uncertain, only the locations of the recorded woodlands are shown on this map. From a comparison with the maps in Chapter 4 the extent of Anglian and Scandinavian clearances may be estimated.

Map 26 reveals that the coal-measure outcrop of south-west Yorkshire was still the most densely forested part of the county in Norman times, the woodland thinning out gradually against the millstone-grit moors on the west and abruptly at the magnesian limestone escarpment on the east. The Vale of York south of that city was well wooded, and to the north the medieval Forest of Galtres extended to the Howardian Hills. Unexpectedly, perhaps, the northern part of the West Riding recorded mainly underwood, the *silva minuta* of Domesday Book, or no timber at all. This situation extends over much of the Vale of Mowbray and the lowlands of the lower Tees.

In the North Riding, wood for pannage for sheep and goats, the *silva pastilis* of Domesday Book, was both scattered and small in area, except for concentrations on the Howardian Hills and the corallian limestone outcrop that forms the southern portion of the North York Moors. There, as in earlier times, the sandstone moors were conspicuously lacking in woodland, except for the coastal belt and in the Esk valley. Generally, however, both the North York Moors and the Pennines continued to stand out as negative

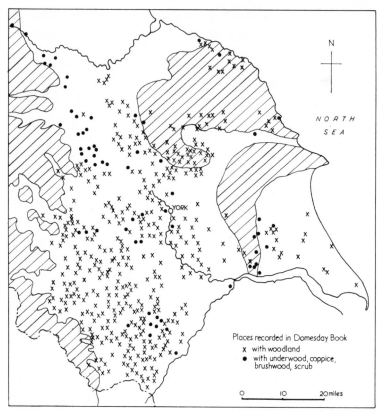

N

NORTH
SEA

YORK

Places recorded in Domesday Book
x with woodland
• with underwood, coppice,
   brushwood, scrub

0   10   20 miles

26 Woodland recorded in Domesday Book (*after H. C. Darby and I. S. Maxwell*)

areas. This is not necessarily evidence that in Norman times such uplands were no longer wooded; it may mean that they were unpopulated and therefore not surveyed and recorded.

According to the Domesday record the East Riding was sparsely timbered. Woodland was concentrated in two areas: in the lowlands of the lower Derwent and Ouse, and around Beverley, where the old Forest of Deira still survived, at least in part. Elsewhere, underwood or no woodland at all was recorded, the Wolds being almost bare of trees. This may mark the result of intensive preconquest clearance, but more likely reflects a lack of settlements and therefore of recordings.

The task of clearance, however, was not over. It continued through Norman times well into the Middle Ages, when it became merged with a broader attack upon the waste – those expanses of uncultivated land, forest, scrubland or heath that lay between the villages. From Norman times onwards it became increasingly the practice of the lords of the manors to enclose portions of this waste, bringing it under cultivation within their manors. For such an operation the Normans introduced their own French word – *assarter*. Any such 'assart' was usually added by the lord to his own home-farm or demesne, though sometimes he would settle a villein family thereon, as described in the previous chapter. As such assarts usually represented enlargements of the cultivated area of existing manors whose names had long been established, any additions they brought to local nomenclature were in field-names rather than in the names of places. The village of Kirkby Malzeard between Ripon and Masham, however, acquired the second part of its name from this practice, for it was recorded in the middle of the twelfth century as *Malassart*, Norman-French for 'a poor assart'.

Often the villagers themselves combined to make a clearing. They would pool their labour and equipment, clear the site and plough it communally, adding the new lands to the communal arable fields of the settlement. Three words were commonly employed in medieval times for such assarts after they had thus been added to the village common fields – *ofnams* (or *afnams*), *brotes* and *brecks*. There are recordings of *ofnams* in the fields at Cayton near Scarborough, and *offnames* at neighbouring Osgodby. Of the places marked in map 21, there are *afnams* recorded at Dromonby, and *ofnams* at Ingleby Greenhow and Hutton Rudby. An *avenam* is recorded at Ormsby, now a suburb of Middlesbrough. Such field-names are found in all parts of the shire. There are *broctes* and *brotes* in the records of Skipton-on-Swale, *brokes* at Upleatham and *brotis* at Skelton near Guisborough. *Northbrockes* are recorded at Hutton Rudby, while from Pockley near Helmsley come *brekz* and *le brotes* in their Norman-French form.

In the West Riding, field-names denoting such medieval intakes from the waste include *aynhems*, *ornams* and *annums*. In the Vale of Pickering there is still a farmhouse known as 'The Brotes'. The first record of this name was not made until the sixteenth century, revealing how late the practice persisted. At the other end of the county there is still a Broaks House, a few miles north of Borough-bridge. This term came from the Old Scandinavian word *broti*, which technically meant 'a heap of trees felled in a wood' and hence a clearing. *Smallbrotes*, *Norbrotes*, *Langbrotes* and other field-names derived from the synonyms *brote*, *breck* and *ofnam* are to be found in all parts of Yorkshire, dating from any time between the twelfth and sixteenth centuries. Collectively, they indicate a major and continuous clearance of woodland, scrub and heath.

To the assarts of the laity must be added the large-scale farming developments fostered by the medieval religious houses. Fountains and Rievaulx Abbeys led the way in widely extending their sheep-runs over the Pennines and North York Moors respectively. They were followed by such smaller foundations as Jervaulx, Kirkstall, Roche and Meaux. Many a Yorkshire name in which 'grange' forms an element marks the site of one of the outlying farms or storage barns established by such abbeys in the course of the Middle Ages.

So, throughout the medieval period what H. C. Darby has called 'the silent revolution' proceeded, village by village assarting patch after patch of its surrounding woodland and waste. By the sixteenth century the cumulative effect had resulted in an actual shortage of timber. Protests arose from both the Lords of the Admiralty, concerned with the lack of oak for the building of warships, and the iron-masters of the Weald and Forest of Dean, who needed wood for the charcoal with which they smelted the ore. By the reign of Elizabeth I the transformation of the York-shire landscape from the prevailing woodland of pre-Domesday times into the modern one of sheep-walks, grouse-moors, cattle pastures and arable fields was beginning to become apparent – a 'silent revolution' indeed, unfolded in the place-names of the county.

Medieval Occupations

No contemporary map of a medieval Yorkshire village exists, even if one were ever made, but map 27 outlines the characteristic features of such a settlement. In general, the houses were grouped around the church or village green, or aligned along the village street, and were far fewer in number than in a village of today. They were constructed on a framework of timber, with thatched roofs and walls of mud-plastered wickerwork. Few possessed an upper storey. Two-storeyed houses were unusual enough for the Scandinavian term for them, *lopt* – a house with a loft or upper floor – to pass into place-names, as at Lofthouse in the West Riding and Loftus near Boulby Cliff in the North Riding. All dwellings, even the most humble, were what the modern house-agent would describe as detached, each in its own plot, thus comprising the toft and croft of medieval place-names. On these plots the villagers kept a goat, perhaps a cow, and a hive of bees to supply honey, their main source of sweetening. At the rear of these garths ran a 'back lane', which can still be traced in Cropton and other villages of today.

Down by the local stream the water-meadows provided a lush pasture, valuable to the villagers for hay and for the grazing of cattle. The Old Scandinavian word for such pastures was *holmr*, which has passed into many a place-name of today as *holme*. A farm called Waterholmes stands on the bank of the River Rye about two miles above its confluence with the Derwent. Sleightholmdale Lodge occupies a site on the water-meadows of Hodge Beck near Kirkbymoorside. A mile further east the River Dove emerges from its limestone gorge to pass the hamlet of Keldholme – the water-meadow by the spring. About three miles north-west of Northallerton there are three farms respectively named Low, Middle and High Brockholme – the *holmr* of the badger. Three miles east of Driffield there is a farm bearing the name Cattleholmes. A little nearer the coast it is surprising to find the place-name Hastem Hills in so flat an area. A thirteenth-century record of the name as *Hestholme* provides the explanation. The present-

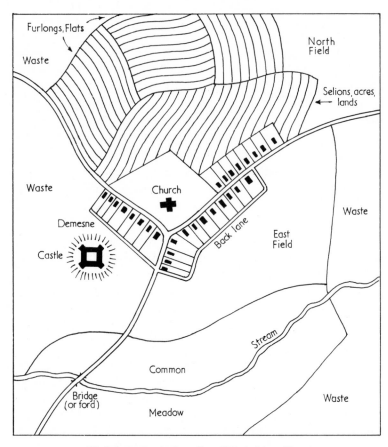

27 A hypothetical medieval Yorkshire village

day name does not refer to hills but comes from the Scandinavian word *hestr*, a horse – the water-meadows where the horses graze would be a fair rendering of the original name.

Still more important were the arable lands, farmed in two huge fields. Each was cultivated in turn while the other remained fallow, enabling the soil to recover and be manured by cattle and sheep turned out to graze there after the harvest had been gathered. This 'two-field' system predominated in the earlier periods, but was later replaced slowly, though by no means universally, by a three-

204

field system. The fields were named, often according to their geographical relation to the village. To this day the byroad near Scarborough from Scalby to Hackness passes between two farms bearing the old names of Northfield and Southfield. Such fields were far larger than those of today, for each had to provide the food necessary to maintain the whole community throughout the coming year. These community fields were divided into strips, allocated among the villagers, each man's holding being scattered in different parts of the field.

Ploughing was done communally, the villagers pooling their equipment and oxen to make up the eight-horse plough-teams. The areas in which the teams were turned at the end of the furrow were called 'headlands' and 'gores', terms which have passed into many a street name in the modern estates that have encroached on former farmland. The sowing was also done communally, wheat or barley in a rotation governed by the ancient 'custom of the manor'. Then the field was divided into strips approximately 220yds long and 22yds wide, measurements dictated by the requirements of ploughing the length a 'furrow-long', roughly a furlong. Our modern word acre is derived from one of the terms then used for these medieval strips, though it then indicated no standard area. The Old English term *aecer* and the Scandinavian *akr* are preserved in several place-names today. Muker in upper Swaledale was first recorded in the thirteenth century as *Meuhaker*, from the Old Scandinavian *mior*, thin or narrow and *akr*, a cultivated strip. East of Doncaster the name Bessacar survives – a rush-grown plot. There is a Stainsacre, near Whitby and an Acredykes Plantation at Bempton near Flamborough Head.

The Norman-French word for such strips was *sillon*, from which the medieval term *selion* was derived. Groups of *selions* were called *lands*, a term which has often entered into field-names, such as Acreland, Westlands and Newlands, frequently found in Holderness. There is a Langland, 'long strips', near Richmond in Swaledale, and a field named Longlands on the fringe of Middlesbrough has given its name to a college there.

No fences or hedges separated the *selions*, which were usually divided by a specially deep furrow, though sometimes by a balk, not unlike the narrow paths between modern allotments. A *Balkendes* was recorded for thirteenth-century Bilsdale in the North York Moors. A. H. Smith quotes one curiosity in the East Riding – a recorded *Nesthesutherrestbalke* – which, by separating out the syllables, he rendered as 'Next to the most southerly balk'. The absence of hedges and fences has given rise to the terms 'open fields' and 'open field farming' for this method of cultivation. It lasted long – into the nineteenth century in places – and it is still carried on at Laxton in Nottinghamshire. It provided the open terrain over which Cromwell's Ironsides and Rupert's Cavaliers in Jacobean days could charge, unobstructed by hedges and fences.

The *selions* were slightly curved into the shape of a reversed 'S', and were ploughed in groups, the direction of the furrows in each group being determined by local conditions, especially by the slope of the ground. Such groups of *selions* were variously termed *furlangs*, *lands* or *aecres*. These terms entered into field-names rather than into settlement names – as Kirkfurlang and Stain-furlang in the West Riding, and Norfurlangs in the North Riding. Another medieval name for a group of *selions* was a *flat*. In Fylingdale parish between Whitby and Scarborough there is a field named in 1236 *Wreckeflatte*, reputedly named from a wreck on the neighbouring coast. South of the railway at Marske-by-the-Sea the farmland at the foot of the Upleatham Hills is still called Cat Flats, originally after a Dane named *Kati* – a nickname meaning 'the cheerful fellow'. Near Helmsley the name Cock Flat comes from *kirkja* and *flat* – the group of *selions* by the church, or owned by the church. Near Hull a field bears the name Haverflats, from the Scandinavian *hafri* – the group of strips growing oats.

Other medieval terms for groups of *selions* included *wandales* or simply *deills*, both of which have entered into local place-names. Many a Yorkshire name ending in -dale has derived that element not from a valley but from this term *deill*, denoting the villagers' shares in the open arable fields. In the East Riding there are fields bearing the names Easedales and Reckendales. The former marked 'the eastern share of the open field', the latter came from

Richardesdaile, Richard's share of strips. There is an Anserdale Lane near Lastingham in the North York Moors, first recorded in the fourteenth century as *Hansterdaile*. Marske-by-the-Sea has preserved several of these ancient terms by applying them to modern residential developments. The comprehensive school there has been called Bydales, while roads on the new estates carry such names as Mordales and Mickledales, all three being drawn from local field-names. The term *wandales* was equally common, the meaning of which passed from denoting an individual's share in the common arable field to cover the *selions* in general. Wandales is found as a field-name near Lastingham and near Rievaulx in the North York Moors; at East Ayton five miles west of Scarborough; around Guisborough; at Middlesbrough; and at several places in the East Riding.

Until recently the village grouped around castle, church or green, such as has so far been described, was thought to have been characteristic of most lowland settlement. But numerous though such villages undoubtedly were in Yorkshire, recent research has shown that there were also many isolated farmsteads that did not fit into the general pattern of collective arable cultivation. The place-name Grassington in upper Wharfedale, for instance, suggests a prime interest in pastoral farming, for the name stems from the Middle English word *gresing*, denoting 'the grazing farm'. The pastoral as distinct from the arable interest of village farming is stressed by other elements in place-names. A common place-name ending today is wick, derived from the Old English *wic*, usually translated as a dairy-farm. In each of the East and West Ridings there is a Butterwick, derived from the *Butruic* of Domesday Book and *Buterwic* of a thirteenth-century record – the butter or dairy-farm. Five miles east of Hull the hamlet of Burstwick originated from '*Brusti*'s dairy-farm'. A little north of Hornsea Mere in Holderness the place-name Atwick marks the site of a former 'dairy-farm of *Atta*'. In the Pennines, Giggleswick has emerged from the Domesday record *Ghigeleswic* – *Gikel*'s *wic*. High up in Wharfedale the name Hawkswick originated from 'the *wic* of the viking *Haukr*'. The widespread distribution of names in

207

-*wic* suggests that such pastoral farms were more common in the Middle Ages than was once thought.

Other place-names indicate the cultivation of crops additional to the wheat and barley grown in the customary farming of the village communities in the Middle Ages. Halifax originated from the twelfth-century *Haliflex* – the holy flax field. The name Linton, of villages near Wetherby and Skipton, probably incorporates the Old English *lin*, which also meant flax. Hayton, five miles towards York from Market Weighton, bears a name that emphasises the importance of the haycrop in medieval farming. In the North Riding, Baysdale, one of the headwater valleys of the River Esk, takes its name from the Old Scandinavian word *bass*, the cowshed. A pastoral development is all the more likely in this moorland valley where corn-growing is still found unrewarding. Pastoral farming is equally stressed in the name Cawton, near Hovingham in the Howardian Hills – from the Old English *calf* and *tun*, 'the calves' farm'.

Medieval sheep-farming has also left its mark on local nomenclature. Many, though not all, place-names beginning with *ship* or *shep* derive this element from the Old English *sceap*, *scep* or *scip*, all meaning sheep. The Pennine foothill towns of Shipley and Shepley are instances, both originating as 'the clearing where sheep are kept'. On the bank of the Ure near West Tanfield the hamlet of Nosterfield has a name that harks back to the Old English *eowestrefelda* – the ewes' or sheep fold.

Medieval urban crafts contributed less to place-name formation than the agricultural practices of the day, for farming employed the overwhelming majority of the population. Further, craftsmen tended to set up shop in towns which already had a name far too strongly established to be displaced or even modified by their small workshops. Some village crafts, however, are recalled in local place-names. Bickerton, three miles east of Wetherby, derived its name from the Old Englih *beocere*, a bee-keeper. Hand querns were used for the home grinding of corn, but the spread of water-mills stimulated a demand for mill-stones. These were termed *cweorn* in Old English, and *kvern* in Scandinavian. The

Pennine summit of Whernside was *Qwernsyd* in the thirteenth century, deriving its name from a form that originally indicated 'the hillside from which mill-stones are obtained'. An association with milling explains the name of Quarmby, now absorbed in Huddersfield, and of Ainderby Quernhow, midway between Boroughbridge and the Leeming service station on the A1(M). Millholme, a field-name on the North York Moors south of Guisborough, recalls the existence of a mill.

The village smith appears early in the records and has left his mark on place-names over the whole county. At Great Smeaton, between Darlington and Northallerton in the Vale of Mowbray, there was a smith as early as the tenth century, for a record of that date refers to the settlement as *Smithatune* – the smith's homestead. Little Smeaton and Kirk Smeaton in the West Riding share the Old English origin.

The once-wooded valley of the Kilton Beck at Skinningrove between Saltburn and Staithes is now occupied by steel-works. The valley was a home of industry as early as the thirteenth century, though the occupation then was tanning. The name first appeared as *Scinergreve*, modifying to *Skynnergreve* later. Both elements are Scandinavian: the second, *gryfa*, referred to the steep slopes of the valley sides, the first is from *skinnari*, a tanner. Other village trades were the drying of corn and the baking of bricks. These occupations required kilns, a word which has entered into several place-names. Kilnsea in Holderness was first recorded in Domesday Book as *Chilnesse*, from the Old English *cyln*, kiln, and *sae*, sea – the kiln by the sea. A similar derivation applied to Kilham, a village in the northern Wolds inland from Bridlington. It was entered in Domesday Book as *Chillun*, from the dative plural, meaning 'at the kilns.'

Place-names also preserve the memory of occupations less closely associated with village life. Five miles south of Malton in the East Riding, the village of Kennythorpe bears a name of which the first element is thought to come from the Old Scandinavian word *kennari*, a teacher, used as a nickname or to denote an occupation. Tollerton, the first station on the railway north of

York, drew its name from the Old English *tollere* – the *tun* of the tax-collector. In upper Swaledale near Grinton, the hamlet of Copperthwaite takes its name from the Middle English word *coupare*, a cooper, or maker of barrels, combined with the Scandinavian *thveit* – the cooper's clearing. Hopperton, a village midway between York and Harrogate, was the *tun* of the hoop-makers.

Long before the Industrial Revolution changed life in the West Riding, iron was needed for ploughshares as well as for swords and armour. Smelting of local ironstone was not unknown in the Middle Ages. There is a Furnace Hill in the West Riding, and a Furnace Farm in the Esk valley near Danby Castle, though these likely date from the nineteenth century. Between Harrogate and Harewood House the name Kirkby Overblow preserves the memory of this medieval smelting, the second element being derived from the Old English *orblaware* – the kirkby of the smelters.

In the towns, small and rural as they were, craft specialisation was more marked. Street-names embodying the names of medieval crafts practised in York have already been quoted in Chapter 8. Bridlington shows a *Fiskergate* and a *Dreggergate*, the former from the Old Scandinavian *fiskari*, fisherman, and the latter from the drag-net used in gathering oysters. Kingston-upon-Hull has a Dagger Lane. Walkergate in Beverley took its name as 'the street of the cloth-fullers', from the Old English word *walcere* and the Scandinavian *gata*. There was a formerly a Tentour Lane, where cloth-makers stretched their cloth on tenter-hooks and tenter-frames.

Medieval Trade and Transport

Trade tended to develop in the towns where routes converged and where some measure of protection and supervision of the weekly markets was possible. In addition to the markets at York outlined in Chapter 8, the names Cornmarket and Cornhill still survive at Beverley. The records of that town refer to Wednesday and

Saturday markets and mention a *fismarketegat* for the fishermen and a *shomarket* for the cobblers there in the fourteenth and fifteenth centuries. Local names in Beverley bear witness to the widespread commercial reputation held by the town. The Landress Lane of today was the Londiners Street of the days of Charles II, when even the wealthy merchants of the City of London found it worth their while to attend the annual trade fair in the town. The fourteenth-century records mention a *Flemyngate*, 'the street of the Flemings' – merchants who at that time held a near monopoly of the Baltic trade.

A medieval trade in coal finds occasional reference in Yorkshire place-names. The largest demand came from London, to where coal was regularly shipped from the Tyne, being unloaded on the north bank of the Thames at Queenhithe, where Cannon Street railway station now stands. To this day, a Sea-Coal Lane links the city to the little yacht harbour that survives there. Yorkshire played a part in this trade. 'Colster' was a medieval term applied to one who dealt in coal, just as we still speak of the dealer in malt as a maltster. The term is preserved in the valley name Colsterdale, on the eastern flank of the Pennines south of Wensleydale.

Several Yorkshire place-names testify to the importance of the trade in salt, a commodity needed throughout the Middle Ages for preserving meat after the autumnal slaughter of most of the cattle, occasioned by the lack of winter feed for the beasts. Salt was worked in distant Cheshire and, more locally, at several spots along the coast. It was distributed among the Yorkshire villages and farms by pedlars with pack-horses travelling the ancient track-ways. One of these crosses the Whitby Moors in the neighbourhood of the Hole of Horcum, that spectacular combe by the Pickering–Whitby road. The track is still known as the Saltergate, from a hybrid word combining the Old English *saltere*, a dealer in salt, with the Scandinavian *gata*, a road or routeway. There is another Saltergate near Harrogate, and near Halifax Salterhebble combines *saltere* with *hebble*, a dialect word meaning footbridge. The place-names Salthaugh Grange and Salts House also refer to this trade. Salthaugh Grange was built by Meaux Abbey near the former shore of the Humber. Its twelfth-century name was *Saltehache*, from the Old English *sealte*, salt, and *haga*, enclosure. It is likely that the tidal waters were evaporated in shallow pools. Salts House was first recorded in the twelfth century as *pasturam de Saltes*, literally 'the salt pastures', a vivid name for the process just mentioned. The name was shortened in the thirteenth century to *le saltes*. Visitors to Whitby will be familiar with the name Saltwick, from a hybrid combination of the Old English *sealt*, salt and the Old Scandinavian *vik*, a creek. There is also Salterforth in the West Riding, marking a former 'ford of the dealers in salt'.

River crossings were essential to the pack-horse trails of medieval England. In an age when wooden bridges were none too common and stone bridges rare, streams had to be forded, and it is therefore not surprising that both the Old English word *ford* and its Scandinavian equivalent *vath* frequently occur in Yorkshire place-names. To the examples in Chapter 5 the following can be added: the main road northwards through the county crossed the River Ure at Castleford. There may be some doubt whether or not the first element referred to the Norman castle or ancient *ceaster* there, but the final element confirms the early establishment of a ford. Bradford originated as 'the broad ford' over the little Bradford Beck, now in the centre of the town. Startforth near Barnard Castle was recorded in Domesday Book as *Stradford*, which had become *Stretteford* by the end of the thirteenth century. From these recordings the name has been traced back to *straet* and *ford*, the *straet* being the Roman road which crossed the River Tees at this point. The change from the Old English *ford* to the modern ending 'forth' illustrates the influence of the Scandinavian cognate term, *vath*.

Fords were often named according to their quality as crossings. Fulford, now a southern suburb of York, deriving its name from the Old English *ful* and *ford*, was condemned as 'the foul, dirty ford'. Stainforth in the West Riding – *Steinforde* in Domesday Book – was 'the stony ford'. Arnford in the West Riding, however, could be recommended, for the name was derived from the Old English *aerne* and *ford* – a ford fit to ride over!

Ampleforth, famous today for its Roman Catholic seminary high on the southern edge of the North York Moors, first drew its name from the local river crossing. The first element came from the Old English word *ampre*, dock or sorrel – the ford where sorrel grows. A ford across the Swale two miles above its confluence with the Ure similarly gave its name to Brafferton. The Domesday clerks recorded it as *Bradfortuna*, from the Old English *brad*, broad, *ford* and *tun* – the farmstead or settlement by the broad ford. In the Vale of Mowbray a bridge carries the road from Northallerton to Richmond over the River Wiske, a tributary of the Ouse, at Yafforth. In Domesday times the stream there was crossed by a ford recorded as *Iaforde*, from the Old English word *ea*, a stream.

The Scandinavian term *vath* has been most commonly preserved in the form of the suffix *wath*. Three hamlets still preserve the term unchanged, being known simply as Wath – one near Hovingham in the Howardian Hills, where the old Roman road through Appleton-le-Street forded the Wath Beck; another two miles up Nidderdale above Pately Bridge; and the third four miles north of Ripon. Motorists travelling to Whitby leave Guisborough by the road that crosses Waterfall Beck through the wooded Slapwath Gap before ascending the moors. The name combines the Scandinavian terms *vath* and *sleipr*, to give the slippery ford. Wassand in the East Riding owes its name to 'the sandy ford', from the Old Scandinavian *vath* and *sand*. Six miles north of Richmond in Swaledale is Sandwath – another 'sandy ford'. In the moors north of Pickering, Grundstone Wath denoted 'the ford made from ground-stones'. Fords were often improved by a layer of flat stones, for which the Scandinavian word was *hella*. This has given us the stream-name Helwath Beck in the moors inland from Robin Hood's Bay. There is a Helwith near Gayles, north of Richmond in Swaledale – the ford paved with flat stones.

In the course of time, especially at much used crossings or where a wealthy benefactor appeared, the earlier ford was replaced by a bridge. Bainbridge, the attractive village in upper Wensleydale, draws its name from such a bridge over the little River Bain which flows from Semer Water to join the Ure in a series of waterfalls. That both bridge and settlement existed here at the beginning of the thirteenth century is suggested by a record of 1219 referring to *Bainebrig(g)*. The bridge over the River Ure which gave the name Boroughbridge was in existence before the middle of the twelfth century, when the name Pons de Burgo first appeared in the records. The '*Burg*' referred to was probably the neighbouring Aldborough, the ancient town that had grown up on the site of the Romano-British town of Isurium. That there was an early bridge at Stamford Bridge is suggested by a reference to *Stanford brycg* in the *Anglo-Saxon Chronicle* for the year 1075. This marked an important crossing on the River Derwent, which had carried the old Roman road from York to the coastal defences. The name indicates the existence of a stone-paved ford here, followed later by a bridge – Old English *stan*, stone; *ford*, ford; and *brycg*, bridge.

Local Government

One of the prime objects of the prosperous burgesses was to free their town from the feudal control of the manorial lord in whose estates it lay. This was achieved by the grant of a charter whereby, in exchange for a fixed annual grant, they were allowed to govern the town, administer justice and supervise trade. As the leading merchants and master-craftsmen took over these duties, the building from which they administered the town usually became known as the Guildhall, a name which has passed into the nomenclature of many a Yorkshire town. The Guildhall at York was first recorded in the late fourteenth century. Nearby stood *le tolleboth*, named from a Danish word *tolboth* – the booth where the tolls were collected. The earliest mention of any municipal building in Kingston-upon-Hull was in 1415, when one is recorded as *le Courthalle*, a name which was changed within a generation to the more usual *Gildhall*. A similar building at Beverley was first recorded as early as 1100 as *le Hanshous*, from the medieval word *hans*, a merchant. This probably referred to the hall of the Merchant Guild, an organisation that preceded the formation of the craft-guilds.

The rural communities remained under the control of the manorial lords until the very end of the Middle Ages. Only the free tenants escaped the jurisdiction of the manorial court and could appeal for justice to the royal courts, or come under the authority of the sheriff, the royal officer in the shire. This ancient title originated in the Anglo-Saxon term *scir reeve*, the shire reeev.

In general, local self-government in rural areas depended on a slender survival of those elements of an ancient freedom that the Angles and Saxons are thought to have brought from the Continent. Yorkshire place-names contain several references to their folk-moots or public assemblies of the freemen of a locality, held at frequent intervals to discuss local affairs with the sheriff, especially those relating to the maintenance of law and order. Such meetings were by immemorial tradition held in the open air, at a spot readily recognisable and accessible to all who as freemen had the right to attend. Such an assembly was known to the Angles and Saxons as a *moot*. The Scandinavians, who shared the custom, used the word *Thyng* or *Thing*. Their term is preserved in such place-names as Tingley near Morley. The records of Whitby Abbey contain a twelfth-century reference to *Tingwall* or *Thing-wala*, though all trace of the site has long since vanished.

Reference has previously been made to the wapentake, the Scandinavian unit of local government, and to the ritual flourishing of weapons from which the term was derived. In the East Riding the Wapentake of Buckrose was recorded in the twelfth century as the *Wapentac de Buccros* – the Wapentake of Bukki's Cross. A. H. Smith has suggested that the base of an old and ruined cross on the ancient road leading to Wharram Percy may mark the site of the meeting-place of this wapentake. The Speeton Cliffs are well known today as the home of countless sea-birds. In Domesday Book the village name was recorded as *Spretone*, from the Old Scandinavian word *sprec*, speech. This suggests that it was then the site of the 'speech *tun*', the folk assembly enclosure.

North-eastern Yorkshire contains three other place-names

indicative of such sites – Malton and Landemoth relating to Anglo-Saxon days and Fingay Hill for Scandinavian times. Old Malton, a settlement on the River Derwent slightly east of the site of the modern Malton, was entered in Domesday Book as *Maltune*. Considering this in connection with the mention of *Madaltune* in a charter of the mid-twelfth century, Smith concluded that the first element is from the Old English word *maethel*, a term applied by the Angles to formal speech. Malton thus indicated the discussion place, site of the Anglian folk-moot.

The other two sites both lie in the gently undulating countryside around Northallerton. About three miles west of the well known Cleveland Tontine Inn on the A19 from Thirske to Middlesbrough, rises a low, round-topped hill known as Fingay Hill. Its thirteenth-century name was *Thynghon*, from a combination of the two Scandinavian words *thing* and *haugr* – 'the hill where the Thing meets'. The third site lies barely five miles away to the south, where the A19 passes the gentle rise of Landmoth Hill. The recording of this name in Domesday Book as *Landemote* gives the clue to its significance. This was the site of the *land-gemot*, the meeting-place of the folk-moot of Anglo-Saxon times. Today, the traffic speeds along the busy A19 within sight of both hills where once the weapons flashed and our ancestors, both Angles and Danes, gathered by foot and on horseback to fashion the beginnings of democracy in England.

Bibliography

Books For Reference

Ekwall, E., *The Concise Oxford Dictionary of English Place-Names* (CUP)

Smith, A. H., *The Place-Names of the North Riding of Yorkshire* (1 vol) (CUP, 1928, 1969)

—, *The Place-Names of the East Riding of Yorkshire and York* (1 vol) (CUP, 1937)

—, *The Place-Names of the West Riding of Yorkshire* (8 vols) (CUP, 1970)

(The above volumes by A. H. Smith, issued by the English Place-Name Society, contain the etymologies, derivations and meanings of most of the place-names of Yorkshire, with excellent introductions.)

General Reading

Cameron, K., *English Place-Names* (Batsford, 3rd ed: 1977)

Copley, G. J., *English Place-Names and Their Origin* (David & Charles, 1968; 2nd impression: 1971)

Ekwall, E., *English River Names* (OUP, 1928)

Gelling, M., *Sign-posts to the Past* (Dent, 1978)

Jensen, Gillian F., *Scandinavian Settlement Names in Yorkshire* (1972)

Mawer, A. and Stenton, F. M., *Introduction to the Survey of English Place-Names* (EPNS, 1924)

Reaney, P. H., *The Origins of English Place-Names* (Routledge & Kegan Paul, 1960)

Stokes, H. G., *English Place-Names* (Batsford, 1948)

(The volumes of Northern History, issued annually by Leeds University, contain helpful articles.)

217

Historical Background

Beresford, M. W., *The Lost Villages of England* (Lutterworth Press, 1954)

Blair, P. H., *Roman Britain and Early England* (Nelson, 1963)

Brooke, C., *From Alfred to Henry III* (Nelson, 1961)

Collingwood, R. G. and Myres, J. N. L., *Roman Britain and the English Settlements* (vol 1 of the Oxford History of England, OUP)

Darby, H. C. and Maxwell, I. S. (eds), *The Domesday Geography of Northern Ireland* (CUP)

Sawyer, P. H., *The Age of the Vikings* (1962; 2nd ed: 1971)

Stenton, F. M., *Anglo-Saxon England* (vol 2 of the Oxford History of England, OUP)

Acknowledgements

I take this opportunity to acknowledge the debt I owe to the authors of the books listed in the bibliography; in particular to the late Sir Frank Stenton. I would like to express my thanks to all who have sanctioned the use of published maps – especially Professor K. Cameron for permission to use maps and information from the volumes published by the English Place-Name Society, and H. C. Darby and the Cambridge University Press concerning maps published in *The Domesday Geography of Northern England*. A special acknowledgement is due to Dr G. F. Jensen, now of Copenhagen University, for her generous and helpful permission to make full use of the maps and information in her scholarly study, *The Scandinavian Settlement Names of Yorkshire*.

Finally, I would like to acknowledge the help I have received from my publishers and their staff, from John Puckrin and Dorothy Arkless of the Cleveland Education Service, from Margaret Doyle of the Redcar Central Library and especially from Joan Davis, Joan Vasey and John Dunne of the Marske Public Library.

R.W.M.

Index

The figures in bold type indicate Abbreviated Etymologies, while those in italics refer to maps.